Aggressive Unilateralism

STUDIES IN INTERNATIONAL TRADE POLICY

Studies in International Trade Policy includes works dealing with the theory, empirical analysis, political, economic, legal relations, and evaluations of international trade policies and institutions.

General Editor: Robert M. Stern

John H. Jackson and Edwin A. Vermulst, Editors. *Antidumping Law and Practice: A Comparative Study*

John Whalley, Editor. *Developing Countries and the Global Trading System.* Volumes 1 and 2

John Whalley, Coordinator. *The Uruguay Round and Beyond: The Final Report from the Ford Foundation Project on Developing Countries and the Global Trading System*

John S. Odell and Thomas D. Willett, Editors. *International Trade Policies: Gains from Exchange between Economics and Political Science*

Alan V. Deardorff and Robert M. Stern. *Computational Analysis of Global Trading Arrangements*

Jagdish Bhagwati and Hugh T. Patrick, Editors. *Aggressive Unilateralism: America's 301 Trade Policy and the World Trading System*

Aggressive Unilateralism

America's 301 Trade Policy
and the World Trading System

Edited by
Jagdish Bhagwati and Hugh T. Patrick

THE UNIVERSITY OF MICHIGAN PRESS
Ann Arbor

Library of Congress Cataloging-in-Publication Data

Aggressive unilateralism : America's 301 trade policy and the world
    trading system / edited by Jagdish Bhagwati and Hugh T. Patrick.
        p.   cm.—(Studies in international trade policy)
    Includes bibliographical references and index.
    ISBN 0-472-09455-6 (alk. paper).—ISBN 0-472-06455-X (pbk. :
alk. paper)
    1. United States—Commercial policy.   2. Foreign trade regulation—
United States.   3. Competition, Unfair—United States.   I. Series.
HF14550.A615   1990
382'.3'0973—dc20   90-43273

Sponsored by the Program on Journalism and International Economics, codirected by Jagdish Bhagwati and James Chace, and by the Center on Japanese Economy and Business, directed by Hugh T. Patrick, and partially supported by the Center on Korean Research, directed by Gari Ledyard, all at Columbia University.

For
the Architects of the GATT-focused
"Fix-rule" Multilateral Trading Regime and
the international community of scholars
whose wisdom and vision are building it anew

Acknowledgments

This volume grew out of an international conference entitled "Super 301 and the World Trading System," held at Columbia University on December 1–2, 1989. The conference was sponsored jointly by Columbia University's Program on Journalism and International Economics, funded by the Ford Foundation and codirected by Jagdish Bhagwati and James Chace, and by the Center on Japanese Economy and Business, directed by Hugh Patrick, and was partially supported by the Center on Korean Research, directed by Gari Ledyard.

The conference could not have been successful without the indefatigable and invaluable support provided by Sheri Ranis, the Associate Director of the Center on Japanese Economy and Business. She managed the conference with perfect planning and total aplomb, leaving us free to focus on its intellectual side without any worries. She also helped us in getting the manuscript to its speedy conclusion: a task that is the most difficult stage in the life of conferences and their resulting volumes. We owe her thanks beyond what that word usually signifies. Her able staff, Charles Curtis, Jennifer Duffy, Karen Tonjes, and Susan Thau, must also be thanked.

Nothing in our financing required that the conference lead to a volume. However, the immense importance and topicality of the subject matter and the high quality of the presentations and the discussion virtually forced us to go the extra mile to put this volume together. The incentive to do so was also provided by the enthusiastic support of Robert Stern and of Colin Day, director of the University of Michigan Press. They reinforced our view that this volume would make a significant contribution to the current debate on U.S. trade policy and the world trading regime. We hope readers will agree.

Contents

CHAPTER 1

Aggressive Unilateralism: An Overview

Jagdish Bhagwati

On May 25, 1989, the United States used Section 301 to name Japan, India, and Brazil as "priority" countries to be put through the process of high-pressure, mandatory-deadlines tactics designed under the Omnibus Trade and Competitiveness Act of 1988 to dislodge, if necessary by retaliation, the trading practices designated by the United States as unacceptable to it. This jolted America's trading partners into fuller awareness that U.S. trade policy had changed to embrace aggressive unilateralism.

Almost uniquely, in view of the threat it seems to pose to an orderly world trading system premised on symmetry of rights defined by mutual consent, this trade instrument has been universally condemned outside the United States. In view also of the continuing need for American leadership on the maintenance and redesign of the multilateral world trading regime at the Uruguay Round, the resort to unilateral tools by the United States in particular has been perceived as a matter of the utmost concern.

Why has the United States embraced such an instrument? What precisely are the dangers it poses? These are the questions that must be answered before anything can be meaningfully said about the desirability of its demise and the strategy for its burial. I proceed to undertake precisely this task, but first delineate and discuss the instrument of concern with the precision it requires.

I. 301, Super 301, and Special 301

Section 301 of the Trade and Tariff Act of 1974 is the original piece of legislation that provides, in popular parlance, the shorthand for the current

---

This chapter has profited from the many excellent contributions in this volume, while also drawing on Bhagwati, *Protectionism* (Cambridge: MIT Press, 1988) and "United States Trade Policy at the Crossroads," *World Economy* 12, no. 4 (December, 1989): 439–79, to provide an overview of the major issues raised by the shift in U.S. trade policy to the use of aggressive unilateralism as constituted by the Section 301 provisions of recent U.S. trade legislation. My intellectual debt to Professor Robert Hudec, in particular, is considerable.

U.S. policy of aggressive unilateralism. Amended repeatedly, its main transformations and elaborations have occurred in Sections 301 to 306 in 1984 and, most notably, in Sections 301 to 310 in the Omnibus Trade and Competitiveness Act of 1988. At issue today is, of course, the current content of this legislation, as reflected particularly in what are known as the new Super 301 and Special 301 provisions, which the contributors to this volume carefully distinguish among when necessary while resorting to the generic Section 301 when the context makes finer distinctions superfluous.[1]

Explanations of Sections 301 through 310 in the 1988 Act are in the appendix to this chapter, with their relationship to Super 301 and Special 301 processes indicated. I shall therefore concentrate here only on their salient aspects as they bear on the analysis to follow.

The 301 legislation of 1974 was broadly directed at foreign restrictions on U.S. trade and used to enforce trade rights as conferred by GATT and by bilateral treaties, if necessary through retaliation against those judged to have violated these rights, with authority to undertake such actions conferred on the President.[2] In the case of GATT-defined rights, or the nullification and impairment of GATT-negotiated benefits, 301 complaints were expected to be pursued by first invoking GATT's dispute settlement machinery. In short, the 301 procedures were GATT-consistent in principle.[3] But while GATT must then (following a favorable finding) authorize a Section 301 retaliation for it to be unambiguously GATT-legal, retaliation had *not* been authorized by GATT in the six GATT-based "Regular 301" cases during 1975–89, based on pre-1988 act procedures.[4]

As Professor Hudec shows, the 1988 legislation now imposes timetables on the steps to be followed in these Regular 301 cases that could conflict with the more leisurely GATT procedures. This would greatly increase the possibility of GATT-illegal Regular 301 retaliations on the part of the United States[5]:

---

1. The transition from Section 301 to its Super 301 and Special 301 amendments in the 1988 Act is described by Judith Hippler Bello and Alan F. Holmer in chapter 2. They also provide insight into the Congressional concerns and perceptions that have prompted the shift to aggressive unilateralism.

2. As Geza Feketekuty notes in chapter 3, legal authority to undertake the retaliation needs to be granted by Congress to the president in the U.S. system of government.

3. See Robert Hudec's extended and careful discussion in chapter 4 of what he calls "Regular 301," i.e., GATT-based, cases.

4. See Hudec, chapter 4, for further details and analysis of the GATT-legality of Regular 301 actions during this period. Note however that: "Only one of the six [retaliations] was clearly GATT-legal, although several others involved general legal breakdowns that would have been difficult to rule on. None of the six actions triggered a legal crisis. GATT complaints were filed against three of the six retaliations. Two of the complaints [EC Wheat Flour and Japan Semiconductors] were not pursued to adjudication; the third [EC Hormones] is being prosecuted, but so far appointment of a panel has been blocked by the United States."

5. See Hudec chapter 4. As usual in legal matters, however, the matter is yet more

If the past is any guide, one or more delays . . . will occur in many cases, and the very tight Section 301 timetable will not be met. In those cases, the current procedures of Section 301 could well require the United States to retaliate before GATT authorizes such action. If so, the U.S. retaliation could well be a violation of GATT law. This is the GATT legal problem with the new 1988 version of Regular 301.

The question of aggressive unilateralism arises however, not in relation to the Regular 301 provisions and actions thereon, but rather with the different categories of 301 actions that are contemplated in regard to other countries' offending trade practices that do not violate any legal obligation.

Section 301, in its original 1974 version, addressed what were called "unreasonable" trade practices that lay outside of GATT rights and obligations. A series of amendments since then have augmented the scope of such unreasonable practices and the likelihood of retaliatory action to secure their removal. Such actions are the true objective of the new Super 301 and Special 301 provisions of the 1988 act.

This act substantially stiffened the process and enhanced the probability of complaints and retaliation by supplying a (not exhaustive) list of such unreasonable practices, including inadequate workers' rights and insufficient anticompetitive policy measures[6] which are not matters traditionally dealt with in trade negotiations and are, in any event, only tenuously trade related at best.

But the main methods by which teeth were put into 301 actions against unreasonable practices were the Super 301 and Special 301 provisions. Super 301 essentially requires the United States Trade Representative (USTR), on schedule, to prepare an inventory of foreign trade barriers, establish a priority list of countries and their unreasonable practices, and then set deadlines for their removal by the foreign countries and, should they fail to comply, for decisions on retaliation by the United States. Special 301 is similar in its time-bound approach but is addressed especially to intellectual property rights.[7]

The actions taken by Ambassador Carla Hills on May 25, 1989, against Japan, India, and Brazil were on the Super 301 time schedule.[8] The United States chose five priority practices among the three countries: quantitative restrictions, citing Brazil for her balance-of-payments restrictions; government procurement restrictions, citing Japanese restrictions on supercomputers and satellites; technical barriers to trade, citing Japanese standards on forest products; trade-related investment measures (TRIMs), citing India for export

---

complex: for instance, unauthorized retaliation may sometimes be GATT-legal. But the quote from Hudec basically hits the nail on the head.

6. Cf. the discussion in Bello and Holmer, chapter 2, of the debate in Congress on these practices.

7. Telecommunications are dealt with separately from Super 301 as well.

8. Actions were announced on Special 301 as well.

performance requirements imposed on foreign investors; and barriers to trade in services, citing India for restrictions on foreign insurance.

It is the exercise of 301 actions in these GATT-unrelated areas, using the threat of trade retaliation against other countries to accept trade practices that the United States has unilaterally decided to consider unreasonable and hence unacceptable, that America's trading partners resent and reject.[9] These actions properly constitute the target of their concerns. They are therefore the principal subject matter of this volume.

II. Objectives behind 301: Unfair Trade, Opening Foreign Markets, and Unrequired Concessions by Others

Why has the current 301, with its defining characteristic of aggressive unilateralism, arisen in the United States? The answer to this question is complex and nuanced.

At the outset, it is useful to distinguish among three ways in which 301 is intended to establish new trade obligations:

  i) opening markets in sectors where GATT already operates, e.g., getting foreign countries to make additional concessions in manufactures;
 ii) opening markets and/or establishing new rules or disciplines in new sectors, e.g., in services and agriculture; and
iii) establishing new rules that may apply to old as well as new sectors, e.g., prohibition of export targeting, prescribing workers' rights, and enforcing intellectual property rights.

These objectives are driven mainly by two underlying motivations: first, to eliminate "unfair" trade practices by others; second, to "open foreign markets." Let me explain.

Unfair Trade

The question of "unfair" trade lies behind virtually all of the three objectives distinguished above. Thus, demands for reciprocity may lead to objective (i). For example, even though the access by South Korean automakers to the U.S. market is greater than U.S. access to the Korean market, by way of tariffs, as a result of obligations adopted earlier and is GATT-legal, it is now considered

---

9. The viewpoints of Minister Chulsu Kim of South Korea, Ambassador Moreira of Brazil, and Ambassador Pirzio-Biroli of the European Community in chapters 8–10 and of Mr. Makoto Kuroda of Japan in chapter 7, are broadly representative of the dismay with which Super 301 actions have been received outside the United States.

unfair, as evident from Congressman Gephardt's campaign pronouncements in the 1988 presidential campaign, and is fair game for 301 pressures on South Korea. Then again, the notion that it is unfair that countries with comparative advantage in manufactures, covered by GATT, have GATT-defined access to U.S. markets while the United States, with its new comparative advantage in services and agriculture, does not have similar access to foreign markets in these sectors, is another potent force fueling objective (ii). Finally, objective (iii) is most explicitly focused on the unfairness of foreign traders: e.g., the South Koreans get unfair advantage by violating workers' rights that the United States supports, whereas the Japanese resort to export targeting that destroys U.S. industry.

Opening Foreign Markets

There is also the distinct sense that the United States is "opening foreign markets" through 301 actions. This focus on *exports* is somewhat novel, compared to traditional preoccupations with regulating or managing *imports* in trade policy. In fact, this is seen as reflecting a benign aspect of 301 policy, if securing freer world trade is seen as a desirable goal.

Of course, not all 301 actions can be interpreted as opening foreign markets and, therefore, trade augmenting. Thus, for instance, the proposed restraints on export targeting would reduce exports and trade. So would workers' rights prompted wage increases if they make exports more expensive, as intended. These are areas of 301 actions and intentions that reflect unfair trade concerns but are trade reducing, not trade expanding, in their effects.

Demanding Unrequited Trade Concessions

The dual concerns with unfair trade practices of others and opening foreign markets, in turn, have arisen as a result of a host of factors that I analyze in section III immediately following. But Section 301 is also characterized by the (wholly distinct) fact that it enables the United States to unilaterally make demands for trade concessions by others without offering any matching, reciprocal concessions of its own that others might demand in turn.[10] These one-way, unrequited concessions, sought through the use of retaliatory threats of reducing existing trade access to foreigners, are a critical aspect of the 301 process. That aspect and the factors prompting the United States to embrace it are discussed in sections IV–VI.[11] "Altruistic" explanations of 301 intentions and actions, on the other hand, are explored in section VII.

---

10. These concessions may be in any of the categories distinguished above.

11. In sections III–VI, I draw extensively on Bhagwati, "United States Trade Policy," 442–63.

III. Factors Underlying the Concerns with Unfair Trade and Opening Foreign Markets

The concerns with fairness of trade and with opening foreign markets arose in the early 1980s and must be traced, in subtle ways (considered at the end of this section), to the acceleration of import protectionism during the first term of the Reagan Administration.

The increased demands for import protection that surged in the U.S. Congress were not the run-of-the-mill kind that arise from time to time as random pressures on specific industries from imports and are translated in the political arena into demands for relief from foreign competition. They were over a much wider spectrum of industries. Their potency derived not merely from the pressure of constituents, reflecting sectional interests, but from the increasing sense in Congress that the social good required support for troubled industries. Let me elaborate.

The Balance of Payments

The overvaluation of the American dollar put significant pressure for adjustment in the traded activities of the American economy—making nontraded activities generally more profitable at the expense of the traded ones.

Mounting constituency pressure for relief from imports was an inevitable political outcome. It was handled inaptly by the Reagan administration during its first term. Until the Plaza Agreement, the appreciation of the dollar was regarded with indifference, seen simply as a consequence of the attractiveness of the U.S. economy for foreign investable funds. The possibility that there could be, even in that case, serious adjustment problems imposed on the economy—as with the "Dutch disease" problem—because of the magnitude of the resource reallocation required was not addressed.

The high-track export restraints that followed were thrown as crumbs to satisfy protectionist demands. But the crumbs turned into loaves, marring the free-trade image, and also the track record, that the Reagan administration wanted.[12]

But the balance-of-payments situation, in the shape of the trade deficit that persisted in spite of the significant post-Plaza realignment of the dollar, fostered a growing feeling that the trade deficit was unsustainable, had to be eliminated, and could not be tackled by exchange-rate realignment. The

---

12. Adjusting for the vastly increased demands for protection, the Reagan administration may be defended as having supplied no more protection than its predecessor under President Carter. But the increased demands for protection were partly a consequence of the administration's own macroeconomic policies.

broader American interest required, therefore, that trade policy had to be deployed to address the trade deficit.

It is true that the unsustainability of the trade deficit and its elimination as a goal for the United States (whether in its own interest or that of countries "more in need of capital") are issues that are arguable, to say the least, and have been argued extensively. But the notion that exchange-rate changes cannot any more have impact on the trade deficit has drawn somewhat greater strength from the empirical observation that the realignment of the dollar failed to reduce the trade deficit as quickly and as much as many had hoped. It accordingly needs commenting upon. Two points should be made.

First, a cliché, but an important one. If excess spending continues, expenditure-switching policies, such as exchange-rate devaluations, will fail to produce more than ripple effects on the trade deficit.[13] If the budget deficit persisted, and no significant reduction in spending occurred in the private sector, the realignment of the dollar could not be expected to work.

Second, a novel consideration. If local prices do not rise, a devaluation cannot induce a switch of expenditure away from imports. Much was made, in the early years after the Plaza Agreement, of the failure of the "pass-through" effects of the currency realignment. Prices of imported goods did not rise by the amount of the dollar devaluation or, at least, not as much as "normal." A search for explanations started among macroeconomists. The more interesting explanation was the notion that investments, once made, would lead to price-setting behavior to hold onto markets. Japanese firms, having invested at the high dollar for sales in U.S. markets, would tenaciously cut prices when the dollar fell, rather than close down and move out. This notion of "hysteresis," and lack of symmetry around a change back and forth, may have some merit insofar as the dollar was high for a long period and investors may not have foreseen the magnitude of the dollar's fall.[14]

But a natural and plausible explanation, pertinent to the discussion of trade policy, is one that the macroeconomists forgot to note, perhaps because their conventional thinking had not caught up with the way nontariff measures are used in developed countries generally and in the United States in particular

---

13. Michael Gavin has alerted me to remind the reader that devaluations may affect excess spending when they successfully switch expenditure toward home goods in a situation of Keynesian unemployment or, secondly, when the rise in import prices increases real savings due to the wealth effect, as in the celebrated Laursen-Metzler-Harberger analysis. The former model is not valid currently; the latter effect does not appear to be important. Also see n. 18.

14. The chief proponents have been Richard Baldwin, "Hysteresis in Import Prices: The Beachhead Effect," *American Economic Review* no. 4 (1988): 773–85; and Richard Baldwin and Paul Krugman, *Persistent Trade Effects of Large Rate Shocks*, NBER Working Paper no. 2017 (Cambridge, Mass.: National Bureau of Economic Research, 1986).

to deal with "disruptive" imports.[15] This was simply that, as the dollar had long remained high, Japanese (and Far Eastern) exports had come to be heavily afflicted by export-restraint arrangements in various forms. This meant that there was often a substantial scarcity premium on Japanese goods. If the dollar was devalued, the devaluation would first cut into this premium, with the final price to U.S. consumers unaffected. Only after the devaluation had exceeded this premium would an impact on final prices be seen. That is to say, the pass-through effects would be abnormally low at the outset, until the premiums were absorbed.[16]

That this hypothesis has explanatory power is supported by the fact that Japanese goods were heavily restrained, that the dollar was devalued mainly against the yen, and that the pass-through effects improved after the dollar devaluation had become substantial. But it is additionally supported by disaggregated industry studies undertaken in Japan.[17]

By ignoring the linkage between protection and exchange-rate inefficacy, analysts have encouraged the erroneous idea that protection is necessary *because* exchange-rate changes are ineffective. We are in danger, then, of experiencing a vicious circle: protection leads to the reduced efficacy of exchange-rate changes; in turn, the inefficacy of exchange-rate changes leads to protection.

---

15. This is evident from a report by Robert Kuttner (of a conference of the leading figures in international macroeconomics in late 1987), "The Theory Gap on the Trade Gap," *New York Times,* 17 January 1988, sec. 3, where the presence of trade barriers as an explanation for the failure of the pass-through effect is not mentioned. This omission is also in the early studies, including Catherine Mann, "Prices, Profits, Margins, and Exchange Rates," *Federal Reserve Bulletin* (June, 1986): 366–79; and Paul Krugman, *Exchange Rate Instability* (Cambridge, Mass.: MIT Press, 1989).

16. This hypothesis is discussed at length in Jagdish Bhagwati, "The Pass-Through Puzzle: The Missing Prince from Hamlet," Department of Economics, Columbia University, 1988, to be reprinted in J. Bhagwati, *Political Economy and International Trade,* ed. Douglas Irwin (Cambridge, Mass.: MIT Press, 1990). The paper was summarized in an Economics Focus column, "Passing the Buck," *The Economist* (London), February 11, 1989, 63.

17. In particular, the experience of the automobile industry bears out this hypothesis. See Kiyohiko Shibayama, Michiko Kiji, Toshihiro Horiuchi, and Kazaharu Kiyono, *Market Structure and Export Prices,* Discussion Paper no. 88-DF-1 (Tokyo: Research Institute of International Trade and Industry, Ministry of International Trade and Industry, 1988). The impact of the trigger-price mechanism on U.S. steel imports on the pass-through effect is also borne out. As Dr. Shibayama communicated to me: "On the aggregate level, pass-through ratios for Japanese exports have been lower during this post-1985 period than during the 1977–78 period of the high yen. More than half of this decline may be attributed to a decrease in the pass-through ratios for Japanese steel and automobiles, two of our country's principal exports" (Letter dated February 14, 1989).

But it is also necessary to remind politicians that if they think exchange-rate changes are inefficacious because "prices no longer matter," the same objection could apply to protection. Both are expenditure-switching policies (although they are not identical insofar as the exchange-rate change affects exports as well). In addition, neither policy can work unless it differentially affects domestic savings and investment, so as to produce an excess of the former over the latter at the margin.[18] Otherwise a lasting impact on the trade deficit is not possible.[19]

The Double Squeeze

The adjustment problem for the traded industries in the United States has been further accentuated by a "double squeeze."[20] The growth of exports from Japan and the Pacific "Gang of Four" (Hong Kong, Singapore, South Korea, and Taiwan) and the less spectacular but still impressive export performance of other newly industrializing countries, such as Brazil, and of the newly exporting countries, such as Malaysia and Thailand, have created problems for specific industries in the developed countries, obliging them to adjust to those changes.

A country that grows more rapidly than others will, on average, export at a volume and rate of growth that is hard for the other countries to accommodate without complaints from the domestic industries that must bear the brunt of the adjustment. Japan has been up against this phenomenon since the 1930s. Even then, when Japan was not yet dominant, Japanese diplomats were scurrying around negotiating "voluntary" export restraints—on pencils, electric lamps, safety matches, and other products—with the United States, Britain, Australia, and other trading partners, partners among whom a bilateral surplus in trade with Japan was common. The present surplus situation

---

18. For a careful analysis of this question, see W. M. Corden, "Trade Policy and Macroeconomic Balance in the World Economy," forthcoming in *Essays in Honor of Isaiah Frank,* ed. Charles Pearson and James Riedel (Oxford: Basil Blackwell, 1990). Also see Richard H. Clarida, "That Trade Deficit, Protectionism, and Policy Coordination," *World Economy* 12, no. 4 (December, 1989): 415–39.

19. Some economic studies show that U.S. protection will improve the trade deficit. But these results come from specific assumptions, such as that the revenues from the tariffs are saved. The implied notion that the United States has become sufficiently underdeveloped to need revenues from tariffs, as many poor countries used to do, would be amusing if it were not so damaging to sensible policy-making. See Rudiger Dornbusch, "External Balance Correction: Depreciation or Protection?" *Brookings Papers on Economic Activity,* Washington, D.C., No. 1, 197, 249–69.

20. See Bhagwati, *Protectionism.*

has compounded Japan's difficulties; but even if her surplus were to disappear, she would continue to attract the protectionist ire of disaffected competitors.[21]

Deindustrialization and National Interest

The protectionist fallout, however, has come not merely from troubled industries seeking relief. There has been the national-interest concern that America is threatened with deindustrialization and that this, in turn, will damage the economic well-being of the United States.

The Democrats, in particular, fell easy prey to these views. For instance, in the 1984 Presidential election campaign in the United States, the Democratic candidate, Walter Mondale, invoked images of Americans reduced to flipping hamburgers at McDonald's while the Japanese overwhelmed the country's industries. He might have invoked, with greater irony, a picture of American kids rolling rice cakes at sushi bars.

The fear of deindustrialization also agitated the leaders of trade unions in declining, protection-seeking industries. Sol Chaikin, for example, of the International Garment Workers' Union, protested in an article in *Foreign Affairs:* "Because there are relatively few well-paying jobs in the service sector, an economy devoid of manufacturing would also necessarily experience a general decline of living standards. . . . Unrestricted trade and the investment practices of the multinationals . . . can only lead to an America ultimately devoid of manufacturing."[22]

The effect was to make life easier for those seeking protection. These views made it less difficult for politicians to respond affirmatively to narrower interests seeking protection: Congressmen voting for protection could feel comfortable in their conviction that they were acting, not as politicians responding to the narrow sectional interests of their constituents, but as statesmen safeguarding the national interest.

From an objective point of view, however, the arguments advanced in support of the view that deindustrialization has deleterious consequences are sufficiently tenuous to make the recent "manufacturing matters" school of worriers in the United States as hard to side with as the members of the better-known and earlier school of deindustrialization in the United Kingdom, led by the late Nicholas Kaldor, the distinguished Cambridge economist and intellec-

---

21. Cf. Jagdish Bhagwati, "A Giant among Lilliputians: Japan's Long-Run Trade Problem," in *Beyond Trade Fiction: Japan-U.S. Economic Relations,* ed. Ryuzo Sato and Julianne Nelson (Cambridge: Cambridge University Press, 1989).

22. Sol Chaikin, "Trade, Investment, and Deindustrialization: Myth and Reality," *Foreign Affairs* 61 (Spring, 1982): 848. Other telling examples are quoted in Bhagwati, *Protectionism,* 99–101.

tual of the Labour Party.[23] I have analyzed these arguments elsewhere at length, and concluded that many are fallacies or unproven assertions.[24]

The "Diminished Giant" Syndrome

The payments difficulties and the "double jeopardy" phenomenon may have produced the conditions for increased demand by sectional interests lobbying for protection and increased supply. They may also have led influential Congressmen to think that protection would also be in the national interest. But the overall ethos favorable to protectionism came from the national psychology produced by America's relative decline in the world economy. I have called this the "diminished giant" syndrome.

While the United States continues to be a dominant power, it has witnessed the erosion of its predominant status in the world economy as Japan has risen from the ashes and, too, as other Pacific countries have come to the fore.

The parallel with Britain at the end of the nineteenth century is dramatic. In both instances, the giant's diminution produced a protectionist backlash, sorely trying the protrade bias of the international regime.[25] Walter Lippmann has characterized ours as the American century. In the same vein, the nineteenth century was Britain's. As the century ended, Britain was gradually losing her political and economic preeminence. The twentieth century is ending similarly for the United States. Staffan Burenstam Linder has already announced the arrival of the Pacific century.[26]

The diminution in Britain's preeminence in the world economy led to a

---

23. The foremost members of the deindustrialization school in the United States are Stephen Cohen and John Zysman, *Manufacturing Matters: The Myth of the Post-Industrial Economy* (New York: Basic Books, 1987). While the British school has virtually become defunct, after an initial splash and having had a temporary impact on British legislation in the form of a Selective Employment Tax designed to create differential incentives for employment in manufacturing at the expense of services (see Bhagwati, *Protectionism*, chap. 5), the American school has recently gained a few academic converts.

Whether and how soon the American school will atrophy like the British school should depend on the different interactions between the manufacturing sector and academics in the two countries. While the Labour Party and generally left-wing British economists who led the deindustrialization school had little to do with the manufacturing corporations who would profit from a promanufacturing policy, this is not so for the academic converts to the deindustrialization school among the new Democrats in the United States. This contrast offers an interesting subject for analysis.

24. Cf. Bhagwati, "United States Trade Policy," 445–50.

25. For a detailed analysis, see Jagdish Bhagwati and Douglas Irwin, "The Return of the Reciprocitarians: U.S. Trade Policy Today," *World Economy* 10 (June, 1987): 109–30.

26. Staffan Burenstam Linder, *The Pacific Century* (Stanford, Calif.: Stanford University Press, 1986).

rise in protectionist sentiments and to demands for an end to Britain's uni-lateralist embrace of free-trade principles. And the United States has followed the same path. The present-day sentiments on trade policy in the United States have been aimed pointedly at the newly successful rivals, just as their nine-teenth-century British counterparts were. The United States and Germany were to Britain what the Pacific nations—Japan in particular—are to the United States today.

Aside, though, from aiding the rise of old-fashioned import protec-tionism, the diminished giant syndrome has prompted a significant shift in United States trade policy toward emphasis on "fair trade." One can argue cynically that words matter, as Orwell taught us, and it is easier to indulge protectionism if it is sold as a response to unfair trade instead of being left undisguised in its true form. The emergence of the fair trade obsession in the United States grew as import competition grew with the rise of the dollar.

But the diminished giant syndrome has also helped. It is relatively easy, when one's premier status is in jeopardy, to think that the success of one's rivals must be due to perfidy. Panic produces petulance.[27] The persistent and pervasive belief that the countries in the Far East are "not playing by the rules" and that "level playing fields" must be established to compete with them, owes much to this syndrome.

In fact, fair trade and reciprocity emerged as issues in an equal degree in Britain when she faced her own relative decline at the end of the nineteenth century. The rise in Britain during the 1870s and 1880s of the National Fair Trade League, the National Society for the Defense of British Industry and the Reciprocity Fair Trade Association are events that make the American senti-ments and actions of the last decade easier to comprehend.[28]

Apart from the rise of concerns over unfair trade, the other dramatic change and, indeed, a novelty in the political economy of trade policy gener-ally, has been the growth of export interests in the United States.[29] This has

---

27. In some instances, contempt has yielded to fear. Who cannot recall President de Gaulle's disdainful remark about the Japanese Prime Minister: "Who is this transistor salesman?" The European Community's frenetic use of antidumping actions to hold Japanese imports down suggests an altogether changed attitude to the subject matter, as documented splendidly by Brian Hindley, "Dumping and the Far East Trade of the European Community," *World Economy* 11 (December, 1988): 445–65; and Patrick Messerlin, "The EC Antidumping Regulations: A First Economic Appraisal, 1980–85," *Weltwirtschaftliches Archiv* 125, no. 3 (1989): 550–71, and "GATT-Inconsistent Outcomes of GATT-Consistent Laws: The Long-Term Evolution of the EC Antidumping Law," paper for the Trade Policy Research Center as part of its program of studies on Regulatory Trade Measures and the Concept of Unfair Trade, London.

28. There are other parallels and contrasts, too, which are analyzed in Bhagwati and Irwin, "Return of the Reciprocitarians."

29. The growth of the export interests in the United States has been noted and analyzed in three independent contributions: Jagdish Bhagwati, *Protectionism;* Helen Milner, *Resisting Pro-*

given a special form, and a sharp edge, to the concerns over unfair trade and to the emphasis on opening foreign markets that characterize American trade policy today, while also explaining the embrace of regionalism and the thrust of positions adopted by the United States in the Uruguay Round negotiations.

Natural Forces: Interests and Ideology

The increasing globalization of economic activity, with the criss-crossing of investments among the major trading countries, has created a spider's web phenomenon. The reaction of multinational enterprises (with global reach) to import pressures does not need to be the old-fashioned demand for import protection. This can, by spreading protection elsewhere and thereby affecting freer trade in the world economy, imperil the open trading system within which they can function best.

They now have another option. If they sell in other markets, as most do, they can also ease the pressure of competition on themselves by asking for not higher import barriers against others, but lower import barriers by others. Aside from providing an option that may equally relieve competitive pressures, it is also in keeping with the general multinational ethos and interests of achieving a freer world trading regime.

It has the added advantage that one might be able to fit it into the unfair trade framework, if applied at the level of products, firms, and industries (as necessary to one's argument). If protection against American exports of automobiles in a particular country is greater than American protection against that country's exports of automobiles, that leads to a plausible claim of unfair competition.

Ideologically, this argument may also be shown to have support from trade theory on grounds of efficiency, not just fairness. International trade theorists have argued that, under large enough scale economies to a firm, import protection can lead to the viability of one's firm at the expense of one's rivals, producing even the paradoxical phenomenon that import protection leads to export promotion.[30] In essence, it is easy to see that if firms are

---

tectionism: Global Industries and the Politics of International Trade (Princeton, N.J.: Princeton University Press, 1988); and I. M. Destler and John Odell, *The Politics of Anti-Protection* (Washington, D.C.: Institute for International Economics, 1987). While all authors consider the benign role of these interests in shifting trade policy away from import protectionism to export expansion and "opening markets," the first considers also the down side of the phenomenon—that these export interests may capture trade policy to foster "export protectionism," as discussed below.

30. For early analyses, see Georgio Basevi, "Domestic Demand and Ability to Export," *Journal of Political Economy*, no. 2 (1970): 330–40; and, in particular, Richard Pomfret, "Some Interrelationships Between Import Substitution and Export Promotion in a Small Open Economy," *Weltwirtschaftliches Archiv* 111, no. 4, (1975): 714–27.

identical, economies of scale yield irreversible gains (as when learning occurs); and if one firm has access to two markets and the other has access to only one (because its market is closed to imports and the other's is not), the firm in the protected market will gain a permanent advantage.[31] This may even be a social advantage (although this is not guaranteed). The sudden popular awareness of this demonstration,[32] brought out of the closet by younger trade theorists and put into the political arena,[33] has lent critical ideological support to the export lobbies seeking outward reach in foreign markets and to Congressmen who see in this a justification for aggressively opening foreign markets.

The combination of export interests and ideology has been a heady brew, enough to provide the momentum for the market opening thrust in U.S. trade policy. But export interests have profited equally from the payments difficulties discussed earlier. Just as the belief that import restrictions will cure the trade deficit refuses to die, rising ever again like Moriarty in Sherlock Holmes mysteries, so does its flip side: that lowering foreign trade barriers will cure the trade deficit. Those who make policy in Congress are doomed to believe it; and those who seek to export willy-nilly have not hesitated to exploit it.

Promoting the Lobbies

The growth of the export lobbies was also encouraged by the administration. Faced with the outbreak of import protectionism in the country and on Capitol Hill, the administration back-tracked—with the Plaza Agreement—on its international, macroeconomic position of benign neglect. The induced, and inevitable, realignment of the dollar was the safety valve that had to be opened.

Equally, the administration saw in the nascent export lobbies the opportunity to provide a political offset to the (import) protectionist lobbies. By nurturing them, and expanding trade through measures aimed at opening markets, the administration would take the political momentum away from the protectionists who would close markets.

In essence, the administration did this in two ways, one consonant with the tradition of multilateralism, the other not quite so. The former was to push

---

31. The permanent advantage exists only in the classroom model. In the real world, countless factors alter the relative fortunes of firms over time, of course. To go from a classroom demonstration of permanent and irreversible advantage to a policy prescription of protection is therefore to make a leap that is not sensible.

32. The scale argument was beautifully formalized in the Brander-Spencer framework by Paul Krugman, "Import Protection as Export Promotion," in *Monopolistic Competition and International Trade,* ed. Henryk Kierzkowski (Oxford, Oxford University Press, 1984).

33. See, in particular, Paul Krugman, ed., *Strategic Trade Policy and the New International Economics* (Cambridge, Mass.: MIT Press, 1986).

energetically for a new GATT round of multilateral negotiations (MTN) where barriers to trade in old and new sectors (agriculture and services) of *export* interest to the United States would be brought down. These efforts culminated in the current Uruguay Round negotiations. The other course was to embrace regionalism in the shape of the Free Trade Agreement with Canada, a dramatic and visible trade-expanding move and one that also, in its inclusion of agreements on services, was supposed to provide a spur to the Uruguay Round negotiations in its deliberations on a compact on trade in services.

IV: Arguments for Unilateral Concessions by Others

None of this necessarily suggests that the United States should pursue the objectives of opening foreign markets and establishing new disciplines by extracting these results as unilateral concessions by others. And yet this is certainly a key feature of the new Section 301, indeed possibly its central characteristic.

Now, the conventional approach to moving toward freer trade, as embodied in GATT for instance, is to trade concessions, fairly and squarely as best one can. While this approach is considered "mercantilist" by those who prefer unilateral trade liberalization by oneself, the pairing of mutual concessions has a fourfold advantage:

i) if I can get you to also liberalize while I liberalize myself, I gain twice over;

ii) if there are second-best macroeconomic considerations such as short-run balance of payments difficulties from trade liberalization, the mutuality of liberalization should generally diminish them;

iii) mutuality of concessions suggests fairness and makes adjustment to trade liberalization politically more acceptable by the domestic losers from the change; and

iv) foreign concessions to one's exporters creates new interests that can counterbalance the interests that oppose one's own trade liberalization.

But the current U.S. policy departs from such requited trade concessions to make demands for one-way concessions by others. Why?

Theoretically, one can think of two sets of reasons why this policy may have been adopted by the United States. They serve the U.S. interest and may therefore be described as *national welfare* reasons; they divide into two, one malign and the other benign.[34]

---

34. I subsequently consider the possibility that 301 is used aggressively, not for extracting

Malign Use of Power for National Interest

The malign national welfare reason is straightforward and, in fact, is one that every informed scholar of the theory of commercial policy teaches in the classroom. As long as trade is voluntary and left to market forces, we know that it will be a nonzero-sum game: it will benefit each party to the transaction. But while each gains from trade, we also teach that power can be used to extract greater gains from trade from the other party. Typically, the examples produced are those of Nazi Germany and Stalin's Soviet Union, not that of the U.S. Congress using American muscle to extract concessions from weaker partners.[35]

The use of power can, however, be argued very quickly to show that power may be used to force another country into making unilateral trade concessions and hence improving one's welfare. In jargon, the economist would say: power is used to improve one's terms of trade by reducing others' use of trade restrictions. This argument goes back to Adam Smith when he discusses (skeptically) the possible use of tariffs to pry open others' tariffs:

> The case in which it may sometimes be a matter of deliberation how far it is proper to continue the free importation of certain foreign goods, is, when some foreign nation restrains by high duties or prohibitions the importation of some of our manufactures into their country. Revenge in this case naturally dictates retaliation, and that we should impose the like duties and prohibitions upon the importation of some or all of their manufactures into ours. Nations accordingly seldom fail to retaliate in the manner.
>
> There may be good policy in retaliations of this kind, when there is a probability that they will procure the repeal of the high duties or prohibitions complained of. The recovery of a great foreign market will generally more than compensate the transitory inconvenience of paying dearer during a short time for some sorts of goods. To judge whether such retaliations are likely to produce such an effect, does not, perhaps, belong so much to the science of a legislator, whose deliberations ought to be governed by general principles which are always the same, as to the skill of that insidious and crafty animal, vulgarly called a stateman or politician, whose councils are directed by the momentary fluctuations of affairs. When there is no probability that any such repeal can be procured, it seems a bad method of compensating the injury done to certain

one-way concessions, but for altruistic reasons. This would serve the interests of the world trading regime and may therefore be described as a *cosmopolitan welfare* or altruistic reason.

35. The only "tolerated" use of muscle in economic discussions is the so-called optimal tariff argument that limits such extraction of gains to the use of one's monopoly power in trade.

classes of our people, to do another injury ourselves, not only to those classes, but to almost all the other classes of them.[36]

Needless to say, the malign use of economic power to force unilateral concessions from others would be welfare improving if these concessions are indeed so extracted. When the British debate at the end of the nineteenth century turned to examine this argument, one of the main objections was that no such power existed in British trade. The willingness to resort to tariff retaliation, contrary to GATT obligations (as discussed by Professor Hudec and others in this volume), and the size of the stake in the U.S. market for the targets of such a tactic, have changed this presumption for today's United States, however. That this malign, self-serving rationale motivates some to embrace Section 301's use of aggressive tactics to extract unilateral concessions from weaker trading partners is not in doubt. Again, the concessions made by countries such as South Korea to avoid Super 301 action on May 25, 1989, should have produced greater converts on Capitol Hill to the cynical view that this is Section 301's principal merit.

Benign Use of Power for National Interest: Illusory Unilateralism, Requited Concessions in Truth

But the United States, which generally prides itself on being fair-minded, is unlikely to embrace the naked use of power to serve its own narrow interests. A careful examination of the debate on 301 suggests, therefore, that a number of arguments produced by its proponents essentially say: the concessions sought by the United States appear unilateral but are, in fact, not so. The mutuality of concessions is in truth preserved. In fact, the securing of such mutuality is the objective of 301 actions, in the absence of which the United States would fail to get the benefits of mutual trade concessions from its trading partners. I consider below the many different such arguments, sorting them out from the confused litany that currently exists. As one may expect, many concern Japan while others are generic.

V: Assessing the Benign National-Interest Arguments for Unilateral Concessions by Others

In the emotionally charged debate underlying the passage of the 1988 trade act, and surrounding the exercise of Super 301 actions on May 25, 1989, and again on April 27, 1990 (against India, with Japan and Brazil exempted this

---

36. Adam Smith, *The Wealth of Nations* (1776), Cannan ed. (New York, Modern Library, 1937), 434–35.

time), a number of rationales have been advanced, justifying the demands for unrequited trade concessions, which I now proceed to differentiate and to scrutinize for their soundness. As one would expect, many are Japan-centered and, in my judgment, seriously flawed. But a few others are either focused on others or more general in scope and have some legitimacy, though not enough to justify serious transgressions of GATT law and procedures that are symmetric among nations and mindful of others' rights.

Japan-focused Arguments

Among the demands made for unrequited concessions from Japan, four seem to be dominant. These relate to the balance of payments, the sense that Japan is cheating in trade, the argument that Japan is different and exotic, and the divergence of ex-ante expectations and ex-post results in previous trading agreements. I will discuss each of these areas in detail.

Balance of Payments

Two arguments related to the payments situation can be distinguished:

i) Japan has an enormous surplus in her trade balance, therefore she should liberalize her trade barriers faster than others; and

ii) The United States has an enormous trade deficit, therefore it is appropriate to ask others, who do not have a similar affliction, to liberalize their trade unilaterally.

These arguments are related but still distinct.[37] The latter, however, serves as the stepping-stone to the former, which is a main driving force behind the pressures directed at Japan.

This contention is not convincing because changes in trade barriers will not generally procure the sustained improvements in trade deficits that are desired unless a differential impact on savings and investment levels in the desired direction can be plausibly argued. In the absence of such impacts, the long-run effect of reduced foreign trade barriers will generally be to increase the trade-to-GNP ratio at which the U.S. deficit will persist.[38]

---

37. Thus, Japan could be asked to reduce her trade barriers, because of the latter argument, even if she did not have a large surplus.

38. There are numerous ways in which one's trade regime can affect investment and savings, in principle. Empirical analysis of many countries' trade and payments policies also suggests many such possibilities, but it also shows that these effects can go in several different directions. Cf. Jagdish Bhagwati, *The Anatomy and Consequences of Exchange Control Regimes,*

But there is a further, systemic objection to the argument. Suppose that one wants to argue that freer world trade is a desirable goal, that it is (in the short run) easier for countries enjoying a large and persistent surplus to reduce trade barriers and that therefore such countries ought to make unilateral moves toward trade liberalization without matching, mutual, reciprocal liberalization by others. Then, one ought to work at GATT and the IMF to introduce such rules into the international institutions. Such a rule could, for instance, be built into the proposed revisions in the Articles (e.g., Article XVIII) of GATT that deal with balance-of-payments related provisions.[39] But to use this notion selectively against Japan and other targeted nations, through a unilateral exercise of muscle and without a corresponding assumption of similar obligation when one's own deficit will turn into a surplus (as it surely will), is to sanction the view that the big dog on the block can bark at the little dogs and also bite them, but the inability of the little ones even to bark back is fine. GATT properly assigns, instead, a symmetry of obligations and rights, establishing the rule of law rather than the law of the jungle.

Japan Is Cheating

There is the argument that Japan is cheating on the trade obligations that it assumed through the reductions of its trade barriers in the successive GATT Rounds in the postwar period. The traded cuts in Japan's trade barriers are not effective. Article XXIII, relating to impairment and nullification of obligations assumed by GATT members, is implicitly invoked.

Thus, Japan can be asked to liberalize unilaterally. This demand, however, is not really for unilateral trade concessions. It is a matter of returning to the true status quo, as defined by obligations assumed earlier as part of the negotiated, reciprocal exchange of trade concessions.

This argument invokes the image of the Japanese jackass refusing to move toward the carrot offered; when you look behind him, you see the samurai holding him by the tail. In short, one has to demonstrate that the effects of reduced trade barriers have been nullified and that this has been caused by governmental interventions targeted at securing such nullification.

The econometric studies aimed at the problem of whether Japan imports "too little," either in the aggregate or in manufactures, were motivated by this problem. For, if Japan is as open as it seems, why are its imports so low? In

---

NBER (Cambridge: Battinger & Co., 1978), chap. 6, which reviews the theoretical and empirical findings on the relationship of trade policy to domestic savings. Also see Clarida, "Trade Deficit," for other theoretical arguments.

39. The "scarce-currency" clause of the IMF is a useful precedent in this regard, although it has never been invoked.

particular, if Japan is significantly off the regression line on import shares, making it an outlier (in econometric jargon), then we can deduce that it is an out-and-out liar (in fulfilling its trade obligations).

There are serious problems however with this case against Japan. As a recent paper by Professors Hamada and Srinivasan argues, the econometric studies have been badly divided on the issue of Japan's import performance, but those that are better crafted and grounded in econometrically appropriate methodology do *not* support the view that it is unduly disappointing.[40]

Even if the econometrics had gone the other way, the results would not tell one that the hand of MITI was responsible for the results or the cause was, instead, a host of other factors, including buyer preferences and institutional features that are conventionally, and for good reasons, treated as part of a nation's "givens," subject to which gains from trade are to be achieved in open markets.

Japan Is Different

In fact, it is interesting that Japan bashing has now shifted increasingly away from the notion of the (malign) efficacy of the Japanese government's visible hand (invisible to us outside) as the culprit to the inefficacy of Adam Smith's invisible hand in this strange country as the source of trouble. Let me explain.

Economists take, for instance, one's tastes as one's own affair. Given your tastes and mine, each sovereign in this regard, we can still engage in profitable, voluntary exchange. Economists do not argue, quite properly, that you must change your tastes to suit my convenience.[41] That is the stuff of coercion and the politics of power. But that is precisely what some seem to want of Japan: for their consumers and producers to shift their tastes.

Thus, a *Newsweek* story typically reflected these sentiments when it reported on Japanese consumers:

---

40. These are by Edward Learner and Gary Saxonhouse. See T. N. Srinivasan and Koichi Hamada, "The U.S.-Japan Problem," paper presented to the Columbia conference on U.S. trade policy, September 8, 1989, mimeo. Surprisingly, the ACTPN Report ignores these studies and concentrates instead on findings, by Robert Lawrence of Brookings, that are favorable to their recommendations for managed trade with Japan.

41. Of course, economists familiar with ethics allow for metapreferences, i.e., preferences about preferences. If you are a racist, I certainly will not take a "value-free" position, allowing you free play. But, to imagine that the Japanese housewife's preference for Japanese goods falls into this class of metapreferences is to invite ridicule.

Again, if one recognizes that tastes can be partly endogenous due to advertising and other forms of diffusion of information, one might argue that Japanese housewives have less access to information about foreign goods than the U.S. housewife. But this would be implausible indeed for postwar Japan and for a period when U.S. cultural hegemony has been a source of worldwide concern.

[Japanese] consumers [do not] seem about to shed their bias against foreign goods. At one of INBIX's NIC stores recently, a 50-year-old salaryman looked at a C.D. player made in South Korea. The price was less than half of what he would pay anywhere else in Tokyo. He shrugged, then put it back. "No," he said. "I'm afraid it might break."[42]

The *Newsweek* reporters could have produced a more effective splash, or I should say backlash, in the United States by repeating instead the story (I hope apocryphal and born [like East European jokes] of the tensions produced by what is perceived as unfair Japan bashing) where a Tokyo housewife walks into a Ginza store looking for a camera. Shown high-quality cameras, she asks: "Don't you have something cheaper?" The answer: "No. But just walk down the block, at the corner you will find a shop selling shoddy American stuff."

But not all tastes, for or against imported goods, are "irrational" if you must depart from the economist's counsel to take them as given data. They can be grounded in reality more than is conceded by those who point accusing fingers. I recall writing, nearly three decades ago from New Delhi, to Harry Johnson on Indian stationery, complaining like V. S. Naipaul about the "craze for foreign." He came back with what could have a lesson for the U.S.-Japan debate: "If the quality of the paper you have written on is any indication, the craze seems quite sensible to me."

The question of buyer preferences among Japanese firms for one another's goods is an even more explosive issue. It has received support recently from Kreinin's study of sixty-two Japanese, European, and American subsidiaries in Australia, examining the comparative way they procure equipment from sources outside Australia.[43]

Again, the issue is not whether such preferences exist, but why. Surely, a large part of the buyer preference in Japanese businesses must relate to the value attached to customer relationships: an idea that is not merely sociological but is now incorporated systematically as a (possibly) rational form of profit-maximizing behavior in the modern theory of industrial organization. Even casual empiricism, based on one's exposure to American firms and products, whether autos or suits, shows that the philosophy underlying the American approach to consumers is caveat emptor. Dissatisfied or, worse, duped consumers must take recourse to litigation, aided by the largest legal establishment in the world; they are also supposed to vote with their feet where repeat buying is involved.

---

42. *Newsweek,* February 13, 1989, 50.

43. Mordechai E. Kreinin, "How Closed is Japan's Market? Additional Evidence," *World Economy* 12 (1989): 529–42.

The Japanese way is evidently different. Their legal establishment is also correspondingly of a piece, small and lean, not large and mean. Consumer loyalty follows. It then becomes hard for American-style competitors to lure customers away by simply offering price discounts that carry no assurance of follow-through and commitment to consumer satisfaction. Large enough discounts could overcome this problem: everything has its price. But complaints of collusive Japanese preferences for their own fill the air when reasonable discounts lead to a failure to find Japanese customers. It is not surprising that U.S. firms that have made the necessary effort to adapt to Japanese ways have done well and are not among the vociferous complaints against "autarkic" Japanese corporate buying preferences.

The buying preferences of Japanese consumers and firms are therefore not grounds for demanding unilateral trade concessions from Japan. The appropriate attitude to the question of different Japanese preferences seems to be conveyed by Paul Samuelson. He tells of encountering a charming old lady at a public lecture on trade policy in Boston. She came up to him and said: "Professor Samuelson, I *would* like to help by buying American, but the Japanese goods are so much better; am I wrong in buying them instead?" Samuelson's answer: "Madam, you should buy what you like; leave it to us economists and the Congress to take care of the balance of payments."

But what then about the question of *access* to these buyers, no matter what their preferences? The Japanese retail distribution system, with its 1.6 million mom-and-pop style stores dotting the country and protected against large stores (recently, even by the Large-scale Retail Store Law passed in the Diet), militates against the distribution of foreign goods.[44]

Nonetheless, it is noteworthy that, faced with strident demands from the United States, the Japanese government has, uniquely among trading nations, recently instituted an import subsidy in the shape of tax credits for imported inputs. It has even forced universities and research institutes to spend grants on foreign equipment and books, not necessarily in conformity with their preferences and perceived interests.

This question is tricky; it needs careful handling at the level of general principles rather than immediate expediency. In particular, we need to ask here (and indeed similarly for other institutional issues) the following questions:

(*a*) are these institutions designed to discriminate in favor of domestic goods and against foreign rivals;

---

44. See, for instance, Paul Blustein, "Finding a Retirement Home for Japan's 'Papa-Mama' Stores," *Washington Post National Weekly,* August 21–27, 1989, 19. However, there is disagreement over how restrictive the Japanese retail distribution system really is.

(*b*) if their unintended fallout is to directly affect trade, can we think of next-best ways in which such effects can be minimized; and

(*c*) in seeking such relief, can we think not just of others accommodating to our needs but of establishing general disciplines and neutral procedures to adjudicate disputes relating thereto, to which we subject ourselves as much as we seek to subject others?

In the case of the Japanese distribution system, the answer to question (*a*) is surely no. The answer to question (*b*) is that it does inhibit, though does not prevent, access for firms that prefer marketing products through large outlets, but that these firms could adapt their sales techniques to include such strategies as mail-order sales, which have begun and offer a possible way out. As for question (*c*), if national distribution systems are to be considered legitimate grounds for foreign scrutiny, the United States should propose procedures under which it becomes possible for other trading nations generally to challenge its own distribution institutions and methods as well.[45] An advantage of such general procedures, applied symmetrically, is that they would also slow down the one-way demands for others to "reform" that are otherwise readily generated by lobbies in the United States. The argument by the administration that one's excesses can come home to roost has traditionally helped to contain such excesses; there is no reason to expect that it would not help in this area too.

It is necessary to observe also that the path down which the United States has gone in its negotiations with Japan under the rubric of Structural Impediments Initiative (SII), where matters such as Japan's retail distribution system and even her "high" savings rate have been discussed as obstacles to trade, is the path of folly. As of the date of completion of this essay, the Japanese have agreed to a number of concessions, among them the promise of action on the Large-scale Retail Store Law, as a result of which they managed to escape being renamed an unfair trader on April 27, 1990. Once one starts bringing into the trade arena issues such as savings rates, one is essentially arguing that everything affects trade, that policy (or absence thereof) on virtually everything will affect trade, and therefore every policy can be put on the line in discussing what is "fair trade" and, hence, a prerequisite for legitimate free trade.

Thus, if Bangladesh has current comparative advantage in textiles, due to

---

45. For example, some nations, and economists, believe that retail price maintenance is a good thing (for reasons such as that consumers do not have to shop around). For foreign firms used to the "orderly" distribution system that also attends such retail price maintenance, the U.S. distribution system may appear too chaotic and difficult to adapt to. Again, within the EC, the retail distribution systems of member countries exhibit substantial variations, reflecting different cultural, historical, and economic factors.

lower wages, we no longer need to worry about being scolded as protectionists when we reject imports of Bangladeshi textiles as unfair trade caused
by her "pauper labor." After all, the low Bangladeshi wages are a result of
inadequate population control policies and of inefficient economic policies
that inhibit investment and growth and, hence, a rise in real wages. Or, if the
United States continues to produce textiles that rely heavily on immigrant
labor, often illegal, this is unfair trade, since American immigration policy
permits this outcome, and therefore a Structural Impediments Initiative demand for changed immigration policy needs to be made against the United
States simply to ensure level playing fields.

In going down this unwise trade route, the American trade policymakers
put the world trading system at great risk. For, if *everything* becomes a
question of fair trade, the only outcome will be to remove, altogether, the
possibility of ever agreeing to a rule-oriented trading system. "Managed
trade" will then be the outcome, with bureaucrats allocating trade according
to what domestic lobbying pressures and foreign political muscle dictate.
Unfortunately, this danger is not seen by many in the United States who fail to
look, in the current psychology attending the diminished giant syndrome, at
the long-run and systemic implications of what they propose as short-term
policy options for the United States.

Divergence Between Ex-Ante and Ex-Post Outcomes

Yet another reason for making demands for unilateral trade concessions by
others can be detected, based on the notions of Japan's anti–foreign goods
biases, "natural" and institutional, that I just discussed but uses them in an
altogether different way.

The argument is that when Japanese cuts in trade barriers were accepted
during the earlier GATT Rounds as "equivalent," "matching," or "balanced"
relative to the U.S. trade barrier reductions the U.S. negotiators overesti-
mated the extent to which, given Japan's buying preferences and institutions,
Japanese imports would rise. But, as we now know, these forces are of such
importance that what Japan gave is way below what America gave. The ex-
post realities show that the trade in concessions was unbalanced, giving
America, therefore, the moral, perhaps even legal, right to reopen the issue
and ask for unilateral concessions from Japan.

This notion that "first difference" reciprocity be negotiated (inevitably)
on ex-ante perceptions of mutual advantages while it can be renegotiated on
the basis of ex-post outcomes is certainly present in some of the sentiments for
unilateralism in U.S. demands for others to move toward new trade concessions without reciprocal concessions by the United States. Let me quote from

Edmund Dell, Secretary of State for Trade in the British Government in 1976–78, who writes cogently on the subject:

> There has been a feeling in the United States that in many cases, whatever the intention or skill of American negotiators, reciprocity has not been achieved. Some of its trading partners have been found to have had the better of the bargain. This is particularly seen to be the case in the trade relations of the United States with Japan . . . Robert Dole, now majority leader in the United States Senate, [has argued] that "reciprocity should be assessed not by what agreements promise but by actual results—by changes in the balance of trade and investment between ourselves and our major economic partners." There is pressure, therefore, to the effect that the United States should withdraw something of what it has conceded—especially, although not entirely, in its relations with Japan.[46]

Or, more importantly, the sentiment and the pressure translate into unilateral demands for unmatched concessions by Japan in particular. There are several things to be said about this sentiment, however.

In terms of GATT laws, is the "reopening" of negotiated barrier reductions in this fashion permissible? Article XXIII relates to impairment and nullification of negotiated GATT obligations. But whether this would extend to alleged ex-post outcomes that depart from expected outcomes is highly dubious. There certainly do not seem to be any precedents in the existing adjudications under Article XXIII that would provide ammunition to the General Counsel to the U.S. Trade Representative, should he take the matter up for an authoritative ruling on the subject.

The reopening of contractual commitments is generally considered destructive of orderly trade and intercourse, with exceptions permitted only when the contract was signed under duress or when the doctrine of "intervening impossibility" can be evoked: both exemptions usually requiring a heavy burden of proof by those who seek relief. If the United States were to argue for nullification of its trade obligations toward Japan, it seems improbable that it could win on either of these two grounds.

Moreover, just imagine what would happen to the trading system if ex-post outcomes, themselves reflecting a host of factors that cannot possibly be isolated and quantified persuasively, were to be used to renege on trade concessions or to demand more from others after deals had been struck at

46. Edmund Dell, "Of Free Trade and Reciprocity," *World Economy* 9, no. 2 (June, 1986): 134.

trade negotiations. The Japan-specific arguments for unrequited concessions are not therefore particularly compelling. But there are others that are not Japan-specific.

Imbalance from Shift in Comparative Advantage

A generic argument for unrequited concessions by others that comes close to the one depending on ex-post realities diverging from ex-ante expectations can be traced to the feeling that shifts in comparative advantage have created an imbalance of mutual advantages from earlier trade concessions.

Thus, the U.S. policymakers, persuaded by lobbies and by independent evidence, feel that the comparative U.S. advantage has shifted in favor of agriculture and services. But these are precisely the sectors that are currently subjected to high trade barriers and even failure of GATT discipline.[47] In consequence, the same structure of trade barriers now produces, in the U.S. view, a lower average barrier in U.S. markets for others than for the United States in the markets of others. Therefore, while the initial reductions of barriers were balanced, they cannot be regarded as such anymore. The United States considers itself therefore justified in asking for changes in trade barriers in these sectors simply to restore the balance of negotiated advantages. While, of course, the United States is willing to have mutual reductions in trade barriers in these new sectors, the fact that they are of principal (export) benefit to the United States means that they amount to an unbalanced trade concession going its way.

The problems with this argument are similar to those raised by such "reopening" of contractual obligations that I considered in regard to the similar argument vis-à-vis Japan.

Moreover, it is not clear at all that the United States has had, ex post, the worse bargain in the concessions on trade in manufactures that the GATT Rounds progressively liberalized.[48] As argued next, Americans cannot fairly maintain that they have given away more than others or that they are today significantly more open than their major trading partners. It is more likely, instead, that the shifting comparative advantage argument was used to promote export lobbies, as discussed earlier, to combat import protectionist lobbies and has come to be an article of faith and a cause for militancy by, and on behalf of, these export lobbies.

---

47. Ironically, the original 1955 waiver granted to agriculture by GATT was to the United States. Equally ironic, the question of trade in services was first raised internationally in UNCTAD rather than in GATT.

48. Developing countries are an exception and are addressed separately below.

I Am More Open Than Thou

There is then the related argument for unrequited concessions by others that rests on the firm belief, in many quarters, that the United States is more open than other developed countries. Combined with another belief that the United States was altruistic in trade policy earlier but, in its age of relative decline, must rejoin the human race and "look after its own interests," this fuels demands for unilateral trade concessions by others.

But the evidence on U.S. trade barriers, especially after the proliferation of high-track as well as low-track protection in the 1980s, certainly does not provide support to the view that it is now significantly more open than other OECD countries.[49]

This is hard to believe since the United States, formed by immigration, is far more open in its cultural attitudes and willingness to experiment with foreign ideas, influences, and goods than most other countries, most of all Japan. But culture does not necessarily translate into corresponding trade policy. The latter reflects equally the play of politics and economic forces. There is in consequence nothing inconsistent, though much that is incongruous, about a culturally open society having access to its markets as restricted by trade policy as a country (such as Japan) which is more inward looking in its citizens' attitudes.

Again, the culturalists find it difficult to believe that protectionism can coexist with a deficit in the balance of trade. Thus, James Fallows has recently written: "Japan and Korean politicians now complain about American 'protectionism,' but how protectionist can a country with a $10 billion monthly trade deficit really be?"[50] Fallows, who is arguably one of the more perceptive of the American journalists today, is unfortunately remiss here: any given degree of protectionism is compatible with any level of trade surplus or deficit.

Perhaps the only countervailing argument in support of the presumption that the United States is more open is that she is most open in regard to receiving foreign investment and that this can give foreign suppliers, in some cases, more effective access to the U.S. market.[51] This asymmetry certainly

---

49. A review of forty U.S. measures that impede EC exports was released, for instance, in May, 1989 by the EC. See *EC News,* no. 13/89 (Washington, D.C.: EC Office of Press and Public Affairs, 1989). The IBRD-UNCTAD index of nontariff barriers also suggests the same conclusion, though the index has well-known conceptual problems.

50. James Fallows, "Containing Japan," *Atlantic Monthly,* May, 1989. In his earlier book, *More Like Us* (Boston: Houghton Mifflin, 1987), Fallows takes the position that the U.S. response to the Japanese challenge should be to improve and strengthen its own institutions along lines more consonant with its flexible and open traditions.

51. This argument has been made by Isaiah Frank.

applies to Japan, and is an argument for pressing Japan for greater mutuality of openness in the matter of foreign investment.

As for the view that the U.S. acted altruistically in trade, that is, as a unilateral free trader of sorts during the postwar period, this too can be exaggerated. It is useful to remember that, unlike Britain through most of the nineteenth century, the United States has never been a unilateral free trader, generally insisting instead on reciprocity in trade concessions. Indeed, this can be seen in the title of the post-Smoot-Hawley-tariff Reciprocal Trade Agreements Act of 1934 and by the later contractarian conception of GATT. Do not forget, either, that the first agricultural waiver from GATT discipline in 1955 was secured by the United States, effectively leading to the chaotic situation in agriculture today. The United States was also among the earliest nations to start restricting textile imports, initiating the descent down the road to the Multi Fibre Arrangement (MFA) that restricts and regulates trade in textiles today. Most important, empirical analysis of even the earliest postwar GATT Rounds of tariff cuts does not support the view that the United States gave significantly more than it took. Altruism is simply hard to practice in the trade area because of constituency pressures.

These matters need to be remembered, not to deny the justly celebrated American leadership (as distinct from altruism) on trade policy and its role in sustaining the concerted reduction of tariff barriers under GATT auspices, but simply to prevent exaggerated notions of past altruism leading to current policies of system-destroying selfishness.

It is perhaps worth remarking that the theme of greater U.S. openness can be used selectively and has not deterred similar pressures being exercised against countries for trade concessions even when they are unambiguously more open than the United States. While greater U.S. openness vis-à-vis Japan is open to doubt, Hong Kong's greater openness vis-à-vis the United States is not. In fact, Hong Kong, aside from nineteenth-century Britain, is a textbook example of (substantially) free trade. Yet U.S. high-handedness in dealing with its legal service sector was a matter of public dispute in early 1989 as the legal profession of Hong Kong was threatened by punitive tariff retaliation for the colony, unless it opened up Hong Kong to American lawyers.[52] In short, the assumed greater openness of the United States has served as a way of demanding unilateral trade concessions from others, used where it can be made without obvious implausibility and discarded when it plays the wrong way.

---

52. See the report in *South China Morning Post,* Hong Kong, February 21, 1989. In particular: "There was clear evidence of threats of retaliation by American law firms that Hong Kong would suffer trade restrictions unless the Government allowed foreign lawyers entry."

Coming of Age

The final, and the most plausible, argument for demands for unilateral concessions applies, not to Japan or other developed countries, but to other countries
of the Far East (and potentially to other newly industrialized countries that are
successful exporters). It is that they had a free lunch so far, having been given
Special and Differential Treatment by GATT, thanks to which they could use
tariffs and other trade barriers but profited from the general reductions in trade
barriers of the developed countries in the postwar period because of unconditional MFN. In terms of "first-difference" reciprocity, these countries secured
unbalanced trade concessions in their favor, making overall access to their
markets significantly less than their access to the markets of the developed
countries. For those countries, such as South Korea and Taiwan which have
come of age in terms of both exports and per capita incomes, this "affirmative
action" is no longer justified. They must now assume their full obligations as
GATT members, as the developed countries do. This means, of course, that
they must unilaterally lower trade barriers or, what is the same thing, provide
greater concessions in future negotiations than they get.

Within the logic of reciprocity, this argument is well taken. Special and
differential treatment for the developing countries was never granted by other
GATT members as a permanent "benefit," simply because GATT is premised
on the assumption of symmetric rights and obligations and on first-difference
reciprocity as a method of negotiation to reduce barriers, and therefore any
exemption from the symmetric obligations has to be legitimated. For developing countries, this legitimacy was provided by infant-industry and balance-of-
payments arguments (as reflected in Article XVIII(b), especially).

But the developmental status of some developing countries has changed
and the theoretical support for exempting any of them from the obligations of
open market access on grounds such as balance-of-payments has also
waned.[53] On both grounds, the coming of age argument for asking unilateral
concessions from South Korea and Taiwan has acquired cogency.

---

53. On these questions, see the splendid analysis by Martin Wolf, "Differential and More
Favorable Treatment of Developing Countries and the International Trading System," and
Shailendra Anjaria, "Balance of Payments and Related Issues in the Uruguay Round of Trade
Negotiations," *World Bank Economic Review* 1, no. 4 (September, 1987). This issue contains a
Symposium on *The MTN and Developing Country Interests*. Also see the excellent articles by
Isaiah Frank, "Import Quotas, the Balance of Payments, and the GATT," *World Economy* 10, no.
3 (September, 1987): 307–18; and Richard Eglin, "Surveillance of Balance-of-Payments Mea-
sures in the GATT," *World Economy* 10, no. 1 (March, 1987): 1–26.

VI. Appropriateness of 301 Framework to Malign and Benign National Welfare–Improving Objectives

It is worth remarking, before I move to consider the altruistic set of considerations possibly underlying 301 actions in section VII, that demands for one-way concessions made it inevitable that U.S. trade policy would move in the direction of 301 and Super 301 with the 1988 trade act. For such one-way demands cannot be satisfied with the conventional techniques and within the framework of GATT. There, trade concessions can be achieved only by offering one's own. By contrast, unilateral concessions must be extracted not by gentle negotiations, but by threat.

Moreover, export interests evidently are at a disadvantage in the GATT framework where trade concessions by others are available on a non-discriminatory basis to all GATT members and, hence, give one no privileged access in the new markets, whereas trade concessions can be captured to one's preferential advantage through voluntary import expansions (VIEs) and trade diversion toward themselves when the concessions are obtained instead in a one-to-one bilateral framework.[54] Section 301, originally enacted in 1974 but suitably endowed with sharper claws in the 1988 act, was evidently a policy instrument that would serve these ends, amounting therefore to what can be described fairly as "export protectionism." The fact that, thanks to economists' efforts at education, the USTR now is explicit in saying that it will call for nondiscriminatory trade concessions under 301 procedures does not invalidate the argument as to why 301 came to acquire its appeal at the outset. Nor does it assuage the worry that, despite the USTR's present policy, the 301 actions will result in VIEs and trade diversion rather than in trade creation, as discussed below.

VII. Altruistic Rationales

The preceding analysis concentrated on the many self-serving rationales for the aggressive unilateralism of recent 301-centered U.S. trade policy. But to leave the matter there would be incomplete.

The use of aggressive tactics in trade policy has also been prompted by assertions that altruistic, rather than self-serving, objectives animate the United States. They relate primarily to the notion that, to save multilateralism,

---

54. The concept of VIEs where the importing countries are asked to increase imports of specific items from particular countries by given amounts is the counterpart of the familiar concept of voluntary export restrictions (VERs) where exports by these countries are restrained. The concept and terminology of VIEs were introduced in Jagdish Bhagwati, "VERs, Quid Pro Quo DFI and VIEs: Political-Economy-Theoretic Analyses," *International Economic Journal* 1, no. 1: 1–12, and are further discussed in Bhagwati, *Protectionism*, 82–84.

one had to depart from it through the use of unilateral threats and even actions that would violate the multilateral obligations defined by GATT. GATT had to be revitalized, and quickly, and the world had to be moved through threats towards this goal.

Managing Domestic Panic

One argument has been that *some* form of aggression had become inevitable in getting other trading nations to accept quickly new rules and disciplines in areas of interest to the United States or else the U.S. commitment to multi-lateralism would erode rapidly in domestic politics and GATT would die.

The U.S. administration certainly faced a sense of crisis in the country, with panic over the trade deficit and petulance resulting from the diminished giant syndrome. Urgency was the order of the day. Evidently, the administration appears to have acted as though, even if the many arguments for extracting something for nothing in trade were seen to be mostly illegitimate, the impatience for quick results on the trade front would have imperiled the commitment to multilateralism in GATT. For, given the indisputable (even if diminished) strength of the United States and a new willingness to wield a crowbar and thus use its muscle, it could certainly go *faster,* even in getting others to make balanced and mutual (rather than unilateral) concessions in matters that she considered essential to her trade interests, if she used one-to-one techniques. In place of GATT, sometimes (naively) denounced as the General Agreement to Talk and Talk, the 301 procedures could guarantee the quicker attention and response that was considered urgently necessary.

The argument is altruistic in the sense that the opting out of multi-lateralism by the United States, still the major player in the world economy, would surely imperil GATT. But it does raise two issues:

i) is the panic that fuels such aggressive threats designed to yield results at the pace set unilaterally by the United States really justified; and

ii) should the U.S. administration not have tried more actively to contain it instead of yielding to it, especially since the threatened tariff retaliations, if implemented, are GATT-illegal and therefore have undesirable consequences?

On the former issue, it is clear that the panic leading to impatience and aggression is grossly exaggerated. The payments deficit has little demonstrated relationship to results in trade policy. It is a non sequitur to translate the urgency of the deficit into an urgency of getting results on trade policy. Nor can it be seriously maintained that U.S. economic (or, more narrowly, industrial) survival is at stake or that, if it is, it is due to unfair competition from abroad and can therefore be addressed only meaningfully by fixing the multi-lateral world trading regime per the U.S. agenda and timetable. On the latter issue, the mismanagement of the lobbying by the Reagan administration to defeat the passage of the 1988 trade act certainly can be faulted.

Getting the Uruguay Round Going

A somewhat different altruistic rationale proceeds by maintaining that Section 301–type unilateralism was necessary to get the Uruguay Round going, without which the desirable reorganization of GATT would fail to materialize. Admittedly, the EC's refusal to launch multilateral trade negotiations, as desired by the United States, at the November, 1982, GATT meetings was a major blow to U.S. efforts to get new disciplines negotiated multilaterally. But three factors other than the new 301 provisions (enacted in 1988, less than two years after the Uruguay Round was launched) were responsible for the EC turning around: (1) there was growing realization by the EC, not present in 1982, that new issues such as services, TRIMs, and TRIPs would benefit them as well as the United States, so that they had much to gain from a new Round as well;[55] (2) the U.S.-Canada FTA suggested that the United States would embrace regionalism more extensively as a substitute for GATT-wide multi-lateralism, also extending this approach to new issues, if the other trading nations did not agree to a new Round; and (3) the mood in Congress, as often before earlier Rounds, was protectionist and ugly enough to make it seem necessary for other nations to begin multilateral trade negotiations (MTN) negotiations to enable the U.S. administration to resist these protectionist pressures.[56] There is very little to suggest that deploying the 301 weapon was necessary or instrumental in any degree in getting the Uruguay Round going.

Bringing the Uruguay Round
to a Successful Conclusion

The exercise of Super 301 against Brazil and India on May 25, 1989, was among the actions that were designed, it seems, to put pressure on those countries not to obstruct agreement at the Uruguay Round on services, TRIMs, TRIPs, and other issues. Since these countries raised objections to the inclusion of several of these new areas and disciplines in GATT, and their "rejectionist" attitude could jeopardize the successful conclusion of the Uru-

---

55. TRIMs are trade-related investment measures and TRIPs are trade-related intellectual property issues, both acronyms happily suggesting good health and gratification to the harried negotiators at the Uruguay Round.

56. The Jenkins bill on textiles was defeated. But the launching of the Uruguay Round did not work to stop the passage of the 1988 trade act.

guay Round, the calculation may have been made to use Super 301 to deliver a firm and clear message to them to fold.

Whether, however, targeting these countries would make them more, rather than less, recalcitrant by compounding their sense of unfair U.S. play in trade negotiations remains to be seen. Brazil, with the dramatic shift in its policies to the right since the last presidential election, is not at issue any more. But India is another matter altogether.

Administration versus Congress

That Congress viewed the 1988 act's strengthening of the 301 provisions as a form of aggressive unilateralism, extracting one-way concessions from abroad that would serve U.S. trading and economic interests, is a hypothesis that is pretty well in conformity with the debate in Congress on the passage of that legislation.

That, however, the administration has instead tried to dilute this central motivation and rationale of the legislation somewhat by trying to name countries and practices where it also sees a need for movement in the rules and disciplines in the world trading regime at GATT, is also a reasonable hypothesis that explains why a country such as India, and a practice such as its export performance requirements on foreign investors, were targeted: they do not add up, as several critics on Capitol Hill have not failed to complain, to a hill of beans as far as U.S. exports are concerned.

Nonetheless, the use of Super 301 and Special 301 provisions represents, overall, a forceful use of U.S. power with a view to obtaining foreign trade concessions, often one-way and unrequited, and always on a U.S. time schedule. What *is* wrong with this?

VII. The Folly of Aggressive Unilateralism

The Question of GATT-Illegality

At the outset, it must be understood that, contrary to the impression of even well-informed commentators, the lack of formal ratification of GATT by the U.S. Senate does not mean that GATT does not have the force of a treaty for the United States. It does.[57]

The attitude that GATT can be disregarded ("Who cares about GATT?") because "we never ratified it" is therefore simply wrong. The GATT-illegality of any contemplated action is no minor matter.

---

57. This was demonstrated in John Jackson, "The General Agreement on Tariffs and Trade in the United States Domestic Law," *Michigan Law Review* 66 (December, 1967): 249–332.

Now, if the United States retaliates, as it did in earlier 301 actions and as it might as a consequence of present Super 301 actions, with its typical 100 percent ad valorem tariff applied selectively to the goods of the targeted country, the GATT-illegality is at several levels. As Professor Hudec notes, the discriminatory nature of such tariffs violates Article I, which imposes the MFN obligation.[58] Also, since the tariff is likely to be bound at a lower level in practice, the 100 percent punitive tariff will generally be in violation of Article II as well. Of course, the GATT-illegality of the retaliation can be avoided by invoking GATT-unrelated measures. Against Japan, for instance, these could include expulsion of the Japanese counsul for trade or dispatching a Delta Force of our best known Japan bashers to land on a Japanese freighter carrying their despised semiconductors and dumping them overboard to "send a clear message" of our resolve. Congress, however, seems to prefer the retaliatory option of closing our markets for goods, choosing GATT-illegality as the technique of choice, underlining perhaps its contempt for multilateralism and its obligations for presumably having served American interests so poorly.

Why GATT-Illegality Matters

Why does GATT-illegality matter? Prima facie, honoring a treaty commitment is to reaffirm one's respect for orderly procedures and the rule of law in dealing with other nation states.

But does *vigilantism* have a place when the sheriff is asleep in the saloon? Or, to rise to a higher principle, is there not a case for "justified disobedience," as Professor Hudec puts it, when the law is not working as it should? In either case, a doctrine of "creative illegality" is being invoked: a breach of law to improve the law is being claimed.

The problem with this defense of GATT-illegality by the United States (to improve an ineffective GATT) is that almost no one else in the trading system quite accepts this justification. Indeed, as Professor Hudec notes, the United States's own record of acting within the rules to respect others' GATT-defined rights has not been exemplary.[59] Nor does the 1988 legislation on 301 provisions accept the principle of symmetric rights. That is, Congress does not propose that others have, in defining (say) unfair trade practices, the same rights vis-à-vis the United States that the United States now arrogates to itself. In short, the justified-disobedience justification for 301 actions to strengthen GATT discipline wears thin since there is no fairness toward others, but

---

58. Hudec, chap. 4, n. 7.
59. See Hudec, chap. 4, appendix 2, on U.S. performance in GATT dispute settlement.

indulgence toward oneself, in the act of disobedience. To quote Professor Hudec:

> (1) There is a plausible case for some degree of justified disobedience here—for some pressure to overcome the inertia toward needed reforms of the GATT system.
>
> (2) The new Section 301 procedures, however, direct the United States to employ disobedience for excessive objectives that cannot be justified, objectives that reflect an even more one-sided view of who must do the reforming.[60]

There is also the problem that means may affect ends. Can the United States seriously maintain that a declared willingness to break GATT commitments, and even the actual breach thereof, cannot spread cynicism toward such commitments by others rather than adherence to them in the future? Also, at another level, there is a possible danger that the professions of U.S. commitment to multilateralism may sound hollow, even hypocritical, and therefore may lack credibility and thus undermine efforts to make the Uruguay Round successful because the United States simultaneously practices aggressive unilateralism.

Trade Diversion

Let me now turn to other dangers inherent in this form of unilateral extraction of trade concessions from others. In particular, since it reflects clout and concentrated pressure from the United States, there is a strong likelihood that the targets of the 301 actions will satisfy American demands by diverting trade from other countries (with less political clout) to the United States, satisfying the strong at the expense of the weak.[61] America seeks to open markets efficiently this way, but in practice she is likely to divert trade. While this serves the interests of the United States and her exporters, it replaces economic efficiency with political clout as the determinant of exports in the world trading system.

Admittedly, the USTR has come to recognize this danger: Ambassador Carla Hills now repeatedly stresses that she will ensure that markets are opened under 301 in a nondiscriminatory fashion. But ex-ante intentions can

---

60. Hudec, chap. 4.

61. For a story on how South Korea planned to do precisely this with its agricultural imports, see *Financial Times*, April 27, 1987. Also see Bhagwati, *Protectionism*, 82–84, for an analysis of this issue; and Rahul Jacob in *Fortune*, February 27, 1989, 88–89, recording these same concerns.

diverge from ex-post outcomes. The lobbies in the United States that drive the USTR do not really care whether markets open generally; their objective is to secure market access for themselves, and their general thrust is to judge openness in terms of their own success. Equally, the countries targeted for action know that the U.S. pressures are therefore more likely to ease if the United States gets a good share than if it does not. The game is set up, therefore, in terms of implicit pro–trade diversion bias rules that all parties recognize as political realities.

Atmospherics

There is also the distinct possibility that the use of muscle to impose one's own views and to extract one-way trade concessions will poison the ethos of fairness in trade relations without which open markets are hard to sustain.[62] A bully can have his way for a while; but he replaces the rule of law by the law of the jungle and reigns, not by consent but by force, and therefore undermines the long-term sustainability of the regime.

As 301 and Super 301 actions are undertaken, unilaterally accusing others of unfair trade practices and demanding their removal, the notion is also reinforced that others are unfair traders, creating a poisoned atmosphere that conventional protectionists can hope to exploit to their own advantage.

A Benign Dictator?

Even if one makes the implausible assumption that 301 is used only for the "altruistic" reasons discussed above, the notion that the United States should serve as a benign dictator, laying down its own definition of a desirable trading regime instead of making (admittedly slower) progress by persuasion and mutual concessions, is frankly an unacceptable one.

The world trading regime should not be built on the assumption that any one player, no matter how dominant, can impose its own rules, unilaterally claiming social legitimacy for them. Institutions cannot be built on notions of benign dictatorship: a lesson the functioning democracy in the United States itself, with all of its slowness and "inefficiencies" that practitioners of realpolitik complain of, amply teaches all of us.

Aside from the fact that dictators will often turn malign, we must confront the fact that trade policy is rarely made in pluralistic democracies by dictators with monolithic objective functions. Instead, it reflects the resolution

---

62. This is manifest from the discussion of the Korean, EC, and Japanese contributions in chaps. 7, 8, and 10.

of sectional interests in the political domain.[63] There is no necessary corre-spondence, therefore, between the triumphant sectoral interests and the na-tional interest and, most important, the international or cosmopolitan interest that must define the world trading regime.[64] It is important therefore to reject the view that even a fair-minded country such as the United States should be permitted to play the roles of a self-appointed "trade cop" and "trade czar."

IX. What Next?

If aggressive unilateralism has no place in a world trading regime reflecting the rule of law and a necessary symmetry of rights and obligations, as GATT fundamentally reflects, how is one to cope with 301?

It will not be repealed by the U.S. Congress: Congress is the problem, not the solution. With the legislation on the books, it can only be restrained, not removed, by the administration as it confronts one 301-mandated deadline after another.

My suggestion is that, since the threatened tariff retaliation is certainly GATT-illegal, and since the threat must be credible for it to work, the best way to defang this monster is to take the United States to the GATT dispute settlement mechanism when a 301 retaliation is undertaken for an "unreason-able" practice and to have such retaliation formally declared GATT-illegal. It is unlikely that the U.S. administration would then explicitly embrace legally determined illegality by failing to exercise the legislated presidential discre-tion to not invoke retaliation. This would then virtually destroy the force of 301 actions.[65]

The problem with this prescription, however, is to find targeted plaintiffs who would do what is necessary. For instance, the Japanese have traditionally failed to think about trade matters in a systemic fashion, bringing a trader's mentality to trade issues rather than that of system builders: the trader strikes deals, settles issues, and accepts the system and works within it. In negotiat-ing its way out of renewed naming as an unfair trader in April, 1990, and in

---

63. See John McMillan's excellent analysis of such political economy considerations in chap. 6.

64. This simple truth is manifest as soon as one takes a clear look at the Uruguay Round positions of the United States on TRIMs and TRIPs, for instance. They reflect dominant corporate interests, important on the U.S. political scene, but are not necessarily consonant with the tenets of economic science in regard to issues such as patents. Surely broader principles, rather than the self-serving arguments of the corporate interests, should determine the socially efficient rules.

65. Jagdish Bhagwati, "Super 301's Big Bite Flouts the Rules," *New York Times*, June 4, 1989, and "Taking the Teeth out of Super 301," in *World Link*, no. 7/8 (July-August, 1989): 7.

failing to pursue a strong anti-301 case on semiconductors against the United States in GATT, Japan can be argued to have played true to form and against the interests of the trading regime. The spunk displayed by the EC on the hormone-fed-beef 301 case, where the EC has persisted with attempts to bring the matter before a GATT panel despite continued U.S. blockage thereof, and in effectively counterthreatening the United States so as to succeed in escaping targeting in the 1989 and 1990 Super 301 actions, suggests on the other hand that the EC is perfectly capable of challenging the United States on the legality of 301 retaliations. But, for that very reason, the United States handles the EC with kid gloves and lets it off the hook.

The minor players, therefore, will succumb; the major players will be spared. The problem with my method to defang 301 is then simple: it may be extremely hard to find nations who will take the offending party to court.[66] If those who worry about the world trading regime also had a locus standi to have 301 adjudicated in GATT, life would be simpler. But they do not.

A similar problem afflicts Professor Hudec's excellent alternate proposal that others do unto the United States what she does unto them through Super 301. He is absolutely right: nothing works as well as "role reversal" to shake one up. The problem is that few have the clout or the gumption to indulge in tit-for-tat against a superpower that is in the grip of the diminished giant syndrome; and the EC, which does have the gumption and the clout, is studiously not the target in Super 301 actions, no matter how protectionist, "obstructionist," or "cussed" it may be in trade matters.

It is difficult, therefore, to foresee how, and when, this instrument will finally be reined in. Evidently, some combination of the proposals advanced by me and by Professor Hudec will have to be deployed. Until they are, we will have to rely on the good sense of the U.S. administration to refrain from the use of this pernicious policy instrument through presidential discretion, keeping in view the larger goals that characterized U.S. trade policy in the postwar period of her economic leadership.[67]

---

66. India, one of the targeted nations in the 1989 Super 301 action, has so far refused to negotiate, and was therefore renamed in April, 1990, and may still have retaliatory tariffs imposed on it eventually. It may well counterretaliate since it firmly rejects unilateral demands by the United States. But a better alternative would be to make this a test case before GATT, even though India does not have the clout of Japan or the EC.

67. I might add that none of what I have argued above means that 301 be altogether abolished, if possible. As Geza Feketekuty notes in chap. 2, something like it is necessary to enforce GATT-defined and other treaty-defined trade rights in the American political system. Also, something like 301 may now be necessary to enforce "fair trade," mutually agreed, in the other country's markets, i.e., for one's exports, just as we have "fair trade" mechanisms for one's imports. It may become inevitable also to worry about such fair trade rules, enforced or policed through some form of legislation like 301, in "third markets," though there are obvious dangers to this ballooning process.

Appendix. The Current Enforcement Authority
and Procedures: 301, Super 301 and Special 301

Chapter 1 of Title III of the Trade and Tariff Act of 1974, as amended, provides the
domestic counterpart to the GATT consultation and dispute settlement procedures and
U.S. domestic authority to impose import restrictions as retaliatory action, if necessary, to enforce rights asserted by the United States against unjustifiable, unreasonable,
or discriminatory foreign trade practices that burden or restrict U.S. commerce. The
broad inclusive nature of Section 301 authority applies to practices and policies of
countries whether or not they are covered by, or are members of, GATT or other trade
agreements. The USTR administers the statutory procedures through an interagency
committee.

Section 301 Authority [301]
Under Section 301, *if* the USTR determines that a foreign act, policy, or practice
violates or is inconsistent with a trade agreement or is unjustifiable and burdens or
restricts U.S. commerce, then action by the USTR to enforce the trade agreement
rights or to obtain the elimination of the act, policy, or practice is *mandatory,* subject
to the specific direction, if any, of the President. The USTR is not required to act,
however, if (1) the GATT Contracting Parties have determined, a GATT panel has
reported, or a dispute settlement ruling under a trade agreement finds that U.S. trade
agreement rights have not been denied or violated; (2) the USTR finds that the foreign
country is taking satisfactory measures to grant U.S. trade agreement rights, the
foreign country has agreed to eliminate or phase out the practice or to an imminent
solution to the burden or restriction on U.S. commerce, or has agreed to provide
satisfactory compensatory trade benefits; or (3) the United States finds in extraordinary
cases that action would have an adverse impact on the U.S. economy substantially out
of proportion to the benefits of action, or action would cause serious harm to U.S.
national security. Any action taken must affect goods or services of the foreign country
in an amount equivalent in value to the burden or restriction being imposed by that
country on U.S. commerce.

If the USTR determines that the act, policy, or practice is *unreasonable or
discriminatory* and burdens or restricts U.S. commerce and action by the United States
is appropriate, then the USTR has *discretionary* authority as under prior law to take all
appropriate and feasible action, subject to the specific direction, if any, of the president, to obtain the elimination of the act, policy, or practice.

As the form of action, the USTR is authorized to (1) suspend, withdraw, or prevent
the application of, benefits of trade agreement concessions to carry out a trade agreement
with the foreign country involved; (2) impose duties or other import restrictions on the
goods of, and notwithstanding any other provisions of law, fees or restrictions on the
services of, the foreign country for such time as the USTR deems appropriate; or (3)

This simple statement of the 301, Super 301, and Special 301 procedures since the 1988
Act comes from *Overview and Compilation of U.S. Trade Statutes,* 1989 ed. (Washington, D.C.:
U.S. Congress, Committee on Ways and Means, 1989) and has been very slightly amended in
places to conform to the needs of this volume.

enter into binding agreements that commit the foreign country to (*a*) eliminate or phase out the act, policy, or practice, (*b*) eliminate any burden or restriction on U.S. commerce resulting from the act, policy, or practice, or (*c*) provide the United States with compensatory trade benefits that are satisfactory to the USTR. The USTR must also take all other appropriate and feasible action within the power of the president that the president may direct the USTR to take.

With respect to services, the USTR may also restrict the terms and conditions or deny the issuance of any access authorization (e.g., license, permit, order) to the U.S. market issued under federal law, notwithstanding any other law governing the authorization. Such action can apply only prospectively to authorizations granted or applications pending on or after the date a Section 301 petition is filed or the USTR initiates an investigation. Before imposing fees or other restrictions on services subject to federal or state regulation, the USTR must consult as appropriate with the federal or state agency concerned.

Action under Section 301 may be taken on a nondiscriminatory basis or solely against the products or services of the country involved and with respect to any goods or sector regardless of whether they were involved in the particular act, policy, or practice.

In taking action, the USTR must give preference to tariffs over other forms of import restrictions and consider substituting, on an incremental basis, an equivalent duty for any other form of import restriction imposed. Any action with respect to export targeting must reflect, to the extent possible, the full benefit level of the targeting over the period during which the action taken has an effect.

Coverage of Authority

The term *unjustifiable* refers to acts, policies, or practices that violate, or are inconsistent with, U.S. international legal rights, such as denial of national or most favored nation treatment, right of establishment, or protection of intellectual property rights.

The term *unreasonable* refers to acts, policies, or practices that are not necessarily in violation of, or inconsistent with, U.S. international legal rights, but are otherwise unfair and inequitable.

In determining whether an act, policy, or practice is unreasonable, reciprocal opportunities in the United States for foreign nationals and firms shall be taken into account to the extent appropriate. Unreasonable measures include, but are not limited to, acts, policies, or practices that (1) deny fair and equitable (*a*) opportunities for the establishment of an enterprise, (*b*) provision of adequate and effective intellectual property right protection, or (*c*) market opportunities, including foreign government toleration of systematic anticompetitive activities by or among private firms that have the effect of restricting on a basis inconsistent with commercial considerations access of U.S. goods to purchasing by such firms; (2) constitute export targeting; or (3) constitute a persistent pattern of conduct denying internationally recognized worker rights, unless the USTR determines the foreign country has taken or is taking actions that demonstrate a significant and tangible overall advancement in providing those rights and standards throughout the country or such acts, policies, or practices are not inconsistent with the level of economic development of the country.

The term *discriminatory* includes, where appropriate, any act, policy, or practice that denies national or most favored nation treatment to U.S. goods, services, or investment. The term *commerce* includes, but is not limited to, services (including transfers of information) associated with international trade, whether or not such services are related to specific goods, and foreign direct investment by U.S. persons with implications for trade in goods or services.

Petitions and Investigations
Any interested person may file a petition under Section 302 with the USTR requesting the president to take action under Section 301 and setting forth the allegations in support of the request. The USTR reviews the allegations and must determine within forty-five days after receipt of the petition whether to initiate an investigation. The USTR may also self-initiate an investigation after consulting with appropriate private sector advisory committees. Public notice of determinations is required and, in the case of decisions to initiate, publication of a summary of the petition and an opportunity for the presentation of views, including a public hearing if timely requested by the petitioner or any interested person.

In determining whether to initiate an investigation of any act, policy, or practice specifically enumerated as actionable under Section 301, the USTR has the discretion to determine whether action under Section 301 would be effective in addressing that act, policy, or practice.

Section 303 requires the use of international procedures for resolving the issues to proceed in parallel with the domestic investigation. The USTR, on the same day as the determination to initiate an investigation, must request consultations with the foreign country concerned regarding the issues involved. The USTR may delay the request for up to ninety days in order to verify or improve the petition to ensure an adequate basis for consultation.

If the issues are covered by a trade agreement and are not resolved during the consultation period, if any, specified in the agreement, then the USTR must promptly request formal dispute settlement under the agreement before the earlier of the close of the consultation period specified in the agreement, if any, or 150 days after the consultation began. The USTR must seek information and advice from the petitioner, if any, and from appropriate private sector advisory committees in preparing presentations for consultations and dispute settlement proceedings.

USTR Unfairness and Action Determinations and Implementation
Section 304 sets forth specific time limits within which the USTR must make determinations of whether an act, policy, or practice meets the unfairness criteria of Section 301 and, if affirmative, what action, if any, should be taken. These determinations are based on the investigation under Section 302, and, if a trade agreement is involved, on the international consultations and, if applicable, on the results of the dispute settlement proceedings under the agreement.

The USTR must make these *determinations:*

- within eighteen months after the date the investigation is initiated or thirty days after the date the dispute settlement procedure is concluded, whichever is earlier, in cases involving a trade agreement, other than the agreement on subsidies and countervailing measures;
- within twelve months after the date the investigation is initiated in cases not

involving trade agreements or involving the agreement on subsidies and countervailing measures; or
- within six months after the date the investigation is initiated in cases involving
  intellectual property rights priority countries, or within nine months if the
  USTR determines such cases (1) involve complex or complicated issues that
  require additional time, (2) the foreign country is making substantial progress
  on legislative or administrative measures that will provide adequate and effective protection, or (3) the foreign country is undertaking enforcement measures
  to provide adequate and effective protection.

The applicable deadline is postponed by up to ninety days if consultations with the
foreign country involved were so delayed.

Before making the determinations, the USTR must provide an opportunity for the
presentation of views, including a public hearing if requested by an interested person
and obtain advice from the appropriate private sector advisory committees. If expedi-
tious action is required, the USTR must comply with these requirements after making
the determinations. The USTR may also request the views of the International Trade
Commission on the probable impact on the U.S. economy of taking the action. Any
determinations must be published in the *Federal Register*.

Section 305 requires the USTR to *implement* any Section 301 actions within 30
days after the date of the determination to take action. The USTR may delay implementation by not more than 180 days if (1) the petitioner or, in the case of a self-
initiated investigation, a majority of the domestic industry requests a delay; or (2) the
USTR determines that substantial progress is being made, or that a delay is necessary
or desirable, to obtain U.S. rights or a satisfactory solution. In cases involving intellectual property rights priority countries, action implementation may be delayed beyond
the 30 days only if extraordinary circumstances apply and by not more than 90 days.

If the USTR determines to take no action in a case involving an affirmative
determination of export targeting, the USTR must take alternative action in the form of
establishing an advisory panel to recommend measures to promote the competitiveness
of the affected domestic industry. The panel must submit a report on its recommendations to the USTR and the Congress within six months. On the basis of this report and
subject to the specific direction, if any, of the president, the USTR may take administrative actions authorized under any other law and propose legislation to implement
any other actions that would restore or improve the international competitiveness of the
domestic industry and must submit a report to Congress within thirty days after the
panel report is submitted on the actions taken and proposals made.

Monitoring of Foreign Compliance; Modification and Termination of Actions
Section 306 requires the USTR to monitor the implementation of each measure undertaken or so-called settlement agreement entered into by a foreign country under Section 301. If the USTR considers that a foreign country is not satisfactorily implementing a measure or agreement, the USTR must determine what further action will be
taken under Section 301. The nonimplementation is treated as a violation of a trade
agreement subject to mandatory Section 301 action as if it is a decision on the original
investigation and is subject to the same time limits and procedures for implementation

as other action determinations. Before making the determination on further action, the USTR must consult with the petitioner, if any, and with representatives of the domestic industry concerned and provide interested persons an opportunity to present views.

Section 307 authorizes the USTR to modify or terminate a Section 301 action, subject to the specific direction, if any, of the president, if (1) any of the exceptions to mandatory Section 301 action in the case of trade agreement violations or unjustifiable acts, policies, or practices applies, (2) the burden or restriction on U.S. commerce of the unfair practice has increased or decreased, or (3) discretionary Section 301 action is no longer appropriate. Before modifying or terminating any Section 301 action, the USTR must consult with the petitioner, if any, and with representatives of the domestic industry concerned, and provide an opportunity for other interested persons to present views.

Any Section 301 action shall terminate automatically if it has been in effect for four years and neither the petitioner nor any representative of the domestic industry that benefits from the action has submitted to the USTR in the final sixty days a written request for continuation. The USTR must give the petitioner and representatives of the domestic industry at least sixty days advance notice by mail of termination. If a request for continuation is submitted, the USTR must conduct a review of the effectiveness of Section 301 or other actions in achieving the objectives and the effects of actions on the U.S. economy, including consumers.

Information Requests; Reporting Requirements
Under Section 308, USTR makes available information (other than confidential) upon receipt of a written request by any person concerning (1) the nature and extent of a specific trade policy or practice of a foreign country with respect to particular goods, services, investment, or intellectual property rights to the extent such information is available in the federal government; (2) U.S. rights under any trade agreement and the remedies that may be available under that agreement and U.S. laws; and (3) past and present domestic and international proceedings or actions with respect to the policy or practice. If the information is not available, within thirty days after receipt of the request, the USTR must request the information from the foreign government or decline to request the information and inform the person in writing of the reasons.

The USTR must submit a semiannual report to Congress describing petitions filed and determinations made, developments in and the status of investigations and proceedings, actions taken or the reasons for no action under Section 301, and the commercial effects of Section 301 actions taken. The USTR must also keep the petitioner regularly informed of all determinations and developments regarding Section 301 investigations.

Identification of Intellectual Property Rights Priority Countries ("Special 301")

Section 182 of the Trade and Tariff Act of 1974, as added by Section 1303 of the Omnibus Trade and Competitiveness Act of 1988, requires the USTR to identify, within thirty days after submission of the annual National Trade Estimates (foreign trade barriers) report to Congress, those foreign countries that (1) deny adequate and effective protection, and (2) those countries under (1) determined by the USTR to be priority foreign countries. The USTR identifies as priorities only those countries that have the most onerous or egregious acts, policies, or practices that have the greatest adverse impact on the relevant U.S. products and that are not entering into good faith negotiations or making significant progress in bilateral or multilateral negotiations to provide adequate and effective intellectual property rights protection. The USTR at any time may revoke or make an identification of a priorty country, but must include in the semiannual Section 301 report to Congress a detailed explanation of the reasons for a revocation.

Section 302(b) requires the USTR to initiate a Section 301 investigation within thirty days after identification of a priority country with respect to any act, policy, or practice of that country that was the basis of the identification, unless the USTR determines initiation of an investigation would be detrimental to U.S. economic interests and reports the reasons in detail to Congress. The procedural and other requirements of Section 301 authority generally apply to these cases except for tighter time limits to make determinations under Section 304 and to implement actions under Section 305.

Identification of Trade Liberalization Priorities ("Super 301")

Section 310 of the Trade and Tariff Act of 1974, as added by Section 1302 of the Omnibus Trade and Competitiveness Act of 1988, requires the USTR, within thirty days after the National Trade Estimates (foreign trade barriers) report to Congress in 1989 and 1990, to identify trade liberalization priorities. This identification includes (1) priority practices, including major barriers and trade distorting practices, the elimination of which are likely to have the most significant potential to increase U.S. exports, either directly or through the establishment of a beneficial precedent; (2) priority foreign countries; and (3) estimates of the total amount by which U.S. exports of goods and services to each foreign country identified would have increased during the preceding calendar year if the priority practices identified did not exist. The statute also lists specific factors that the USTR must take into account in identifying priority practices and priority foreign countries. The USTR must submit a report to the House Committee on Ways and Means and the Senate Committee on Finance listing the priority countries, the priority practices with respect to each of the priority countries, and the trade amounts estimated with respect to each of the priority countries.

Within twenty-one days after submission of the report, the USTR must initiate Section 301 investigations with respect to all of the priority practices identified for each of the priority foreign countries. The USTR may, but is not required to, initiate Section 301 investigations with respect to all other priority practices identified.

The normal Section 301 authorities, procedures, time limits, and other requirements generally apply to these investigations. In the consultations with the country under Section 303, the USTR must seek to negotiate an agreement that provides for the elimination of, or compensation for, the priority practices within three years after the initiation of the investigation, and the reduction of these practices over three years with the expectation that U.S. exports to the country will increase incrementally during each year as a result. Any investigation will be suspended if such an agreement is entered into with the country before the date on which any Section 301 action may be required to be implemented under Section 305. If the USTR determines that the country is not in compliance with such an agreement, the USTR must continue the investigation as though it had not been suspended.

On the date the National Trade Estimates report is due in 1990, and on that date in succeeding years, the USTR must submit a report that includes (1) revised total export estimates for each priority foreign country; (2) evidence that demonstrates, in the form of increased exports to each priority country during the previous year, substantial progress during each of the three years toward the goal of eliminating priority practices in the case of countries that have entered into an agreement, and the elimination of such practices by countries that have not entered into an agreement; and (3) to the extent this evidence cannot be provided, any actions that have been taken by the USTR under Section 301 with respect to the priority practices of each priority country. The USTR may exclude from the report in any year after 1993 any foreign country identified if the evidence submitted in the previous two reports demonstrated that all the priority practices identified with respect to that country have been eliminated.

Foreign Direct Investment

Section 307(b) of the Trade and Tariff Act of 1984 requires the U.S. Trade Representative to seek the reduction and elimination of foreign export performance requirements through consultations and negotiations with the country concerned if the USTR determines, with interagency advice, that U.S. action is appropriate to respond to such requirements that adversely affect U.S. economic interests. In addition, the USTR may impose duties or other import restrictions on the products or services of the country involved, including exclusion from entry into the United States of products subject to these requirements. The USTR may provide compensation for such action subject to the provisions of Section 123 of the Trade and Tariff Act of 1974 if necessary or appropriate to meet U.S. international obligations.

Section 307(b) authority does not apply to any foreign direct investment, or to any written commitment relating to a foreign direct investment that is binding, made directly or indirectly by any United States person prior to October 30, 1984 (date of enactment of the act).

Part 1
The History of 301 and
Current U.S. Policy

CHAPTER 2

The Heart of the 1988 Trade Act: A Legislative History of the Amendments to Section 301

Judith Hippler Bello and Alan F. Holmer

In 1985, over 300 trade bills were introduced in Congress. The message was loud and clear: Congress was dissatisfied with the direction and results of U.S. trade policy. Many congressmen complained that "trade is the hand-maiden of all other considerations of the U.S. Government,"[1] and that considerations of foreign relations, national security, foreign and domestic economics, and domestic politics "have crowded trade off the agenda."[2] They noted their "festering frustration" that "all administrations sort of have to be dragged kicking and screaming into trade retaliation . . . because of the desire to use trade to barter for other nontrade issues. . . ."[3] The pending bills were rattled like sabers, pressuring the administration at least to increase its pace, if not change its direction.

Several omnibus bills emerged and evolved over the next three years, culminating on August 23, 1988, in the enactment of H.R. 4848, the Omnibus Trade and Competitiveness Act of 1988 (1988 Trade Act).[4] Throughout the three-year debate, the heart of the trade provisions of these bills was amendments to Section 301 of the Trade Act of 1974 (Section 301),[5] the main U.S. trade law designed to pry open foreign markets to U.S. investment and

---

Reprinted with the permission of the *Stanford Journal of International Law*. Copyright © 1988 by the Board of Trustees of the Leland Stanford Junior University. 25 *Stanford J. Int'l Law* 1 (1988). The authors would like to thank Bruce Hirsch for his assistance with this article.

1. *Comparing Major Trade Bills: Hearings on S. 490, S. 636, and H.R. 3 Before the Senate Committee on Finance,* 100th Cong., 1st sess., 1987, pt. 1, 10 (statement of Chairman Lloyd Bentsen [D-Texas]); hereinafter *April Hearings on S. 490.*

2. Id.

3. *Presidential Authority to Respond to Unfair Trade Practices: Hearing on Title II of S. 1860 and S. 1862 Before the Senate Committee on Finance,* 99th Cong., 2d sess., 1986, 64 (statement of Chairman Bob Packwood [R-Oregon]); hereinafter *Hearing on S. 1860.*

4. Omnibus Trade and Competitiveness Act of 1988, Pub. L. No. 100-418, 102 Stat. 1107; hereinafter 1988 Trade Act.

5. Trade and Tariff Act of 1974, 88 Stat. 1978, 19 U.S.C. § 2411 et. seq. (1982 and Supp. IV 1986) (prior to 1988 amendment); hereinafter 1974 Trade Act. As used in this article,

exports of goods and services, and to achieve adequate and effective protection abroad for intellectual property rights.[6]

This article traces the evolution of the major 1988 amendments to this key weapon in America's trade arsenal, and assesses their significance.

I. Transfer of Authority from the President to the U.S. Trade Representative

During 1985, a contentious debate of strategic and symbolic importance developed over whether Congress should transfer any of the authority of the president under Section 301 to the United States Trade Representative (USTR), the cabinet official responsible for trade policymaking.[7] Prior to the 1988 Trade Act, Section 301 authorized the president to (1) determine whether foreign government practices were unfair, and therefore actionable, within the terms of Section 301, and (2) take in response all appropriate and feasible action within his power, including increasing duties or other restrictions on imports of goods or services.[8] The motive behind the transfer of this authority to USTR was to increase the USTR's importance and power[9] and thus reduce the likeli-

---

"Section 301" refers to Sections 301–6 as amended through 1984, and to Sections 301–9 as amended in 1988.

6. Section 301 amendments may be characterized as the "heart" of the bills based on, for example, the statement of Senator Packwood (R-Oregon), then chairman of the Committee on Finance, that "(Section) 301 is a critical statute, particularly at this time." *Hearing on S. 1860,* supra n. 3, 10. In fact, during Ambassador Yeutter's confirmation hearing before the Senate Committee on Finance, Senator John C. Danforth (R-Missouri) offered his opinion that effective enforcement of Section 301 should be one of the trade representative's top two priorities (the other being policies related to the value of the dollar). *Nomination of Dr. Clayton K. Yeutter to be U.S. Trade Representative: Hearing Before the Senate Committee on Finance,* 99th Cong., 1st sess., 1985, 88; hereinafter *Yeutter Nomination Hearing.* Senator Danforth later claimed (in 1987) that "correcting Section 301 . . . is perhaps the most important aspect of the [omnibus trade] legislation [S. 1420] that is before us" (133 *Cong. Rec.* S8657 [daily ed., June 25, 1987]).

7. Ambassador Clayton Yeutter has served as U.S. Trade Representative since 1985. The Office of the United States Trade Representative was originally called the Office of the Special Representative for Trade Negotiations (called STR for "Special Trade Representative"), which was established by the Trade Expansion Act of 1962, § 241, Pub. L. No. 87-794, 76 Stat. 872, 878. In implementing the agreements reached in the Tokyo Round of Multilateral Trade Negotiations, the Congress directed the president to "upgrade" the responsibilities of the STR. Trade Agreements Act of 1979, § 1109, Pub. L. No. 96-39, 93 Stat. 144, 314. This upgrading was accomplished through Reorg. Plan No. 3 of 1979, 3 C.F.R. 513, 1980, reprinted in 19 U.S.C. § 2171, 1982, 963 and Executive Order No. 12,188, 3 C.F.R. 131, 1981, reprinted in 19 U.S.C. § 2171, 1982, 968, which redesignated the Office of the Special Trade Representative for Trade Negotiations as the Office of the United States Trade Representative. The 1988 Trade Act essentially codifies the provisions of Reorganization Plan No. 3 and the 1980 Executive Order. 1988 Trade Act, supra n. 4, § 1601.

8. 19 U.S.C. § 2411(a) (1982 and Supp. IV 1986).

9. As Senator Lloyd Bentsen (D-Texas) put it, the transfer "gives [USTR] some extra

hood of trade benefits for foreigners being exchanged for nontrade benefits.[10]

The Reagan administration consistently opposed proposals to transfer Section 301 authority. Speaking on behalf of the administration, USTR argued first that a transfer of authority would make no constructive difference in trade policy outcomes, since the trade representative serves at the pleasure of the president. Consequently, no trade representative who wishes to remain in office would contradict the president's policies.[11] Second, USTR argued that the transfer could actually reduce Section 301's effectiveness with foreign governments by removing the president's personal involvement from the process.[12] Trading partners could perceive the transfer as signaling *less* rather than more interest in trade issues at the highest levels of the U.S. government.[13]

Third, USTR argued that decisions in Section 301 cases should be made and actions should be taken by the president, because of their potentially broad effects on national interests. The president is in a better position than USTR to weigh competing interests, with advice from all of his principal

---

muscle" (134 *Cong. Rec.* S10,674 [daily ed., August 3, 1988]). Senator William Roth (R-Delaware) stressed that it enables the USTR to "speak with a loud, clear voice" (id., S10,672). Senator Max Baucus (D-Montana) concurred that it "gives the USTR just a little bit more clout, a little bit more authority" (id. S10,671). See also House Committee on Ways and Means, *Trade and International Economic Policy Reform Act of 1987: Report to Accompany H.R. 3,* H.R. Rep. No. 40, 100th Cong., 1st sess. 1987, 59 (the transfer of authority "will strengthen the negotiating authority and credibility of the USTR").

10. Senator Bob Packwood (R-Oregon) called such bartering trading of "blacks versus reds" (*Hearing on S. 1860,* supra n. 3, 65). See also 134 *Cong. Rec.* S7,381 (daily ed., June 8, 1988) (statement of Sen. Timothy Wirth [D-Colorado]) (the transfer of authority "will ensure that when decisions are made under Section 301 authority, these decisions will be made primarily for reasons of trade policy"); and 134 *Cong. Rec.* H5,532 (daily ed., July 13, 1988) (statement of Rep. Bill Richardson [D-New Mexico]) (the change is "intended to enhance USTR's position as the lead trade agency and to make it less likely that trade retaliation would be waived because of foreign policy, defense, or other considerations").

11. See e.g., *Hearing on S. 1860,* supra n. 3, 51–52 (testimony of Ambassador Clayton Yeutter, U.S. Trade Representative), and id., 57 (USTR's section-by-section analysis, title II of S. 1860). But see 134 *Cong. Rec.* S10,661 (daily ed., August 3, 1988) (statement of Senator Malcolm Wallop [R-Wyoming]) ("There is not a soul in this body who has not seen people appointed who did not do what the president of the United States wished to have him do, in both parties, in every administration."); hereinafter statement of Senator Wallop.

12. *Hearing on S. 1860,* supra n. 3, 52 (testimony of Ambassador Clayton Yeutter, U.S. Trade Representative); *Improving Enforcement of Trade Agreements: Hearing on S. 490, S 539 and H.R. 3 Before the Senate Committee on Finance,* 100th Cong., 1st sess., 1987, 33, 44 (testimony of Alan F. Holmer, General Counsel, USTR); hereinafter *March Hearing on S. 490.*

13. *Hearing on S. 1860,* supra n. 3, 57 (USTR's section-by-section analysis, title II of S. 1860). See also 134 *Cong. Rec.* H5,545 (daily ed., July 13, 1988) (comments of Rep. Jim Kolbe [R-Arizona]) ("Section 301 also dilutes our bargaining power by shifting authority for action from the president to the USTR.").

economic advisers.[14] Ambassador Yeutter argued that "the buck should stop in the office of the president of the United States."[15] He continued: "Section 301 is the H-bomb of trade policy; and in my judgment, H-bombs ought to be dropped by the president of the United States and not by anyone else."[16]

Despite the administration's opposition, sentiment in the Congress to transfer some or all of the president's authority under Section 301 remained strong. S. 1860, the principal Senate omnibus trade bill in 1986, would have transferred *all* the functions of the president under Section 301 to the trade representative.[17] H.R. 4800, the omnibus trade bill passed by the House of Representatives in 1986,[18] transferred to the trade representative only the authority to determine whether a foreign government practice was unfair,[19] leaving to the president the power to take action under Section 301.[20] H.R. 4800 was reintroduced in the 100th Congress on January 6, 1987, as H.R. 3.[21]

H.R. 3's partial allocation of Section 301 authority to USTR remained

---

14. *Hearing on S. 1860,* supra note 3, at 57 (USTR's section-by-section analysis, title II of S. 1860); see also id., 52 (statement of Ambassador Clayton Yeutter, U.S. Trade Representative) ("decisions under Section 301 should be reserved for the president, who can best weigh interests within and without the government"). Some members of Congress wholeheartedly shared the administration's views. For example, Representative Jack Kemp (R-New York) denounced the transfer because:

It takes authority in very delicate trade negotiations with the rest of the world out of the hands of the president who is responsible not only for the good of the international trading system, but also for the public good. And it puts it in the hands of a czar, an unelected bureaucrat. (134 *Cong. Rec.* H5,535 [daily ed., July 13, 1988])

Senator Malcolm Wallop agreed, arguing that "it is critical for the president to retain some discretion to weigh trade versus nontrade interests." 134 *Cong. Rec.* S10,661 (daily ed., August 3, 1988).

15. *April Hearings on S. 490,* supra n. 1, 19 (statement of Ambassador Clayton Yeutter, U.S. Trade Representative).

16. Id. See generally Letter and Attachment from Ambassador Yeutter to Committee on Ways and Means Chairman Dan Rostenkowski (D-Illinois) and Subcommittee on Trade Chairman Sam M. Gibbons (D-Florida) (March 18, 1987) (unpublished, on file at USTR); hereinafter Yeutter-Rostenkowski-Gibbons Letter.

17. S. 1860, 99th Cong., 2nd sess., § 203, 131 *Cong. Rec.* S15,960 (daily ed., November 20, 1985). Although S. 1860 was introduced in 1985, it is referred to as a 1986 bill because all significant deliberation on it occurred in 1986. The Senate never passed S. 1860.

18. H.R. 4800, 99th Cong., 2d sess., 132 *Cong. Rec.* H3,025 (daily ed., May 21, 1986) was passed May 22, 1986, by a vote of 295 to 115. 132 *Cong. Rec.* H3,225 (daily ed., May 22, 1986).

19. H.R. 4800, supra n. 18, § 116.

20. Id., § 112.

21. 132 *Cong. Rec.* H101 (daily ed., Jan. 6, 1987). The text of H.R. 3, 100th Cong., 1st sess., as introduced, is available on Superintendent of Documents, Government Printing Office, microfiche no. 249.

unchanged through its early March, 1987, markup in the Subcommittee on Trade of the House Committee on Ways and Means.[22] However, on March 24 during the full Committee markup, Congressman J. J. Pickle (D-Texas) proposed an amendment to also transfer the president's authority for action under Section 301 to the trade representative. The chairman of the Subcommittee on Trade, Sam M. Gibbons, (D-Florida) then proposed an amendment to the Pickle amendment, providing for action by the trade representative "subject to the direction of the president." The committee approved the Gibbons amendment, but then rejected the entire Pickle amendment as amended by Gibbons.[23]

Congressman Pickle then proposed to transfer to the trade representative the authority for action in those Section 301 cases in which H.R. 3 required retaliation—i.e., in response to violations of trade agreements, violations of other agreements that burdened or restricted U.S. commerce, or a foreign government's export targeting.[24] Again, Subcommittee on Trade Chairman Gibbons introduced an amendment to the Pickle amendment, calling for such action by the trade representative "at the direction of the president." The Committee once again approved the Gibbons amendment, but this time the Pickle amendment (as amended by Gibbons) also passed.[25] The House omnibus bill had thus changed in a very significant respect.

H.R. 3 was subsequently changed in this regard by the consent of the Committee on Ways and Means without any further official markup. The bill that was debated and passed by the House of Representatives on April 28–30, 1987,[26] transferred authority for action in *all* Section 301 cases to the trade

---

22. House Subcommittee on Trade Press Release no. 1-A, The Honorable Sam M. Gibbons (D-Florida), Chairman, Subcommittee on Trade, Committee on Ways and Means, House of Representatives, Announces Subcommittee Action on H.R. 3, Comprehensive Trade Policy Reform Legislation, 100th Cong., 1st sess., 3 (March 13, 1987); hereinafter Subcommittee on Trade Press Release.

23. Modified Transfer of Authority Amendment (March 24, 1987) (unpublished, on file at USTR).

24. See H.R. 3, supra no. 21, § 112. See also infra n. 51–83 and accompanying text.

25. The Committee on Ways and Means approved H.R. 3, as marked up, by a vote of 34 to 2 on March 25, 1987. House Committee on Ways and Means Press Release no. 5-A, The Honorable Dan Rostenkowski (D-Illinois), Chairman, Committee on Ways and Means, U.S. House of Representatives, Announces Committee Action on H.R. 3, the Trade and International Economic Policy Reform Act of 1987, 2 (March 25, 1987); hereinafter Press Release no. 5-A. This press release notes that as amended in Committee, H.R. 3 transferred authority for action to the trade representative in all cases for which retaliation is required, but left with the president the authority to take action, based on the trade representative's recommendation, in other cases.

26. As amended on the floor, the bill was passed by a vote of 290 to 137. 133 *Cong. Rec.* H2,981 (daily ed., April 30, 1987).

representative, without distinguishing cases in which retaliation would be required from those in which it would be discretionary.[27]

Meanwhile, on the Senate side, change occurred in precisely the opposite direction. Although S. 1860 in 1986 would have transferred all Section 301 authority to the trade representative,[28] S. 490, the Senate's principal 1987 trade bill, transferred to USTR only the authority to determine whether a foreign government's practices were unfair within the meaning of Section 301.[29] Although the Senate Committee on Finance approved Senator Bob Packwood's (R-Oregon) comprehensive amendments to Section 301[30] at its markup of S. 490, the Packwood amendments made no change with respect to the transfer of Section 301 authority. The Committee approved S. 490, as amended in markup, on May 7, 1987.[31]

The Senate debated the omnibus trade bill[32] from June 25 until July 21, 1987, finally approving it by a vote of 71 to 27.[33] The final bill passed by the Senate thus transferred to the trade representative only the authority under Section 301 to determine whether foreign government practices were unfair, *not* authority to take action in response.[34]

A trade conference met in August, 1987, to resolve differences between the two bills.[35] This conference established seventeen subconferences; all core trade provisions were assigned to Subconference 1, composed principally of Ways and Means and Finance Committee members.[36] On October 22, 1987,

27. H.R. 3, (May 8, 1987 print), 100th Cong., 1st sess., § 121, 1987, Superintendent of Documents, Government Printing Office, microfiche no. 258.

28. S. 1860, supra n. 17, § 203.

29. S. 490, 100th Cong., 1st sess., § 304, 133 *Cong. Rec.* S1,852 (daily ed., February 5, 1987).

30. Packwood Proposal on Section 301, April 29, 1987 (unpublished, on file at USTR); hereinafter Packwood Proposal. See infra text accompanying n. 71. The vote was 14 to 2. The dissenting votes were Senators John Heinz (R-Pennsylvania) and Donald W. Riegle, Jr. (D-Michigan).

31. The vote was 19 to 1. Senate Committee on Finance Press Release M-9, Senate Finance Committee Completes Action on Omnibus Trade Bill, May 7, 1987. The dissenting vote was cast by Senator Malcolm Wallop (R-Wyoming).

32. The Senate leadership had combined S. 490, the Finance Committee bill, with a number of other bills to create S. 1420, the omnibus bill. See 133 *Cong. Rec.* S8,587, S8,631 (daily ed., June 24, 1987). S. 1420 was then substituted entirely for H.R. 3.

33. 133 *Cong. Rec.* S10,372 (daily ed., July 21, 1987).

34. S. 1420, 100th Cong., 1st sess., 1987, § 308 (on file at USTR).

35. *See* 133 *Cong. Rec.* S11,321 (daily ed., Aug. 5, 1987) (partial list of Senate conferees). An initial meeting was held on August 7, at which Representative Dan Rostenkowski (D-Illinois) was elected conference chairman and Senator Lloyd Bentsen (D-Texas), vice-chairman. Both stressed that everyone, including the president, would need to be flexible and open-minded. Opening Statement of Chairman Dan Rostenkowski before the Conference on H.R. 3 (undated, but in fact August 7, 1987) (unpublished, on file at USTR).

36. *H.R. 3, Omnibus Trade and Competitiveness Legislation: Comparison of House and*

Subconference 1 conferees began proceedings with an agreement on non-controversial provisions on trade agreements authority and a host of miscellaneous tariffs.[37] House conferees made an offer regarding trade agreements authority on October 27,[38] but no further action was taken until February 23, 1988, when the House subconferees launched "phase 1" of Subconference 1 with a new offer on trade agreements authority and a host of peripheral (often foreign relations–related) issues.[39] Senate subconfereees largely accepted the House offer on February 25,[40] and the subconference entered "phase 2," covering the bread-and-butter trade law provisions.

The conferees did not exchange offers on the Section 301 amendments until virtually the end of the conference. On March 15, 1988, Senate subconferees made the first proposal, which included a request that the House recede to the Senate on the issue of transfer of authority to take action.[41] On March 21, House subconferees counterrequested the Senate to recede.[42] A week later on March 30, subconferees remained at a stalemate on this issue. Senate subconferees again asked the House to recede on the Section 301 transfer issue, leaving authority to act under Section 301 exclusively with the president.[43] On March 31, the final day of Subconference 1, offers and counteroffers were exchanged throughout the day.[44] The issue was not resolved until

---

Senate Provisions, 100th Cong., 2d sess., 2–7 (Committee print, October 6, 1987 [on file at USTR]). In addition to House Ways and Means and Senate Finance Committee members, Subconference 1 included representatives of the Senate Committee on Agriculture, and the House Committees on Agriculture; Banking, Finance, and Urban Affairs; Energy and Commerce; Foreign Affairs; the Judiciary; and Rules.

37. Trade Agreement Negotiating Authority (Oct. 22, 1987) (unpublished, on file at USTR); Miscellaneous Tariff Bills (Oct. 22, 1987) (unpublished, on file at USTR).

38. House Offer on Trade Agreement Negotiating Authority (October 27, 1987) (unpublished, on file at USTR).

39. H.R. 3, Omnibus Trade Legislation, Subconference 1, House Offer on Phase I Issues (February 23, 1988) (unpublished, on file at USTR). Phase I issues included advice and consultation on national trade policy, section 337 protection of intellectual property rights, organization and functions of trade agencies, appropriations, national security import relief, and miscellaneous other provisions (id.).

40. H.R. 3, Omnibus Trade Legislation, Subconference 1, Senate Response to House Offer on Phase I Issues (February 25, 1988) (unpublished, on file at USTR).

41. H.R. 3, Omnibus Trade Legislation, Subconference 1, Senate Offers to House on Phase II Issues, 1 (March 15, 1988) (unpublished, on file at USTR); hereinafter March 15 Senate Offer. The phase II issues were Section 301, telecommunications, international intellectual property 'protection, antidumping, and countervailing duty laws, Section 406, and tax law provisions.

42. H.R. 3, Omnibus Trade Legislation, Subconference 1, Proposed House Counteroffer on Section 301 Amendments (March 21, 1988, 5:30 PM) (unpublished, on file at USTR); hereinafter March 21 House Counteroffer.

43. Senate Offer, Document A, 3 (March 30, 1988, 6:30 PM) (unpublished, on file at USTR); hereinafter March 30 Senate Offer.

44. H.R. 3, Omnibus Trade Legislation, Subconference 1, House Counteroffer to Senate

that evening, when Ways and Means Committee Chairman Dan Rostenkowski and Finance Committee Chairman Lloyd Bentsen met in the Capitol.[45] Chairman Rostenkowski held firm on the House position. The final outcome, therefore, was to transfer to the trade representative authority under Section 301 not only to determine whether foreign government practices are unfair, but also to take action.[46] This provision eventually was enacted into law in Section 1301 of the 1988 Trade Act.[47] As amended, Section 301 today authorizes the trade representative to determine whether foreign government practices are unfair and, subject to the specific direction (if any) of the president, to take action under Section 301.

What is the impact of this transfer likely to be? The Congress made an important symbolic statement[48] in insisting upon the transfer of authority

Offer on Remaining Issues, 5 (March 31, 1988, 9:00 AM) (unpublished, on file at USTR); hereinafter March 31, 9 AM House Counteroffer. H.R. 3, Omnibus Trade Legislation, Subconference 1, House Counteroffer to Senate Offer on Remaining Issues, 5 (March 31, 1988, 11:00 AM) (unpublished, on file at USTR); hereinafter March 31, 11 AM House Counteroffer. H.R. 3, Omnibus Trade Legislation, Subconference 1, Senate Counteroffer to House Offer on Remaining Issues, 5 (March 31, 1988, 2:00 PM) (unpublished, on file at USTR); hereinafter March 31, 2 PM Senate Counteroffer.

45. Ambassador Clayton Yeutter, U.S. Trade Representative, Ambassador Alan F. Holmer, Deputy U.S. Trade Representative, and Judith H. Bello, General Counsel, USTR, were in an adjacent room but were not allowed into the meeting until after three hours of discussion.

46. Proposed Final Agreement on Remaining Phase II Issues, H.R. 3, Omnibus Trade Legislation, Subconference 1, 3 (March 31, 1988, 8:00 PM) (unpublished, on file at USTR); hereinafter Proposed Final Agreement. See also H.R. *Rep. No. 576,* 100th Cong., 2d sess., 1988, 551; hereinafter *Conference Report.*

47. The H.R. 3 conference outcome was adopted by the House on April 21 by a vote of 312 to 107, and by the Senate on April 27 by a vote of 63 to 36. 134 *Cong. Rec.* H2,375 (daily ed., April 21, 1988), S4,926–27 (daily ed., April 27, 1988). The text of H.R. 3 as reported by the Conference Committee is reprinted in *Conference Report,* supra n. 46, 1. However, on May 24, 1988, the president vetoed the bill. 134 *Cong. Rec.* H3,531 (daily ed., May 24, 1988). This veto was overridden that same day in the House by a vote of 308 to 113. 134 *Cong. Rec.* H3,552 (daily ed., May 24, 1988). However, the veto was sustained in the Senate on June 8 by a vote of 61 to 37. 134 *Cong. Rec.* S7,385 (daily ed., June 8, 1988).

H.R. 3 was reintroduced in the House of Representatives one week later on June 16 with only two modifications (eliminating the plant closings provisions of sections 6401–10, and modifying the Alaska oil provisions of section 2424) as H.R. 4848. 134 *Cong. Rec.* H4,427 (daily ed., June 16, 1988). It was passed by the House on July 13 by a vote of 376 to 45. 134 *Cong. Rec.* H5,694 (daily ed., July 13, 1988). For the text of H.R. 4848 as passed by the House, see id., H5,547. The Senate then passed H.R. 4848 on August 3 by a vote of 85 to 11. 134 *Cong. Rec.* S10,731 (daily ed., August 3, 1988). An amendment to the section 301 transfer of authority provisions offered by Senator Malcolm Wallop (R-Wyoming) to "place the president . . . back into the [Section] 301 decision-making process" was tabled on a 69 to 26 vote during this debate. Id., S10,660, S10,675. The president signed H.R. 4848 on August 23, 1988. See 1988 Trade Act, supra n. 4, 102 Stat. 1107, 1107 (1988).

48. But see the assertion of Representative Dick Schulze (R-Pennsylvania) that the Section 301 transfer of authority is "more than a merely symbolic gesture." 134 *Cong. Rec.* H5,534 (daily ed., July 13, 1988).

despite the administration's strong and repeated objections. Many members of Congress believe that the transfer will significantly increase the power of the USTR, although they disagree over the benefits and disadvantages of USTR's greater authority.[49] However, the change is unlikely to be particularly significant. The trade representative still serves at the pleasure of the president, and therefore is unlikely to take actions of which the president disapproves.[50] The only question—which will be answered in time with experience under the new Section 301—is whether there may occasionally be cases in which the president may permit the trade representative to take actions that he himself would not take.

II. Mandatory Retaliation

By 1985, many in Congress, in both parties, believed that the president was not using Section 301 effectively.[51] They pointed to the president's discretion

---

49. On the one hand, some believe the transfer makes "it easier for protectionist interests to maneuver the United States into a self-defeating cycle of retaliatory measures." 134 *Cong. Rec.* H5,536 (daily ed., July 13, 1988) (remarks of Representative Jack Kemp [R-New York]). Representative Philip M. Crane (R-Illinois) likewise argued:

> In general, Congress tends to side with the various special interests while the president has the position and ability to make a fair assessment of the overall national interest. H.R. 4848 would unsettle this balance by wrenching away some of the president's decision-making authority and placing it with the USTR who, the thinking goes, will be more susceptible to arm twisting by special interest lobbies. (Id., H5,537)

Representative Jim Kolbe (R-Arizona) noted that "it would be easier for Congress to browbeat [the trade representative] with our parochial concerns than it would be the president." Id., H5,545. Senator Malcolm Wallop (R-Wyoming) concurred, expressing his extreme nervousness "about placing as [*sic*] much authority in the hands of an unelected, albeit appointed, official like the U.S. Trade Representative." 134 *Cong. Rec.* S10,661 (daily ed., August 3, 1988). Senator Mark O. Hatfield (R-Oregon) summarized that such a "wholesale delegation of presidential discretion and flexibility is bad precedent and bad policy," id., S10,719, and Senator Daniel J. Evans (R-Washington) agreed that it is "simply foolish, silly, unnecessary, and unwise." 134 *Cong. Rec.* S7,348 (daily ed., June 8, 1988).

On the other hand, proponents of the transfer believe it will strengthen the hand of the trade representative, see, e.g., 134 *Cong. Rec.* S10,671 (daily ed., August 3, 1988) (statement of Senator Max Baucus), and make it more likely that trade objectives will not be compromised by nontrade objectives. See supra n. 1–3 and accompanying text.

50. But see statement of Senator Wallop, supra n. 11.

51. Most members of Congress have recognized the vigorous and effective use of Section 301 since 1985. For example, Finance Committee Chairman Bentsen noted in 1987: "President Reagan began in 1985 to use Section 301 more vigorously than he had in the past. And I commend him for that." *March Hearing on S. 490*, supra n. 12, 8. Senator John Chafee (R-Rhode Island) noted in 1986: "I am pleased with the use the administration has made of this statute in recent months." *Hearing on S. 1860*, supra n. 3, 7. Representative Dick Schulze (R-Pennsylvania) commented to Ambassador Clayton Yeutter, U.S. Trade Representative, in February, 1987:

> Mr. Ambassador, when you first came to this job I suggested it was a lot like a new fire chief being hired by a town when the town was already burning down. I have got to say that you

to take action as the main source of the failure of Section 301. Senator John C. Danforth (R-Missouri) voiced this complaint to Clayton Yeutter at his confirmation hearing in June, 1985:

> Since Section 301 has been on the books it has been underutilized in the minds of some people. . . .
> . . . [U]nless we at least sometimes actually enforce the law, there is no credibility. . . . I think that if you never retaliate, I think that if the referee never blows the whistle on a foul, there is no way to stop fouls.[52]

Senator Danforth led this refrain again in 1986: "A lot of people feel that by and large Section 301 of the Trade Act has been a dead-end street; that cases brought under Section 301 will probably go nowhere."[53] Senator George J. Mitchell (D-Maine) agreed:

> Section 301 of the 1974 Trade Act is the mechanism intended to address the increasing foreign use of unfair trade practices. But it does not work. The history of Section 301 is a history of administration after administration of both parties refusing to implement the law. Instead, this president and his predecessors have used the wide discretion provided in the law to deny or to delay taking action sometimes for close to a decade.
> . . . The administration will claim that [proposed Section 301] reforms limit their discretion. *But it is this very discretion which has led to the disastrous record of enforcement under Section 301.*[54]

---

have been able to put out more fires than I thought you could. (*Comprehensive Trade Legislation: Hearings on H.R. 3 Before the House Committee on Ways and Means and Its Subcommittee on Trade*, 100th Cong., 1st sess., 1987, 187; hereinafter *Hearings on H.R. 3*. Ambassador Yeutter himself said in February, 1987: "I am not sure how we can get much tougher than we have been over the last eighteen or twenty-four months." Id., 152. And again in April, 1987: "I don't see how we can be a whole lot more aggressive than we have been in recent months." *April Hearings on S. 490*, supra n. 1, 58.

52. *Yeutter Nomination Hearing*, supra n. 6, 81, 85. Ambassador Yeutter expressly agreed that the Section 301 remedy "has been underutilized even by industry itself in the formulation and submission of complaints, that there have been a good many cases when Section 301 action or submissions by industry groups or firms would have been appropriate, and they have not availed themselves of that prerogative." Id., 82.

53. *Hearing on S. 1860*, supra n. 3, 11.

54. Id., 14, 15 (emphasis added). Such concerns were widely shared in Congress. For example, Senator Heinz complained that U.S. industries "haven't gotten a fair deal . . . because the administration by and large has another agenda, and their trade policy is a de facto mish-mash of afterthoughts designed to try and limit the political fallout through the series of nondecisions, bad decisions." Id., 12–13. He concluded that "the only tool we have available is to remove the discretion currently afforded the U.S. Trade Representative." Id., 9. Senator John Chafee (R-Rhode Island) said, "We want the 301 process to be more useful and more routine." Id., 7.

Concerns over the president's discretionary authority to retaliate continued despite the vigorous use of Section 301 in the 1985–88 period.[55] For example, in April, 1987, Chairman Lloyd Bentsen (D-Texas) opened hearings of the Senate Finance Committee with the following statement:

> We need a trade policy that our trade partners can predict, and I maintain that requires limits on the President's discretion *not to act*. He needs plenty of discretion on what action to take, but limits have to be placed on his discretion to take no action. . . .
>
> The fact is, if you insist on total discretion, it comes out being do-nothing.[56]

The ranking Republican and former chairman of the Finance Committee, Senator Bob Packwood (R-Oregon), summarized as the committee began its markup of S. 490: "Whether to mandate retaliation against foreign unfair trading practices under Section 301 is the issue with which we have probably struggled the most during our hearings."[57] Many Senators supported the advice of former Special Trade Representative Robert Strauss that retaliation under Section 301 should be "mandatory . . . but not compulsory."[58]

Senator Charles E. Grassley (R-Iowa) summarized: "[T]here exists a broad consensus in this body that modifications of the statute are needed to ensure that it will be used vigorously and that it will present a credible threat of retaliation against any unfair trade practices both in the context of this administration and in future administrations." Id., 10. Testifying at the Finance Committee hearing, Representative Don J. Pease (D-Ohio) agreed: "Clearly, presidents past and present have failed to implement Section 301 in the manner Congress originally intended. There is a broad consensus in Congress on modifications to ensure that the statute will be used vigorously and that it will present a credible threat of retaliation." Id., 19.

55. See supra n. 51. See also *Hearing on S. 1860*, supra n. 3, 40–44 (testimony of Ambassador Clayton Yeutter, U.S. Trade Representative); *March Hearing on S. 490*, supra n. 12, 11, 28–29, 39–40 (testimony of Alan F. Holmer, General Counsel, USTR).

56. *April Hearings on S. 490*, supra n. 1, 4, 6 (emphasis in original). See also *March Hearing on S. 490*, supra n. 12, 8 (statement of Senator Bentsen).

57. Senator Bob Packwood, Opening Statement for Trade Markup 2 (April 22, 1987) (on file at USTR). Several months later Senator Packwood concluded: "I think you have to have that [retaliation] arrow in your quiver. . . . You have to go to the edge of the cliff every now and then and, perhaps, one time in twenty, one time in fifty, one time in ten, you have to retaliate." 133 *Cong. Rec.* S8,650 (daily ed., June 25, 1987).

58. While this advice is widely attributed solely to former Ambassador Strauss, Senator Packwood contributed to it. The exchange took place as follows:

> Sen. Packwood: Do you think any trade [bill] that we have should require mandatory retaliation?
>
> Mr. Strauss: Well, I am a little hesitant to require mandatory retaliation. . . . I hate to make [Section 301] mandatory. I think somewhere in between. . . . [M]ore mandatory is a bum choice of words—
>
> Sen. Packwood: But not compulsory. (*Mastering the World Economy: Hearings Before the*

Throughout the three-year debate, the administration strongly opposed any mandate to retaliate under Section 301. One argument was that Section 301 was not broken, and therefore did not need to be fixed. As proof of the efficacy of Section 301, the administration pointed to its vigorous implementation of the section from 1985 to 1988, including unprecedented self-initiated investigations, self-initiated action even without formal preceding investigations, and numerous trade-liberalizing settlement agreements.[59]

The administration's second argument was that mandatory retaliation ties the president's hands.[60] An inflexible and rigid requirement to retaliate could easily do more harm than good by provoking nationalistic reactions in other countries and thereby reducing a foreign government's political ability and willingness to negotiate a satisfactory settlement. Too often threatening a trading partner could provoke that government to stonewall or retaliate rather than to satisfy American demands, thereby closing, rather than opening, markets around the world.[61]

Senate Committee on Finance, 100th Cong., 1st sess., 1987, pt. 1, 44–45 [statement of Robert Strauss, former Special Trade Representative])

While "mandatory but not compulsory" could mean different things to different people, it implies at least greater pressure on USTR to act in response to unfair foreign government practices, but also implies significant discretion to tailor any U.S. government response to fit particular circumstances. The advice to make retaliation mandatory but not compulsory was frequently referred to throughout the debate on mandatory retaliation. See, e.g., *March Hearing on S. 490,* supra n. 12, 9 (statement of Sen. Chafee): 133 *Cong. Rec.* S8,649, S8,716 (daily ed., June 25, 1987) (statements of Sens. Packwood and Chafee).

59. See, e.g., *Hearing on S. 1860,* supra n. 3, 40–44 (statement of Ambassador Clayton Yeutter, U.S. Trade Representative); *March Hearing on S. 490,* supra n. 12, 11, 28–29 (statement of Alan F. Holmer, General Counsel, USTR); Bello and Holmer, "Significant Recent Developments in Section 301 of the Trade Act of 1974: Cases," *International Lawyer* 21 (1987): 211; Bello and Holmer, "Section 301 of the Trade Act of 1974: Requirements, Procedures, and Developments," *Northwest Journal of International Law and Business* 7 (1986): 633; Office of the United States Trade Representative, *Annual Report of the President of the United States on the Trade Agreements Program 1988* (Washington, D.C.: U.S. Government Printing Office, 1988), 42–50. See also supra n. 51. But cf. the comments of Senator Tom Daschle (D-South Dakota) to Ambassador Holmer:

The frustration that most of us have . . . is the lack of assurance, the lack of confidence that perhaps after you leave, the same kind of diligence in utilizing [Section] 301 will be present as it appears to be now. . . . What is it . . . that will give us the confidence that after you leave and for all perpetuity 301 will be used a lot more effectively and aggressively in the future? (*March Hearing on S. 490,* supra n. 12, 28)

60. *March Hearing on S. 490,* supra n. 12, 24 (testimony of Alan F. Holmer, General Counsel, USTR). See also 133 *Cong. Rec.* S8,699 (daily ed., June 25, 1987) (statement of Senator Evans).

61. *Hearing on S. 1860,* supra n. 3, 48 (testimony of Ambassador Clayton Yeutter, U.S. Trade Representative), 59 (USTR's section-by-section analysis, title II of S. 1860); *March Hearing on S. 490,* supra n. 12, 24, 41–42 (testimony of Alan F. Holmer, General Counsel, USTR);

Finally, the administration argued that any rigid time schedule for retaliation could be counterproductive. It claimed that the executive branch needs the discretion to act when the timing is right for overall U.S. economic interests. For instance, proposals for mandatory retaliation could require action against a country just as a large export sale was pending for a major U.S. exporter.[62]

As this debate unfolded, the proposals for mandatory retaliation evolved significantly from the automatic approach in Senate bills, to the more modest and tailored approach of the House. The first major Senate omnibus trade bill, S. 1860, would have required retaliation within fifteen months of initiation of an investigation under Section 302 of the Trade Act of 1974[63] in almost every case in which an unfair practice was determined to exist. S. 1860 provided only two exceptions to this mandate: if (1) the unfairness determination were subsequently determined to be incorrect or no longer valid; or (2) a settlement agreement was reached that was satisfactory to USTR *and* the industry or petitioner concerned.[64] Under the latter exception, U.S. producers effectively had veto power over any proposed settlement agreement.

On the other hand, successive House bills generally took a more moderate approach.[65] H.R. 4800 as passed by the House in May, 1986, and H.R. 3 as introduced in the House on January 6, 1987, required retaliation only in cases involving violations of trade agreements, unjustifiable practices that

---

April Hearings on S. 490, supra n. 1, 18–19, 27–29 (statement and testimony of Ambassador Clayton Yeutter, U.S. Trade Representative); Yeutter-Rostenkowski-Gibbons Letter, supra n. 16, 1–2; Letter to Speaker of the House Jim Wright from Secretary of the Treasury James A. Baker III, U.S. Trade Representative Ambassador Clayton Yeutter, Secretary of State George P. Shultz, Secretary of Commerce Malcolm Baldrige, Secretary of Agriculture Richard E. Lyng, Secretary of Labor Bill Brock, Secretary of Defense Caspar Weinberger, Secretary of Transportation Elizabeth H. Dole, Secretary of Energy John Herrington, Secretary of Education William Bennett, Director, Office of Management and Budget, James E. Miller, and Chairman, Council of Economic Advisers, Beryl W. Sprinkel, 2 (April 27, 1987) (unpublished, on file at USTR); hereinafter Cabinet Letter.

62. *Hearing on S. 1860,* supra n. 3, 48–49 (testimony of Ambassador Clayton Yeutter, U.S. Trade Representative), 59 (USTR's section-by-section analysis, title II, S. 1860); *March Hearing on S. 490,* supra n. 12, 13–14, 41, 45 (testimony of Alan F. Holmer, General Counsel, USTR); *April Hearings on S. 490,* supra n. 1, 28–30 (testimony of Ambassador Clayton Yeutter, U.S. Trade Representative).

63. 19 U.S.C. § 2412 (1982 and Supp. IV 1986).

64. S. 1860, supra n. 17, § 205(b)(3).

65. Such relative moderation in the House bill provisions on mandatory retaliation prompted Representative Pease to state at Senate Finance Committee hearings in July 1986: "If anything, the Senate bill is tougher, more mandatory than the House bill in this respect. I don't know how we in the House could have let this happen!" *Hearing on S. 1860,* supra n. 3, 18.

burden or restrict U.S. commerce, or export targeting.[66] Thus, the scope of the mandate to retaliate was far narrower in H.R. 3 than in S. 1860. Moreover, H.R. 3 also provided broader exceptions. No retaliation was required if the contracting parties to General Agreement on Tariffs and Trade (GATT) found the practice not to be unfair, or if the president found that:

- satisfactory measures were being taken by the foreign country to grant the United States its rights under a trade agreement;
- the foreign government had agreed to eliminate or phase out the practices concerned, or had agreed to an imminent solution to the burden or restriction on U.S. commerce;
- it was impossible to achieve such elimination, phase out or imminent solution, but the foreign government agreed to provide adequate compensatory trade benefits; or
- the national economic interest would be more adversely affected if action was taken than if it was not.[67]

Thus even in the more limited area of its application, the House mandate to retaliate included, most importantly, a national economic interest exception.

In the Subcommittee on Trade's markup of H.R. 3 during the week of March 13, 1987, the only significant amendment to the mandatory retaliation provisions eliminated the requirement in export targeting cases for an injury determination by the International Trade Commission (ITC), and substituted instead a requirement for a USTR finding that the export targeting causes a *significant* burden or restriction on U.S. commerce.[68] In its markup on March 24–25, 1987, the full committee rejected a series of amendments offered by Representative Hal Daub (R-Nebraska) that would have allowed the president or the trade representative *not* to take action under Section 301, even if otherwise required, if such action would be inconsistent with the international obligations of the United States or would be likely to result in reduced foreign markets for U.S. agricultural exports.[69]

---

66. H.R. 4800, supra n. 18, § 112; H.R. 3, supra n. 21, § 112. These provisions required retaliation only if the ITC determined that imports caused or threatened injury or materially retarded the establishment of a U.S. industry. For a definition and discussion of export targeting, see infra n. 109–36 and accompanying text.

67. H.R. 3, supra n. 21, § 112.

68. Subcommittee on Trade Press Release, supra n. 22, 3.

69. Amendments Offered by Representative Daub (R-Nebraska) (unpublished, on file at USTR). The final Ways and Means Committee action on H.R. 3 is reflected in Press Release no. 5-A, supra n. 25, 2–3. See H.R. 3 (May 8, 1988 print), supra n. 27, § 121. See generally H.R. *Rep. No. 40,* supra n. 9, 60–62. Support for mandatory retaliation was not unanimous within the committee. For example, Representative Philip Crane (R-Illinois) called it "patently foolish" to create "a self-propelled mechanism to mount trade assaults on our best customers. . . ." 134 *Cong. Rec.* H3,551 (daily ed., May 24, 1988).

The analogous Senate omnibus trade bill remained substantially less flexible on mandatory retaliation than the House bill. S. 490 continued to mandate retaliation in all Section 301 cases where the trade representative found unfairness, although it added a limited national economic interest exception, not included in S. 1860, available in all cases except those found to be "unjustifiable" as defined in the bill.[70] During the Finance Committee's markup of S. 490 in April and May, 1987, Senator Bob Packwood (R-Oregon) offered a package of amendments to the Section 301 provisions.[71] The administration inferred that Senator Packwood had proposed—and that in adopting the Packwood proposals, the Finance Committee had voted—to restrict the scope of the mandate so as not to apply to "unreasonable" and "discriminatory" cases. However, in fact, the proposal as finally drafted applied the mandate in *all* Section 301 cases, but provided a national economic interest exception in unreasonable and discriminatory cases.[72] Senator Packwood also proposed—and the committee agreed—to add two exceptions to the mandate to retaliate: (1) where it was "impossible" to eliminate the practice, but the foreign government agreed to provide fully compensatory trade benefits;[73] and (2) where action under Section 301 would cause serious harm to national security. The Packwood proposals were adopted by the Finance Committee, 14 to 2, on April 29.[74]

The Senate floor debate in June and July, 1987, resulted in only one amendment regarding mandatory retaliation. This amendment, offered by Senator Pete V. Domenici (R-New Mexico), made the use of subsidies to create excess capacity to produce nonagricultural, fungible goods an unreasonable practice for purposes of Section 301. This practice was uniquely exempted entirely from the mandate to retaliate.[75] Thus the mandatory retalia-

70. S. 490, supra n. 29, § 304.

71. Packwood Proposal on Section 301, supra n. 30.

72. See S. 490 (June 12, 1987 print), § 305 (on file at USTR). The temporary confusion over the scope of the Packwood proposals resulted from the conceptual description of the proposals, which indicated that the provisions in S. 490 mandating retaliation in unjustifiable cases would be retained.

73. See S. *Rep. No. 71*, 100th Cong., 1st sess., 1987, 83 ("[T]he standard of impossibility . . . is a high one; however, it is not meant to connote physical impossibility.").

74. See supra n. 30.

75. Amendment no. 433, offered by Senator Pete V. Domenici (R-New Mexico), 133 *Cong. Rec.* S9,367 (daily ed., July 8, 1987). The amendment was adopted by a vote of 71 to 28. Id., S9,384. It had been thought that members of the Congressional Copper Caucus would offer a similar amendment to H.R. 3 during the Trade Subcommittee or Ways and Means Committee markup in March, 1987. However, no such amendment was ever introduced. See Letter to Sam Gibbons, Chairman, Subcommittee on Trade, from Congressmen Jim Kolbe, Morris K. Udall, Bob Stump, Beau Boulter, Joe Skeen, Richard Stallings, Robert W. Davis, Bill Richardson, Howard C. Nielson, Barbara F. Vucanovich, Jon L. Kyl, and Ronald D. Coleman (March 11, 1987) (unpublished, on file at USTR).

tion provisions in the final Senate substitute bill, S. 1420,[76] closely tracked the Finance Committee bill.

During the trade conference, the Senate and House conferees went through the same series of offers and counteroffers on mandatory retaliation as they had on transfer of authority.[77] They finally reached agreement at the March 31, 1988, Rostenkowski-Bentsen meeting in the Capitol.[78] Essentially the Senate receded, adopting the House provisions on mandatory retaliation modified by the deletion of the House national economic interest exception and the addition of exceptions (1) where action under Section 301 would cause serious harm to the national security, and (2) "[i]n extraordinary cases, where action would have an adverse impact on the U.S. economy substantially out of proportion to the benefits of action, taking into account the impact of not acting on the credibility of Section 301."[79]

Thus the final bill takes the more moderate House approach, limiting the scope of the mandate to retaliate to those Section 301 cases involving a violation of, or denial of benefits under, a trade agreement, or a breach of any other agreement, that burdens or restricts U.S. commerce. Even in these cases, the bill contains the limited national economic interest exceptions drafted by Chairman Bentsen.[80] The mandate does not apply to unreasonable or discriminatory cases.[81]

What is the significance of the mandatory retaliation provisions likely to be? Proponents of mandatory retaliation hope that the establishment of a statutory mandate will enhance the credibility of the threat of retaliation under Section 301, and thereby increase the administration's negotiating leverage and the prospects for favorable, trade-liberalizing resolutions of trade disputes.[82] They also hope that the existence of the mandate will have a chilling effect on the establishment of new trade barriers by U.S. trading partners.[83]

76. S. 1420, supra n. 34, § 306.

77. See supra n. 41–44.

78. Proposed Final Agreement, supra n. 46, 3; see also supra text accompanying n. 45.

79. Proposed Final Agreement, supra n. 46, 3; *Conference Report*, supra n. 46, 559. Finance Committee Chairman Bentsen personally drafted the second exception in his own handwriting.

80. See 1988 Trade Act, supra n. 4, § 1301, amending 1974 Trade Act, supra n. 5, § 301(a); *Conference Report*, supra n. 46, 557–60.

81. The mandate does not apply to targeting, which in the final bill was defined as an unreasonable practice. See infra n. 109–36 and accompanying text. *Conference Report*, supra n. 46, 560, states: "In 'unreasonable' cases there is a presumption that the USTR would take action on such cases where it has a reasonable indication that such action will be effective in changing the foreign country's practice or barrier." This language was agreed to in the final Rostenkowski-Bentsen meeting the evening of March 31. See Proposed Final Agreement, supra n. 46, 3.

82. See, e.g., H.R. *Rep. No. 40*, supra n. 9, 62.

83. For example, Senator Bill Bradley (D-New Jersey) expressed his hope that mandatory retaliation would maximize efficiency by forcing the free flow of goods and serve as a disincentive for a country to put up new trade barriers. *March Hearing on S. 490*, supra n. 12, 36.

Even opponents of the retaliation mandate readily recognize that it increases pressure on USTR to act decisively, and makes it far harder for the executive not to respond to Section 301 violations. On the other hand, the mandate preserves sufficient discretion in the USTR to ensure that such action can be judicious and trade-liberalizing, rather than protectionist. According to this view, the effect of the mandatory retaliation amendments in the 1988 Trade Act is essentially to ensure the perpetuation of the aggressive, effective use of the Section 301 program by the Reagan administration during 1985–88. While the provisions could be used in a protectionist manner, they allow ample discretion to avoid any necessarily protectionist application.

III. Unfair Practices: Worker Rights, Targeting and Private Anticompetitive Activity

Another major debate throughout the 1985–88 period was which practices, if any, specifically to enumerate as potentially actionable under Section 301.

Worker Rights

Many members of Congress were concerned about denial of internationally recognized worker rights: the right of association, the right to organize and bargain collectively, freedom from any form of forced or compulsory labor, establishment of a minimum age for the employment of children, and standards for minimum wages, hours of work, and occupational safety and health of workers. Following several amendments to the Generalized System of Preferences (GSP), designed to promote respect for such rights,[84] members of Congress seeking to promote worker rights issues in other trade remedies wished to include specific provisions in Section 301 as well.

The principal architect of the Section 301 amendments on worker rights, Congressman Donald Pease (D-Ohio), explained his support for these provisions by asking three questions:

> Don't the governments of some trading nations systematically deny fundamental rights to their workers in order to gain [a] competiti[ve] advantage in world trade?
>
> Since trading rules already exist against capital subsidies and dumping, shouldn't labor repression (perhaps the oldest and least talked-about unfair trade subsidy) be renounced as well in an effort to promote fair competition in world trade?
>
> Shouldn't fair competition in world trade be structured by rule and in

---

84. See Trade and Tariff Act of 1984, title V (Generalized System of Preferences Renewal Act of 1984), 19 U.S.C. § 2461–66 (Supp. IV 1986).

practice to improve the living standards of workers as well as consumers and manufacturers?[85]

The administration opposed proposals to amend Section 301 expressly to cover denials of worker rights. The main reason was its belief that the unilateral adoption of a worker rights standard, without any basis in internationally agreed trade rules, would subject U.S. exports to counterretaliation, and would block trade rather than improve worker rights practices.[86] Communist countries would be most unlikely to change their labor practices, which are fundamental to their economy and ideology, in response to a Section 301 proceeding. Therefore, the routine application of Section 301 to such countries for denying worker rights would result in either (1) widespread U.S. retaliation, likely to precipitate Communist counterretaliation and thus virtually halting trade with such countries; or (2) U.S. toleration of such worker rights denials and nonuse of Section 301 authority to retaliate, undermining the credibility of Section 301. If the United States failed to apply the Section 301 worker rights provision systematically against Communist countries but applied it selectively against an ally, the United States could not readily explain to its allies why it was treating the Communists more favorably.

On the House side, H.R. 4800, in 1986, and H.R. 3, in 1987, both included amendments providing that the denial of specified internationally recognized worker rights[87] is "unreasonable" and therefore actionable under Section 301 if the denial causes a burden or restriction on U.S. commerce.[88] Retaliatory action was discretionary rather than mandatory in these bills.[89] Two significant changes were made to the worker rights provisions in H.R. 3 during the Trade Subcommittee's markup in March, 1987, both at staff's suggestion. First, the subcommittee agreed to authorize the trade representative to determine that the denial of certain worker rights is not unreasonable if the foreign country concerned has taken or is taking steps that demonstrate significant and measurable overall improvement with respect to such rights.[90] Second, the subcommittee agreed to permit the trade representative to take the foreign country's level of economic development into account in determining

---

85. *Hearing on S. 1860,* supra n. 3, 21 (statement of Representative Pease).

86. Id., 39, 52 (testimony of Ambassador Clayton Yeutter, U.S. Trade Representative). See also Yeutter-Rostenkowski-Gibbons Letter, supra n. 16; Cabinet Letter, supra n. 61, 3.

87. I.e., denial of the right of association, denial of the right to organize and bargain collectively, tolerance of any form of forced or compulsory labor, failure to provide a minimum age for the employment of children, and—taking into account a country's level of economic development—failure to provide standards for minimum wages, hours of work, and occupational safety and health of workers. H.R. 3, supra n. 21, § 112.

88. H.R. 4800, supra n. 18, § 112(5)(B); H.R. 3, supra n. 21, § 112(5)(B).

89. See supra nn. 66–69 and accompanying text.

90. Subcommittee on Trade Press Release, supra n. 22, 4.

whether it provided acceptable conditions of work with respect to minimum wages, hours of work, and safety and occupational health of workers.[91] There were no further changes to the bill during the full committee markup[92] or on the House floor.[93]

In the Senate, the 1986 bill, S. 1860, did not contain any worker rights amendments to Section 301;[94] nor did its 1987 successor, S. 490, as introduced.[95] During markup of S. 490 in the Finance Committee in April-May, 1987, however, Senators Riegle (D-Michigan) and Heinz (R-Pennsylvania) offered an amendment to include denials of worker rights as an unreasonable practice under Section 301.[96] Two amendments to the Riegle-Heinz provision were then proposed, patterned on the H.R. 3 amendments as passed by the House Subcommittee on Trade. These amendments required a "persistent pattern" of denial of worker rights before a practice could be potentially actionable under Section 301, and permitted the trade representative to take into account the level of economic development of the country concerned. Unlike the House version, the Senate amendments extended the "level of development" exception to every category of specified worker rights, rather than solely to standards for minimum wages, hours of work, and safety and occupational health of workers. The Finance Committee adopted the Riegle-Heinz proposal as amended by a vote of 15 to 2.[97] In doing so, it rejected a substitute amendment offered by Senator Chafee (R-Rhode Island) to not include denials of worker rights in the definition of unreasonable, but instead to establish a "blue ribbon" commission to study the worker rights issues and report its findings within a year.[98] The worker rights provisions of the bill approved by the Finance Committee[99] were not changed during the debate on the Senate floor.[100]

---

91. See H.R. 3 (May 8 print), supra n. 27, § 121.

92. Press Release no. 5-A, supra n. 25, 4. See generally H.R. *Rep. No. 40,* supra n. 9, 67–68.

93. H.R. 3 (May 8 print), supra n. 27, § 121, § 124.

94. S. 1860, supra n. 17. In the hearings on S. 1860, the Trade Representative opposed such provisions nonetheless, recognizing their inclusion in H.R. 3 and anticipating possible future inclusion in an analogous Senate bill. *Hearing on S. 1860,* supra n. 3, 39, 52 (statement and testimony of Ambassador Clayton Yeutter, U.S. Trade Representative).

95. S. 490, supra n. 29, § 305, expanded the definition of "unreasonable" practices but did not cover worker rights denials.

96. Riegle-Heinz Worker Rights Amendment (undated, but in fact April 30, 1987) (unpublished, on file at USTR).

97. The dissenting votes were Senators Chafee and Wallop.

98. Worker Rights "Blue Ribbon" Commission (undated, but in fact April 30, 1987) (unpublished, on file at USTR). The vote on the Chafee amendment was 4 to 12 (the yeas were Senators Packwood, Roth, Chafee, and Wallop).

99. See S. 490 (June 12, 1987 print), supra n. 72, § 306; S. *Rep. No. 71,* supra n. 73, 88–89.

100. S. 1420, supra n. 34, § 307(c).

The worker rights amendments to Section 301 then lay untouched until the Senate and House conferees of Subconference 1 began exchanging offers. On March 15, 1987, the Senate conferees offered to strike these provisions from the bill altogether and include them instead in a report of managers.[101] The House conferees counteroffered to retain in the bill three forms of unreasonable practices, including the worker rights provisions.[102] On March 30 and 31, Senate and House conferees held to their respective positions on these three unreasonable practices[103] until the final Rostenkowski-Bentsen meeting, when it was agreed that the Senate would recede to the House position retaining worker rights provisions in the statute. The worker rights language would, however, be drawn from the Senate bill, thus requiring a persistent pattern of denials of worker rights, and allowing the trade representative more broadly to take into account the foreign country's level of economic development in considering the alleged unfairness of such denials.[104] The Subconference 1 agreement was included in H.R. 3 as approved by the House[105] and Senate,[106] and is reflected in the Conference Report,[107] and the final 1988 Trade Act.[108]

Export Targeting

Export targeting had been the subject of an extensive debate for a number of years. Although the Trade and Tariff Act of 1984 did not amend any trade remedies expressly to cover targeting,[109] it did require a number of comprehensive studies of foreign industrial targeting, thus setting the stage for further debate and action in the next trade bill.[110] Proponents of adding targeting

101. March 15 Senate Offer, supra n. 41, 5–7. A report of managers is a legislative history in which the managers of a bill state their intentions with respect to certain provisions of the bill.

102. March 21 House Counteroffer, supra n. 42, 4. The other two unreasonable practices were export targeting and anticompetitive behavior.

103. See supra nn. 43–44.

104. Proposed Final Agreement, supra n. 46, 5.

105. 134 *Cong. Rec.* H2,375 (daily ed., April 21, 1988). The conference report was agreed to by a vote of 312 to 107.

106. 134 *Cong. Rec.* S4,926–27 (daily ed., April 27, 1988). The final vote on the conference report was 63 to 36.

107. *Conference Report,* supra n. 46, 568–69. For subsequent history of H.R. 3 and H.R. 4848, see supra n. 47.

108. 1988 Trade Act, supra n. 4, § 1301, amending 1974 Trade Act, supra n. 5, § 301(d).

109. See Holmer and Bello, *"The Trade and Tariff Act of 1984: The Road to Enactment,"* *International Lawyer* 19 (1985): 287, 294–304.

110. Trade and Tariff Act of 1984, supra n. 5, § 625, required the Secretaries of Commerce and Labor, the Trade Representative, and the Comptroller General each to undertake comprehensive analyses of: "(A) whether foreign industrial targeting should be considered . . . an unfair trade practice under United States law; (B) whether current . . . law adequately address[es] the

provisions to Section 301 argued that foreign governments were distorting trade, to the detriment of U.S. producers of targeted products, by marshaling their resources to enhance artificially the export competitiveness of selected industries.[111]

The administration, however, opposed these targeting proposals. First, it argued that any amendment to Section 301 was unnecessary, since targeting practices already were actionable under this trade remedy, as reflected by actions in the *Japan Semiconductors*[112] and *Brazil Informatics*[113] cases. Second, the administration asserted that any amendment could inadvertently narrow the scope of Section 301's application, since the statute was already quite broad. Third, and most important, the administration maintained that reciprocal action by U.S. trading partners could be detrimental to U.S. exports, since foreigners could claim that the U.S. engaged in targeting practices of its own.[114] U.S. exports could then be excluded from foreign markets, as a result

---

subsidy element of foreign industrial policy measures; and (C) the extent to which foreign industrial targeting practices are significantly affecting United States commerce. . . ." The resulting studies are as follows: U.S. Trade Representative, *Report on Foreign Industrial Targeting* (July 15, 1985); Department of Commerce, *Study of Foreign Government Targeting Practices and the Remedies Available under the Countervailing Duty and Antidumping Duty Laws* (July, 1985); Department of Labor, *Trade and Employment Effects of Foreign Industrial Targeting: Results of Three Case Studies* (July, 1985); Quick Finan and Associates, *An Analysis of the Effects of Targeting on the Competitiveness of the U.S. Semiconductor Industry* (1985) (prepared for USTR, Commerce, and Labor); The Futures Group, *The Impact of Foreign Industrial Practices on the U.S. Computer Industry* (1985) (prepared for USTR, Commerce, and Labor); Booz-Allen and Hamilton, Inc., *The Effects of Foreign Targeting on the U.S. Automotive Industry* (May, 1985) (prepared for USTR and Labor).

111. See e.g., S. *Rep. No. 71,* supra n. 73, 86; H.R. *Rep. No. 40,* supra n. 9, 64–67.

112. See Initiation of Investigation, 50 *Fed. Reg.* 28,866 (USTR 1985) (initiating an investigation in response to the petition of the Semiconductor Industry Association complaining of Japanese targeting of semiconductor production); Presidential Memorandum of July 31, 1986, Determination under Section 301, 3 C.F.R. 263 (1987), reprinted in 51 *Fed. Reg.* 27,811 (1986) (approving the U.S.-Japan Semiconductor Agreement, and noting that any failure by Japan to meet the commitments and objectives of the agreement would be inconsistent with a trade agreement or would be an unjustifiable act that burdened or restricted U.S. commerce); Proclamation No. 5,631, 3 C.F.R. 41 (1988), reprinted in 52 *Fed. Reg.* 13,412 (1987) (raising duties on specified imports of Japan to 100 percent in response to Japan's breach of the Semiconductor Agreement); Suspension of Some Sanctions, 52 *Fed. Reg.* 22,693 (USTR 1987), and Suspension of Some Sanctions, 52 *Fed. Reg.* 43,146 (USTR 1987) (suspending some sanctions based upon Japan's improved conformity with the Semiconductor Agreement).

113. See Initiation of Investigation, 50 *Fed. Reg.* 37,608 (USTR 1985) (self-initiating an investigation of Brazilian practices targeting the informatics, or computer and computer-related, industry); Presidential Memorandum of October 6, 1986, Determination under Section 301, 3 C.F.R. 270 (1987), reprinted in 51 *Fed. Reg.* 35,993 (1986) (determining that Brazil's informatics practices are unreasonable and a burden or restriction on U.S. commerce).

114. See, e.g., *April Hearings on S. 490,* supra n. 1, 13, 43 (statements of Senator Durenberger [R-Minnesota]).

of either retaliation by foreign governments against U.S. actions under Section 301, or foreign mirror actions against products allegedly targeted by the U.S. government.[115]

Given the extensive debate on export targeting, it was not surprising that the 1986 House omnibus trade bill, H.R. 4800, established targeting as a new form of unfair practice under Section 301, actionable if the ITC found that it caused or threatened injury to U.S. producers. Targeting was defined as:

> any government plan or scheme consisting of a combination of coordinated actions, whether carried out severally or jointly, that are bestowed on a specific enterprise, industry, or group thereof the effect of which is to assist the enterprise, industry, or group to become more competitive in the export of a class or kind of merchandise.[116]

H.R. 4800 required the trade representative to determine whether a foreign government was engaging in targeting within only 180 days of initiating an investigation. If USTR found that targeting existed, action was mandatory rather than discretionary, and had to reflect the full benefits to beneficiary industries over the period during which targeting had an effect on U.S. commerce.[117]

The H.R. 4800 targeting provisions were incorporated into H.R. 3, as introduced on January 6, 1987.[118] At the staff's suggestion, the Subcommittee on Trade modified these proposals at its markup of H.R. 3 in March, 1987. The subcommittee dropped the ITC injury determination and instead made targeting actionable only if it *significantly* burdened or restricted U.S. commerce, as determined by the trade representative.[119] Action was mandatory in cases where the targeting was determined *currently* to be such a significant burden or restriction, unless the national economic interest would be more adversely affected if action were taken than if not. Action was discretionary where targeting only *threatened* to cause a significant burden or restriction.[120] Finally, if the trade representative declined to take action in a targeting case

---

115. See, e.g., *Hearing on S. 1860,* supra n. 3, 52 (testimony of Ambassador Clayton Yeutter, U.S. Trade Representative); see also id., 56–57 (USTR's section-by-section analysis, title II of S. 1860); *March Hearing on S. 490,* supra n. 12, 17, 45–46 (testimony of Alan F. Holmer, General Counsel, USTR); *April Hearings on S. 490,* supra n. 1, 44; Yeutter-Rostenkowski-Gibbons Letter, supra n. 16, 2.

116. H.R. 4800, supra n. 18, § 112.

117. Id., §§ 112–13.

118. H.R. 3, supra n. 21, §§ 112–13.

119. In requiring a *significant* burden or restriction on U.S. commerce, the committee "does expect the USTR to apply a higher, somewhat more rigorous 'injury' test than in other Section 301 cases." H.R. *Rep. No. 40,* supra n. 9, 66.

120. Subcommittee on Trade Press Release, supra n. 22, 3–4.

based on the national economic interest exception, he or she was required to appoint a panel of experts from the private sector to advise how to promote the competitiveness of the affected industry.[121] The subcommittee provisions were not significantly modified either during the full committee markup[122] or on the House floor.[123]

On the Senate side, S. 1860 had included amendments to Section 301's definition of unreasonable to cover "any combination" of acts, policies, and practices denying fair and equitable market opportunities, and "protection of any industry in its formative stages."[124] S. 490 was far more comprehensive than S. 1860 in its coverage of targeting. S. 490 specifically made targeting, as defined in H.R. 3, unreasonable, and incorporated an illustrative laundry list of prohibited targeting practices, including (1) protection of the home market (which the GATT expressly permits in some instances[125]), (2) promotion or tolerance of cartels, (3) special restrictions on technology transfer imposed for reasons of commercial advantage, (4) discriminatory government procurement, and (5) use of export performance requirements or subsidization.[126] S. 490 mandated action against these targeting practices and required an unfairness determination on an expedited basis within only six months.[127]

The Finance Committee debated the targeting provisions of S. 490 extensively during its markup of the bill in April-May, 1987. A proposal by Senator Durenberger (R-Minnesota) to delete the provisions was defeated, 9 to 1.[128] On the other hand, the committee unanimously approved a proposal by Senator Chafee (R-Rhode Island) to adopt certain provisions of H.R. 3.[129] In targeting cases where the president invoked the national economic interest exception and declined to act under Section 301, the Chafee amendment required the establishment of a private sector advisory panel to recommend how to restore or improve the international competitiveness of the industry affected by the export targeting. While the amendment did not require the president to act on the panel's recommendations, the president would have to transmit those recommendations to Congress and report the actions he took in

---

121. Id., 4; see also H.R. 3 (May 8 print), supra n. 27, § 121.

122. Press Release no. 5-A, supra n. 25, 3. See generally H.R. *Rep. No. 40,* supra n. 9, 63–67.

123. H.R. 3 (May 8, 1987 print), supra n. 27, § 121.

124. S. 1860, supra n. 17, § 204(c).

125. General Agreement on Tariffs and Trade, opened for signature Oct. 30, 1947, Articles XI, XII, XVIII, XIX, 61 Stat. pts. 5 and 6, T.I.A.S. No. 1700, 55 U.N.T.S. 187.

126. S. 490, supra n. 29, § 305(c).

127. Id., §§ 304–5.

128. Targeting Amendment Offered by Senator Dave Durenberger (undated, but in fact April 30, 1987) (unpublished, on file at USTR). See *April Hearings on S. 490,* supra n. 1, 13, 43 (statements of Senator Durenberger).

129. H.R. 3 (May 8, 1987 print), supra n. 27, § 121.

response.[130] No significant amendments were made to the Section 301 targeting provisions on the Senate floor.[131]

Although the House and Senate bills treated targeting differently (the House establishing it as a new practice, the Senate defining it as an "unreasonable" practice), the outcomes were quite similar. Both bills required an unfairness determination within six months, required action (subject to specified exceptions), and required a private sector panel if action otherwise mandated was not taken on the basis of the national economic interest exception.[132]

As with the other Section 301 issues, the Senate and House conferees of Subconference 1 did not take up the targeting provisions until March, 1988. As already indicated, the initial Senate offer was to strike all the unfair practices from both bills and include them instead in a report of managers.[133] The House subconferees counteroffered, instead, to retain export targeting, worker rights, and anticompetitive practices in the bill.[134] The final agreement within Subconference 1 included targeting in the statute, defined it as unreasonable without the illustrative list of targeting practices from the Senate bill, and deleted the requirement for a private sector panel if the president declined to take Section 301 action on the basis of the national economic interest exception.[135] However, as finally drafted and approved, H.R. 3 and the 1988 Trade Act do include the private sector panel provisions.[136]

Anticompetitive Practices

A third major unfair practice addressed in the 1988 trade act's amendments to Section 301 is the toleration by a foreign government of systematic, anticom-

---

130. Amendment on Export Targeting, Amendment to S. 490 Offered by Senator Chafee (undated, but in fact April 30, 1987) (unpublished, on file at USTR).

131. S. 1420, supra n. 34, §§ 306–8.

132. See H.R. 3 (May 8, 1987 print), supra n. 27, § 121, § 124; S. 490 (June 12, 1987 print), supra n. 72, § 304.

133. March 15 Senate Offer, supra n. 41, 5–7. See also supra n. 101 and accompanying text.

134. March 21 House Counteroffer, supra n. 42, 4; see supra n. 102. See also subsequent offers and counteroffers, supra n. 43–45.

135. Proposed Final Agreement, supra n. 46, 5. The House offer to delete the private sector panel requirement is most clearly apparent in the March 21 House Counteroffer, supra n. 42, 5.

136. H.R. 3 (Final), § 1301, amending 1974 Trade Act, supra n. 5, § 301(d)(3), § 305(b), reprinted in *Conference Report,* supra n. 46, 1, 65, 71; 1988 Trade Act, supra n. 4, § 1301, amending 1974 Trade Act, supra n. 5, § 301(d)(3), § 305(b). See also *Conference Report,* supra n. 46, 566–68. Initially omitted in the final agreement, the private sector panel provision was later restored by the staff with the approval of Chairmen Bentsen and Rostenkowski.

petitive practices by private firms that restrict access of U.S. companies to purchasing by such private firms in that foreign country. Various members of Congress were concerned that market-restrictive behavior on the part of private firms, when coupled with the failure of a foreign government to intervene to eliminate such behavior, can be as great a barrier to market access as any formal governmental act, policy, or practice. To the extent such behavior creates a burden or restriction on U.S. commerce, they proposed that it be actionable under Section 301.[137]

The administration opposed the specific inclusion of anticompetitive practices within the scope of Section 301 on two primary grounds. First, it argued that the amendment was unnecessary, since Section 301 already could be used in such circumstances, provided a sufficient nexus existed between private and governmental activity. Second and more important, the administration feared that the amendment would increase pressure to use Section 301 authority in response to principally private behavior—a fundamental departure from Section 301's traditional focus on unfair foreign *government* acts, policies, or practices.

The administration pointed to the relation of Section 301 and the international obligations of the United States to explain the significance of such a departure. Actions under Section 301—such as raising tariffs or imposing quantitative restrictions on imports—are covered by GATT.[138] Article I of GATT generally requires parties to provide most favored nation treatment with respect to tariff matters; Article II prohibits increases in tariffs beyond the GATT-approved rates; and Article XI generally prohibits the imposition of quantitative restrictions. As a result, action under Section 301 on products[139] could be inconsistent with GATT, unless GATT approval were obtained in advance. Because use of Section 301 authority could entail breaches of U.S. international obligations under GATT to other governments, the administration opposed any such use in response to solely private activity. Unless a foreign government itself had engaged in an unfair practice, the administra-

---

137. U.S. exports of soda ash, semiconductors, and automobile parts were believed to have suffered from such foreign anticompetitive practices. S. *Rep. No. 71*, supra n. 73, 85; *March Hearing on S. 490*, supra n. 12, 29–30 (statements of Senator Wallop [R-Wyoming]).

138. See supra n. 125.

139. This concern does not exist for retaliation on services, since services are not currently covered by GATT. However, in the ongoing Uruguay Round of Multilateral Trade Negotiations, the United States has proposed to extend GATT discipline to cover services, as well as other frontier areas, such as trade-related investment measures and intellectual property protection. M. Samuels, "The Prospects for a Strengthened General Agreement on Tariffs and Trade," 5–8 (speech by Ambassador Michael A. Samuels, Deputy U.S. Trade Representative, American Club of Brussels and the International Trade and Investment Committee of the American Chamber of Commerce, Brussels, Belgium, December 10, 1987) (unpublished, on file at USTR).

tion believed that breaching U.S. obligations to that government was not warranted or appropriate.

Neither H.R. 4800,[140] nor H.R. 3 as introduced in the House in 1987,[141] included anticompetitive behavior as an unfair practice actionable under Section 301. During the Ways and Means Committee markup, however, Representative J. J. Pickle (D-Texas) circulated a proposed amendment on March 18, 1987,[142] and Representative Sander M. Levin (D-Michigan) offered it formally on March 24.[143] As amended by Representative Gibbons (D-Florida),[144] the amendment included within the term *unreasonable* the "toleration by a host government of systematic anticompetitive activities by private firms or among private firms in the foreign country that have the effect of restricting, on a basis that is inconsistent with commercial considerations, access of United States goods to purchasing by such firms. . . ."[145] The committee adopted the provision, and there were no amendments to it on the House floor.[146]

On the Senate side, the proposals concerning foreign government toleration of systematic private anticompetitive activity originated in S. 1860. This 1986 bill would have amended the definition of unreasonable to include a foreign government's failure to provide adequate and effective protection against anticompetitive practices.[147] While this concept was not originally included in the 1987 bill, S. 490,[148] it was added during the Finance Committee's markup on April 29. Senator Riegle proposed to include the H.R. 3 provision that had been offered by Representative Levin in the House.[149] Following the administration's intervention explaining its concerns, the committee unanimously approved the Riegle amendment. However, the committee required the conference report to clarify that the administration could continue to exercise discretion by taking into account, among other things, the following factors: (1) the flagrancy of the anticompetitive acts, (2) the degree of the effect on U.S. commerce, and (3) whether the acts are inconsistent with

---

140. H.R. 4800, supra n. 18.

141. H.R. 3, supra n. 21.

142. Congressman Pickle, Proposed Amendment to Section 301 (undated, but in fact March 18, 1987) (unpublished, on file at USTR).

143. Amendment by Representative Levin (undated, but in fact March 24, 1987) (unpublished, on file at USTR).

144. The Gibbons amendment, which was proposed orally only, not in writing, specified that the requisite toleration of systematic private anticompetitive activity had to be by the host government.

145. H.R. 3 (May 8, 1987 print), supra n. 27, § 121(5)(B).

146. Id., § 121. See generally H.R. *Rep. No. 40,* supra n. 9, 68–69.

147. S. 1860, supra n. 17, § 204(c)(5).

148. S. 490, supra n. 29.

149. Riegle Amendment to S. 490, Government Toleration of Anticompetitive Practices (undated, but in fact April 29, 1987) (unpublished, on file at USTR).

local (rather than U.S.) law.[150] No amendments were made to this provision on the Senate floor.

Like denials of worker rights and export targeting, the trade conference did not review the anticompetitive practices amendment until March, 1988. The Senate conferees in Subconference 1 initially offered to strike all the specifically enumerated unfair practices from the bill;[151] the House conferees counteroffered to retain worker rights, export targeting, and anticompetitive practices (as defined in the House bill) in the statute, along with most of those provisions already in current law.[152] Ultimately the Senate receded,[153] so that H.R. 3[154] and the 1988 Trade Act[155] both contain this provision.

Significance of Unfair Practices Amendments

Although denial of worker rights, export targeting, and anticompetitive practices already fell within the broad compass of unreasonable practices under Section 301, their specific enumeration could increase the pressure on the trade representative formally to find such practices to be unfair and to take action in response.[156] However, even if the unreasonable criteria are satisfied, each practice still must cause a burden or restriction on U.S. commerce in order to be actionable. And even if the trade representative makes an affirmative unfairness finding, he or she is not required to take any action in response.[157] These amendments thus appear to be evolutionary refinements of the law rather than revolutionary changes.

---

150. See S. *Rep. No. 71*, supra n. 73, 86. This report also clarified that this provision is "not intended to apply broadly to any and all purchasing decisions by private firms. It is intended to apply to government toleration of pervasive or egregious activities in a foreign country . . . which result in a persistent pattern of restricted market access by U.S. firms in a particular industry" (id., 85). The report continued: "The Committee wishes to emphasize . . . that its intent is not to regulate the business practices of foreign firms or to enforce upon foreign governments U.S. concepts of antitrust law. This provision [applies] . . . only when the foreign government is in essence at least a silent partner to the restrictive practice" (id., 86).

151. March 15 Senate Offer, supra n. 41, 5.

152. March 21 House Counteroffer, supra n. 42, 5. For the ensuing sequence of House and Senate proposals, see supra n. 43–45. See supra n. 101–2 and accompanying text for an explanation of the House and Senate offers with respect to worker rights, export targeting, and anticompetitive practices.

153. Proposed Final Agreement, supra n. 46, 5.

154. H.R. 3 (Final), § 1301, reprinted in *Conference Report*, supra n. 46, 1, 65.

155. 1988 Trade Act, supra n. 4, § 1301(a), amending 1974 Trade Act, supra n. 5, § 301(d).

156. See S. *Rep. No. 71*, supra n. 73, 74, stating that "this title specifies several additional types of foreign practices as actionable . . . *in order to provide more concrete direction to the USTR and the President*" (emphasis added).

157. But cf. *Conference Report*, supra n. 46, 560 (there "is a presumption that the USTR

IV. The Gephardt Amendment and Super 301

A prominent feature of the House omnibus trade bills was Representative Richard A. Gephardt's (D-Missouri) amendment on countries with excessive and unwarranted trade surpluses. Included in both H.R. 4800[158] and H.R. 3 as introduced,[159] this amendment was intended to provide a mechanism "sufficiently broad to deal with the full spectrum of a country's acts, policies, and practices as they affect that country's overall international trade position."[160] Its proponents hoped that it could be used to "induce large surplus countries to take immediate steps to remove their trade barriers in a manner which will cause substantial reductions in their trade surpluses. . . ."[161]

The Gephardt proposal was complex. First, it called on the ITC to identify countries that have an "excessive" bilateral trade surplus with the United States, using a mathematical formula.[162] Then, within fifteen days of the ITC decision, the trade representative would determine whether countries with excessive surpluses also engage in a pattern of unjustifiable, unreasonable, or discriminatory trade policies or practices having a significant adverse effect on U.S. commerce and contribute to the countries' trade surpluses. In addition, USTR would be required each year to quantify the cost of all barriers blocking U.S. exports to major trading partners.

Once USTR identified those excessive and unwarranted trade surplus countries, it would have six months in which to negotiate bilateral agreements with each country to: (1) eliminate such country's unwarranted acts, policies, and practices, or eliminate the significant adverse effects of such acts, policies, or practices on U.S. commerce, (2) reduce the U.S. bilateral deficit by the amount attributable to the unfair practices, and (3) achieve at least an annual 10 percent reduction in the foreign country's bilateral surplus. If no

would take action on such cases where it has a reasonable indication that such action will be effective in changing the foreign country's practice or barrier").

158. H.R. 4800, supra n. 18, § 119.

159. H.R. 3, supra n. 21, § 119.

160. H.R. *Rep. No. 40,* supra n. 9, 80.

161. Id.

162. An "excessive trade surplus country" was defined as any major exporting country (i.e., any country for which the aggregate value of merchandise trade with the United States is more than $7 billion, adjusted to reflect inflation since 1985) which has a bilateral trade surplus with the United States exceeding $3 billion and whose nonpetroleum exports to the United States are 175 percent of its nonpetroleum imports from the United States. No ITC determination was required with respect to a country for a certain year if the U.S. merchandise trade deficit with that country was less than 1.5 percent of U.S. GNP in that year. H.R. 4800 and H.R. 3, supra n. 18 and 21, § 119. Based on 1986 data, excessive trade surplus countries would have included Brazil, Hong Kong, Italy, Japan, South Korea, Taiwan, and West Germany.

agreement was reached, the president would be required to take specific trade-restricting actions against *all* the unjustifiable, unreasonable, or discriminatory acts, policies, or practices in an amount necessary to achieve the deficit reduction goals in that year. If negotiated agreements or presidential actions failed to achieve such reduction goals, the president would have to take further actions to the extent necessary to meet those goals. Two exceptions were provided: (1) for countries with balance of payments difficulties, if the president considered that the country could not meet the surplus reduction goal without suffering significant economic harm; and (2) if the president determined that enforcement would cause substantial harm to the national economic interest of the United States. However, both exceptions were subject to a sixty day "fast-track" Congressional veto; and even where the president waived mandatory action, he would be required to pursue an alternate plan to meet the deficit reduction goals. A similar process would be followed in each year through 1990.[163]

The Gephardt proposal was controversial from its inception, and the administration argued vigorously against it. The first argument was that the amendment made no economic sense. It contemplated (1) a correction of bilateral trade imbalances through trade policy actions; and (2) a measurement of the success of trade policy actions through improvements in bilateral trade imbalances. Because foreign unfair trade practices constitute only a small part of the cause of the trade deficit, the fundamental premise of the amendment was fatally flawed.

Second, the administration argued that the Gephardt amendment was unfair. Even if the United States took action fully offsetting the unfair trade practices concerned, the Gephardt amendment nonetheless required further action if the arbitrary, annual trade surplus reduction goals were not met. Thus the United States would unjustifiably overreact to unfair foreign government practices.

Third, the administration contended that the Gephardt amendment was counterproductive. Its stated purpose was to open up foreign markets. Yet its measurement of success was annual reduction in a country's bilateral trade surplus with the United States. Under the Gephardt provision, a foreign government would be more likely to restrain exports to the United States, since that is far easier than eliminating unfair trade practices. Foreign restraints on exports to the United States would not boost U.S. exports, and would undermine U.S. industrial competitiveness by increasing costs to domestic consumers. In short, the administration argued, the Gephardt amendment was an unacceptable approach to the trade deficit and unfair trade

---

163. H.R. 3, supra n. 21, § 119.

practices problems. It would put U.S. trade policy on automatic pilot by denying the president the discretion he needs to determine whether a trading partner has satisfactorily eliminated or offset its unfair trade practices.[164]

Perhaps not surprisingly, the Gephardt provisions were modified in the bill prepared by staff for markup by the House Subcommittee on Trade in early March, 1987. The subcommittee-approved provisions differed from the original proposal principally in their elimination of the requirement for action to meet the 10 percent trade deficit reduction goal. Retaliation was still required if negotiations (on a very short deadline) failed to result in a substantial reduction either of the foreign country's unfair trade practices or of effects on U.S. commerce. The success of any agreement resulting from those negotiations or, in the event no agreement were reached, the retaliation, would not be measured by changes in such country's bilateral trade surplus.[165]

The subcommittee bill also modified the available exceptions. Whereas the original Gephardt provisions provided a national economic interest waiver only where enforcement would cause *substantial* harm to U.S. economic interests, the subcommittee bill established this standard only for unjustifiable acts. For unreasonable or discriminatory acts, a waiver would be available if the economic harm of retaliation would simply outweigh the harm caused by the foreign policy or practice.[166]

When the full Ways and Means Committee left the subcommittee's amended Gephardt provisions unchanged,[167] Representative Gephardt indicated that he would seek an amendment to the bill on the House floor more nearly to reflect his original proposal for mandatory, annual 10 percent surplus reduction goals.[168] The issue in the House then became whether to replace the Ways and Means provisions on excessive and unwarranted trade surplus countries with the original Gephardt provisions. On April 22, Chairman Rostenkowski circulated a "Dear Colleague" letter in which he urged support for the Ways and Means Committee substitute. He stressed that the committee had not dropped the Gephardt amendment, but rather had modified it "in light of all the criticism we have received since last year in order to make it a fairer,

---

164. Talking Points on Gephardt Amendment (undated) (unpublished, on file at USTR). See also Cabinet Letter, supra n. 61, 2; attachment to Yeutter-Rostenkowski-Gibbons Letter, supra n. 16, 3; and 133 *Cong. Rec.* H2,781 (daily ed., April 29, 1987) (statement of Representative Frenzel [R-Minnesota]).

165. Subcommittee on Trade Press Release, supra n. 22, 5–6.

166. Id.

167. Press Release no. 5-A, supra n. 25, 5–6. See generally H.R. *Rep. No. 40,* supra n. 9, 77–85.

168. Outline of Proposed Gephardt Amendment (undated, but in fact March 25, 1987) (unpublished, on file at USTR).

more workable, and more realistic approach to foreign unfair trade practices."[169]

A substantial portion of the House floor debate on H.R. 3 was devoted to the Gephardt amendment.[170] Opponents of the original Gephardt amendment (some of whom also did not support the Ways and Means substitute) argued that it was a "loaded gun,"[171] "protectionism in reciprocity's clothing,"[172] and in the "spirit of retrenchment, reversal, and retreat."[173] Chairman Rostenkowski (D-Illinois) denounced it as "too draconian to be effective."[174] Representative Kemp (R-New York) summarized: "[W]hen you have a problem with your neighbor and you pull a gun, do you expect him to carry on a reasonable discussion? Does anyone seriously believe that our allies will lower their trade barriers if we raise our tariffs and quotas?"[175] Gephardt amendment supporters argued to the contrary that it was "an American ace in the hole" in the "international poker game."[176] Representative Gephardt himself stressed that "[t]he amendment is reasonable. It is flexible. It sets standards. It makes sense." He added that his amendment provided more pressure on foreign governments, and established a standard of accountability.[177] The House adopted the Gephardt amendment by a vote of 218 to 214.[178]

On the Senate side, the 1986 Senate omnibus trade bill included no provisions comparable to the Gephardt amendment.[179] The original 1987 bill, S. 490, included a provision that some considered the analogue of the Gephardt amendment, although it operated quite differently. As introduced, S. 490 included a provision entitled "Negotiations in Response to Adversarial Trade,"[180] that called for USTR to identify countries that maintain a consistent pattern of barriers and market-distorting practices—"as in the case of Japan"[181]—as described in the National Trade Estimates Report.[182] The pres-

---

169. Letter from Chairman Dan Rostenkowski to House colleagues on H.R. 3, the Gephardt Amendment (April 22, 1987) (unpublished, on file at USTR).

170. See 133 *Cong. Rec.* H2,755–90 (daily ed., April 29, 1987).

171. Id., H2,760 (remarks of Representative Crane).

172. Id., H2,777 (remarks of Representative Schumer).

173. Id., H2,787 (remarks of Representative Michel).

174. Id., H2,789.

175. Id., H2,764.

176. Id., H2,780 (remarks of Representative Williams [D-Montana]).

177. Id., H2,757 (statement of Representative Gephardt).

178. Id., H2,789–90. The Gephardt amendment became § 126 of H.R. 3 as amended on the House floor. H.R. 3 (May 8, 1987 print), supra n. 27, § 126.

179. S. 1860, supra n. 17.

180. S. 490, supra n. 29, § 302.

181. Id.

182. This report is prepared annually pursuant to 19 U.S.C. § 2241 (1982 and Supp. IV 1986).

ident was then required to enter into negotiations with each such country to eliminate all such practices. Moreover, the president was required to submit a report to Congress describing, in detail, any agreements reached and commitments made as a result of such negotiations, and any evidence that U.S. exports had increased as a result.

The administration opposed the "adversarial trade" provisions of S. 490 as the "rough analogue" to the Gephardt amendment.[183] The fundamental objection was that, like the Gephardt provisions, the Senate measures contemplated a balancing of bilateral trade through trade policy actions rather than through macroeconomic policies. Moreover, they mandated retaliation, and required USTR to "dub a country as an unfair trader," provoking, in all likelihood, a nationalistic backlash that would reduce prospects for negotiating a satisfactory solution.[184]

At Senator Donald Riegle's (D-Michigan) initiative, the Finance Committee discussed, but did not vote, on the Gephardt amendment during its markup of S. 490 on May 7, 1987. The committee did agree to modify the title of the original S. 490 provision, so that the reported bill included a section on "Countries Maintaining a Consistent Pattern of Trade Distortions."[185]

The issue then became whether Senator Riegle would introduce the Gephardt amendment, or a "son of Gephardt" amendment, on the Senate floor. Staff to Senators Riegle, Danforth, Dole, Byrd, and others worked late nights as the bill was debated on the Senate floor to reach agreement on an amendment. After a particularly long night, the "World Markets Opening Initiative" was offered as an amendment on July 10, 1987.[186] Most simply stated, this Super 301 amendment required USTR to: (1) identify—based on the National Trade Estimates Report—countries that maintain a consistent pattern of import barriers and market-distorting practices; (2) self-initiate investigations under Section 302 with respect to those major barriers and market-distorting practices, the elimination of which would be likely to have the most significant potential to increase U.S. exports, either directly or through the establishment of a beneficial precedent;[187] and (3) seek negotia-

---

183. *March Hearing on S. 490*, supra n. 12, 48 (statement of Alan F. Holmer, General Counsel, USTR).

184. Id.

185. S. 490 (June 12 print), supra n. 72, § 303. This provision still singled out Japan as a country maintaining a consistent pattern of trade distortions. See also S. *Rep. No. 71*, supra n. 73, 77.

186. 133 *Cong. Rec.* S9,636–37 (daily ed., July 10, 1987) (text of amendment).

187. There was a considerable difference of opinion about the appropriate number of such self-initiated investigations, which was left unspecified. See, e.g., comments of Senators Dole ("as many or as few") and Danforth ("in quantity and number to be determined by the admin-

tions to eliminate all such major barriers and market-distorting practices. In addition, the amendment called for estimates of effects on U.S. exports if such barriers and practices were eliminated and for reports on actual effects.[188] Moreover, it authorized the Senate Finance and House Ways and Means Committees to file petitions with USTR for the initiation of an investigation under these provisions.[189]

The kinship, if any, between Super 301 and the H.R. 3 Gephardt amendment was extensively debated. Senators Byrd, Danforth, Bentsen, and Baucus all stressed repeatedly that the initiative was not a Gephardt amendment, a "son of Gephardt," or any other relative of Gephardt.[190] Rather, it was intended to "transform a sporadic, unpredictable, occasional, ad hoc use of Section 301 . . . into a systematic attempt to get at those situations which [have been] described as being like peeling layers off an onion. It is an effort aimed not at closing markets, but at opening markets."[191] Not everyone agreed. For example, Senator Daniel Evans (R-Washington) denounced Super 301's focus on bilateralism and mandatory negotiations.[192] Senator John McCain (R-Arizona) warned: "[I]t may well backfire, prompting nationalistic responses around the world that will ignite the very trade war we must avoid."[193] Nonetheless, the Senate passed the initiative by a vote of 87 to 7.[194]

---

istration"), id., S9,639, 9,647–48. See also 134 *Cong. Rec.* H5,535–36, H5,537, H5,545 (daily ed., July 13, 1988) (statements of Representatives Kemp, Crane, and Kolbe). There were considerable differences as well regarding the nature and scope of such self-initiated investigations. Senator Danforth clearly envisioned "super" or "all-embracing" cases, broader than the traditional product- or service-specific Section 301 case (id., at S9,648). However, the initiative did not require investigations any different in nature or scope than traditional investigations.

188. However, the initiative did not require any action by USTR or the president in the event that the actual effects on U.S. exports, after the elimination of the unfair barriers or practices, fell short of the estimates of such effects. See id., S9,651 (dialogue between Senators Danforth and Evans).

189. Id., S9,637 (text of amendment). See also S. 1420, supra n. 34, §§ 303–4.

190. For example, Senator Byrd began his remarks: "[T]his is not a Gephardt amendment. Let us get that straight right here and now" (133 *Cong. Rec.* S9,638–39 [daily ed., July 10, 1987]). Senator Dole confirmed that "what we have here is an alternative to Gephardt, not a son or a cousin or a stepchild but a clear alternative" (id., S9,639). Senator Bentsen agreed: "I would oppose the Gephardt amendment. . . . What they have brought us is not the son of Gephardt" (id., S9,640). Senator Danforth stressed that the initiative "is truly a milestone in American trade policy," "a very meaningful provision," but "not the Gephardt amendment. . . . I would oppose [the Gephardt amendment] with every ounce of energy I have" (id., S9,641–42). Senator Baucus echoed: "This is not, as they say, the Gephardt amendment" (id., S9,645).

191. Id., S9,643 (remarks of Senator Danforth). Senator Danforth continued: "Is this not the real option? Is this not the real alternative to the defeatism of the protectionist and the passivity of those who would turn our borders into a doormat?" (Id.).

192. 133 *Cong. Rec.* S7,347–48 (daily ed., June 8, 1988).

193. Id., S7,379.

194. 133 *Cong. Rec.* S9,664 (daily ed., July 10, 1987).

Even more than other Section 301 provisions, the Gephardt and World Markets Opening Initiative provisions were untouched until the very end of Subconference 1. In their initial offer, the Senate conferees proposed for the House to recede.[195] The House counteroffer deferred a response to the Senate offer until the basic Section 301 issues were resolved.[196] Finally on the morning of the last day of the subconference, the House conferees caucused on the issue in the library adjacent to the Ways and Means Committee hearing room in the Longworth building. Representatives Gephardt and Pease offered a substitute amendment to replace both Gephardt and Super 301, which was broader in concept than the original Gephardt amendment, After considerable discussion, the assembled House conferees voted not to insist on the Gephardt amendment or the new Gephardt-Pease proposal, but instead to give Chairman Rostenkowski latitude to accept something more nearly along the lines of Super 301.

That evening Chairman Rostenkowski agreed to accept the Senate initiative with modifications.[197] The title of the initiative was changed to "Identification of Trade Liberalization Priorities" and the terminology in the body of the provisions was modified to reflect this change.[198] In addition, the final agreement deleted the authority of the Finance and Ways and Means Committees to file Section 301 petitions. The 1988 Trade Act incorporates the final agreement in Section 1302.[199]

It is still too early to tell what the impact of the "trade liberalization priority" provisions will be. Some members of Congress predicted that they would have a serious impact. Representative Phil Crane (R-Illinois), for example, denounced Super 301 as a "helter-skelter, vigilante-like procedure" that would have the dual disadvantage of "inciting the ire of our trading partners" without improving access to foreign markets.[200] The actual signifi-

---

195. March 15 Senate Offer, supra n. 41, 7.

196. March 21 House Counteroffer, supra n. 42, 6. The March 30 Senate Offer, supra n. 43, 4, was again for the House to recede. The March 31, 9 AM House Counteroffer, supra n. 44, 7, was marked "blank." The 11 AM House Offer, supra n. 44, 7, was marked "open." The 2 PM Senate Counteroffer, supra n. 44, 7, remained "House recedes."

197. Proposed Final Agreement, supra n. 46, 5. The modifications were not merely described conceptually, but were attached as a comprehensive marked-up version of the S. 1420 provisions.

198. H.R. 3 (Final), § 1302, reprinted in *Conference Report*, supra n. 46, 1, 75; H.R. 4848, supra n. 47, § 1302.

199. 1988 Trade Act, supra n. 4, § 1302.

200. 134 *Cong. Rec.* H5,537 (daily ed., July 13, 1988) (statement of Representative Crane). See also, e.g., 134 *Cong. Rec.* S10,662 (Aug. 3, 1988) (statement of Senator Wallop: "It propels the President into a series of no-win bilateral trade negotiations under impossible deadlines and almost certainly results in highly nationalistic anti-U.S. trade restrictions."); 134 *Cong. Rec.* H5,545 (daily ed., July 13, 1988) (statement of Representative Kolbe: "This is the Gephardt

cance, however, is unclear, and depends largely on the way the provisions are administered in 1989 and 1990.

V. Other Amendments

Several other amendments to Section 301 in the 1988 Trade Act merit attention, albeit less so than the above provisions. They are described briefly below.

Mandatory Self-Initiation

Under Section 301 (both prior to and following enactment of the 1988 Trade Act), investigations may be begun either in response to a petition filed by an interested party or on the initiative of the trade representative.[201] USTR's authority to self-initiate investigations was added by the Trade and Tariff Act of 1984,[202] which also required USTR to identify trade barriers in an annual National Trade Estimates Report.[203] The purpose of this trade barrier identification "was to encourage a more active use of the president's power to self-initiate Section 301 investigations."[204] The 1984 Act did not require USTR to self-initiate investigations.

The administration opposed mandatory self-initiation. It argued first that inflexible self-initiation requirements would hinder the administration's ability to resolve trade problems, by tying its hands and dictating policy without regard to the particular facts of each case. Second, the administration argued that cases self-initiated by USTR currently had clout because they were extraordinary. Foreign governments knew that the administration meant business when USTR self-initiated a Section 301 case. The regular, routine self-initiation of investigations, however, would lessen their impact on, and importance to, foreign governments. Third, routine self-initiation would relegate all other trade disputes, including those on which interested U.S. parties petitioned USTR to take action under Section 301, to second class status. Self-initiation requirements

---

amendment all over again. . . . [I]t is not only unwise and totally unnecessary, but it needlessly invites a trade war. . . . [It] extends the doctrine of mutually assured destruction to trade policy, with us launching the first salvo in response to even the most isolated regional conflict.").

201. 19 U.S.C. § 2412(b), (c) (1982 and Supp. IV 1986); 1988 Trade Act, supra n. 4, § 1301, amending 1974 Trade Act, supra n. 5, § 302.

202. Trade and Tariff Act of 1984, § 304(d)(1), Pub. L, No. 98-573, 98 Stat. 2948, 3003, 19 U.S.C. § 2412 (1982 and Supp. IV 1986).

203. See supra n. 182.

204. S. *Rep. No. 71,* supra n. 73, 75. This report characterizes the self-initiation power as the president's; it was presumed that the president had the power to self-initiate investigations, before the 1984 amendment that specifically gave this authority to the Trade Representative as well.

would devalue all trade issues on which the trade representative does not self-initiate an investigation.[205]

Although H.R. 4800 and H.R. 3 as introduced included requirements for self-initiated investigations,[206] H.R. 3 as transformed by the Subcommittee on Trade and Committee on Ways and Means did not.[207] On the Senate side, several Senate bills introduced during the 1985–86 session would have required annual self-initiation of investigations under Section 302 of the Trade Act. In fact, Senator Danforth noted his concern about the lack of any self-initiated investigations at Ambassador Yeutter's confirmation hearing in 1985: "The whole theory of the reciprocity title in the 1984 Trade Act was to place more initiative in the hands of the administration. . . . Do you intend to address the intent of Congress seriously? Or do you intend to be dragged kicking and screaming into 301 enforcement?"[208]

Not surprisingly, despite the self-initiation of four investigations in 1985,[209] S. 1860, the 1986 bill, included a requirement to self-initiate investigations.[210] S. 490, as introduced in February, 1987, contained a sweeping scheme requiring extensive annual self-initiation of investigations based upon the National Trade Estimates Report.[211] This requirement was modified as it made its way through the Finance Committee[212] and the full Senate.[213] As finally passed by the Senate, the bill called for the annual self-initiation of investigations of "those acts, policies, and practices . . . the pursuit of which is most likely to result in the greatest expansion of United States exports, either directly or through the establishment of a beneficial precedent."[214]

---

205. *March Hearing on S. 490*, supra n. 12, 42–43 (testimony of Alan F. Holmer, General Counsel, USTR). See also *Hearing on S. 1860*, supra n. 3, 50–51 (testimony of Ambassador Clayton Yeutter, U.S. Trade Representative); id., 56–57 (USTR's section-by-section analysis, title II of S. 1860); and *April Hearings on S. 490*, supra n. 1, 29 (testimony of Ambassador Clayton Yeutter, U.S. Trade Representative).

206. H.R. 4800, supra n. 18, § 115; H.R. 3, supra n. 21, § 115.

207. H.R. 3 (May 8 print), supra n. 27. H.R. 3 did include a specific, tailored requirement to self-initiate "fast-track" investigations of priority intellectual property cases, described infra nn. 221–22 and accompanying text. And it also included the Gephardt amendment, supra nn. 158–63 and accompanying text. But it did not include a generic mandate to self-initiate investigations.

208. *Yeutter Nomination Hearing*, supra n. 6, 83.

209. Brazil Informatics Policy, 50 *Fed. Reg.* 37,608 (USTR 1985) (initiation of investigation under Section 301); Korea's Restrictions on Insurance Services, 50 *Fed. Reg.* 37,609 (USTR 1985) (initiation of investigation under Section 301); Japan's Practice with Respect to Tobacco Products, 50 *Fed. Reg.* 37,609 (USTR 1985) (initiation of investigation under Section 301); and Korean Protection of Intellectual Property Rights, 50 *Fed. Reg.* 45,883 (USTR 1985) (initiation of investigation under Section 301).

210. S. 1860, supra n. 17, § 202.

211. S. 490, supra n. 29, § 303.

212. S. 490 (June 12 print), supra n. 72, § 304.

213. S. 1420, supra n. 34, § 305.

214. S. 490 (June 12 print), supra n. 72, § 304; S. 1420, supra n. 34, § 305.

The Senate conferees of Subconference 1 initially proposed to retain the self-initiation requirement.[215] The House objected.[216] But unlike most Section 301 amendments, the conferees reached agreement early, in the very next round of exchanged offers. The Senate offered to recede on this issue on March 30,[217] and the House accepted.[218]

What is the explanation for this relatively early agreement to drop a broad requirement for annual self-initiated investigations? The answer probably is that Super 301 was perceived as serving much the same function (at least in 1989 and 1990), and that special expedited intellectual property investigations were already required as well.[219] At any rate, aside from Super 301 and the fast-track intellectual property cases, the final bill does not mandate annual self-initiated investigations.

Priority Intellectual Property Rights Cases

Both H.R. 4800 and H.R. 3 required the trade representative to identify "those foreign countries that . . . maintain the most significant barriers . . . to market access for United States persons that rely on intellectual property protection."[220] These bills required the president to direct USTR to enter into negotiations with such countries to obtain fair and equitable market access. If the President was unable to achieve an agreement providing for fair and equitable market access within two years, he was required to take some action, which could include action under Section 301.[221] As marked up in the Ways and Means Committee and passed by the House, H.R. 3 required more-expedited action, including self-initiated investigations under Section 302 of the trade act of countries identified by USTR as intellectual property priorities.[222]

---

215. March 15 Senate Offer, supra n. 41, 1.
216. March 21 House Counteroffer, supra n. 42, 1.
217. March 30 Senate Offer, supra n. 43, 3.
218. March 31 9 A.M. House Counteroffer, supra n. 44, 5.
219. See infra nn. 221–31 and accompanying text.
220. H.R. 4800, supra n. 18, § 143; H.R. 3, supra n. 21, § 143.
221. H.R. 4800, supra n. 18, § 143; H.R. 3, supra n. 21, § 143.
222. H.R. 3 (May 8, 1987 print), supra n. 27, § 173. Priority countries were defined as those

> (A) that have the most egregious acts, policies, or practices that deny adequate and effective protection of intellectual property rights;
>
> (B) whose acts, policies, or practices that deny adequate and effective protection of intellectual property rights have the greatest adverse impact in their own markets, or in other international markets, for the affected United States items; and
>
> (C) that have not entered into good faith negotiations, or are not making significant progress in bilateral or multilateral negotiations, to provide adequate and effective protection of intellectual property rights. (Id.)

S. 490 as introduced did not contain any provision analogous to H.R. 3's intellectual property section. During the Finance Committee markup, however, Senator Mitchell offered an amendment along the lines of the House bill, providing for expedited investigations of priority intellectual property rights cases. The amendment required USTR, based on the National Trade Estimates Report,[223] to identify priority countries that do not provide adequate and effective protection of intellectual property rights, or that deny fair and equitable market access to U.S. companies that rely on intellectual property protection. The trade representative was required to self-initiate investigations of such priority countries and, usually within six months (extendable in special circumstances to twelve months), to make recommendations to the president on what action, if any, he should take to achieve adequate protection of intellectual property rights and to improve market access for U.S. companies relying on such protection. The president would be required to act within thirty days, unless he determined that action was not in the national economic interest.[224] The Finance Committee initially approved only the part of the Mitchell amendment calling for priority investigation of failure to provide adequate protection of intellectual property rights, and rejected the market access portions. However, the next day the Committee approved the entire Mitchell amendment, including the market access provisions.[225]

The final 1988 Trade Act contains a merger of the House and Senate provisions.[226] USTR must annually identify intellectual property priority countries, defined as in H.R. 3,[227] except that such countries also include those with the most egregious policies denying "fair and equitable market access to United States persons that rely upon intellectual property protection."[228] The USTR must self-initiate investigations of such priority countries within thirty days of identification unless he or she determines such an initiation would be detrimental to U.S. economic interests.[229] The USTR must determine whether the foreign activity is actionable, and if so, what action to

---

223. See supra n. 182.

224. Mitchell Amendment: Intellectual Property Protection and Market Access (undated, but in fact April 28, 1987) (unpublished, on file at USTR). This amendment was adopted in the Finance Committee prior to its adoption of the Packwood amendments, supra n. 30, which required changes in the Michell amendment.

225. See S. 490 (June 12, 1987 print), supra n. 72, § 302; and S. 1420, supra n. 34, § 303, § 305.

226. 1988 Trade Act, supra n. 4, § 1301, § 1303, amending 1974 Trade Act, supra n. 5, § 302(b), § 182.

227. See supra n. 222.

228. 1988 Trade Act, supra n. 4, § 1303, amending 1974 Trade Act, supra n. 5, § 182.

229. 1988 Trade Act, supra n. 4, § 1301, amending 1974 Trade Act, supra n. 5, § 302(b)(2).

take, within six months of the initiation,[230] and must implement Section 301 action within thirty days of an affirmative determination.[231] These are the only open-ended annual self-initiation requirements in the Act.

Mandatory Unfairness Determination

The old Section 301 did not require the president to determine whether foreign practices under investigation were unfair unless he decided to take action.[232] Now, under the 1988 Trade Act, the president must determine in *all* Section 301 cases whether the foreign government practices complained of are actionable under Section 301.[233]

The administration consistently opposed any requirement to make such findings in every case. Administration representatives argued that they would have better results under Section 301 if they could continue to decide in each case whether such a determination increases their leverage and, if so, when and how to play this negotiating chip. They further noted that a trading partner occasionally feels so threatened by the stigma of an unfairness label that it is willing to grant more concessions if USTR simply refrains from branding its conduct unfair. In other cases, USTR might wish to make a determination on a time schedule different from the statutory deadline. In still other cases, there could be serious disagreement over whether the practice is unfair. Compelling the trade representative to make a formal determination could result in a negative decision, allowing the foreign government to continue its practices without fear of U.S. reprisals.[234]

Despite the administration's objections, both House and Senate bills from their inception required an unfairness determination in every case.[235] The 1988 Trade Act thus requires such determination in all Section 301 cases.[236]

---

230. 1988 Trade Act, supra n. 4, § 1301, amending 1974 Trade Act, supra n. 5, § 304(a)(3).

231. 1988 Trade Act, supra n. 4, § 1301, amending 1974 Trade Act, supra n. 5, § 305.

232. See S. *Rep. No. 71*, supra n. 73, 79.

233. 1988 Trade Act, supra n. 4, § 1301, amending 1974 Trade Act, supra n. 5, § 304, 19 U.S.C. § 2414 (1982 and Supp. IV 1986).

234. *March Hearing on S. 490*, supra n. 12, 42–43 (testimony of Alan F. Holmer, General Counsel, USTR). See also *April Hearings on S. 490*, supra n. 1, 30 (testimony of Ambassador Clayton Yeutter, U.S. Trade Representative).

235. S. 1860, supra n. 17, § 205 (requiring an unfairness determination within only 90 days!); S. 490, supra n. 29, § 304; S. 490 (June 12, 1987 print), supra n. 72, § 305; S. 1420, supra n. 34, § 308; H.R. 4800, supra n. 18, § 116; H.R. 3, supra n. 21, § 116; H.R. 3 (May 8, 1987 print), supra n. 27, § 124.

236. 1988 Trade Act, supra n. 4, § 1301, amending 1974 Trade Act, supra n. 5, § 304, 19 U.S.C. § 2414 (1982 and Supp. IV 1986).

Deadlines

All omnibus trade bills prescribed differing deadlines for various stages of proceedings and actions under Section 301. The most significant deadline is the establishment of a definite date for USTR's recommendations in disputes arising under trade agreements, such as GATT. Previously the only deadline for the trade representative's recommendations to the president in these cases was thirty days following the conclusion of dispute settlement.[237] As amended by the 1988 Trade Act, the deadline for decisions whether the foreign practice is unfair and, if so, what action to take is thirty days following the conclusion of dispute settlement *or* eighteen months after initiation of the investigation, whichever occurs first.[238]

VI. Conclusion

It has been said that U.S. trade law arises half from the rules of international law, and half from the law of the jungle[239]—although some have suggested a more accurate allocation would give far more weight to the jungle.[240] In the eyes of many foreigners, this is particularly true of Section 301, which authorizes the trade representative (subject to the specific direction, if any, of the president) to take action in response to foreign practices even if they do not violate any international agreement.

Clearly the 1988 amendments to Section 301 are significant. They are likely to ensure that future administrations continue to apply this trade remedy in the vigorous manner of the Reagan administration from 1985 through 1988. In making this trade remedy more predictable and systematic, establishing a specific deadline in trade agreements cases, and requiring the self-initiation of some investigations, the 1988 amendments enhance confidence that outcomes will be achieved on a timely basis. This should encourage the business community to believe that pursuit of a Section 301 case is worth any time and trouble that it takes. Increased confidence in Section 301 as a useful trade remedy in turn is likely to generate more petitions and more reliance on Section 301.

Perhaps the greatest domestic significance of the 1988 Trade Act amend-

---

237. 19 U.S.C. § 2414 (a)(1)(C) (1982 and Supp. IV 1986).

238. 1988 Trade Act, supra n. 4, § 1301, amending 1974 Trade Act, supra n. 5, § 304(a)(2)(A), 19 U.S.C. § 2414 (1982 and Supp. IV 1986).

239. R. Herzstein, "Remarks upon the Dedication of the U.S. Court of International Trade (December 19, 1980), 5 (unpublished, available at Arnold & Porter, Washington, D.C.) (Mr. Herzstein was Undersecretary of Commerce for International Trade).

240. E.g., David E. Birenbaum of the Washington, D.C., office of Fried, Frank, Harris, Shriver & Jacobson.

ments to Section 301 lies largely outside the Section 301 program itself. The enactment of these changes was a catharsis for the Congress's "festering frustration"[241] with the way past and present administrations had conducted trade policy. It also enabled congressmen to take (and report to constituents) some coherent action in response to the United States trade deficit situation. And finally, it permitted many who generally support freer trade to continue to do so. As members of both parties had noted,[242] the consensus in the United States for free trade is more likely to be preserved when the public is confident that the government is "taking regular, swift, and tough action" against unfair trade practices abroad.[243]

Abroad, the significance of the 1988 Trade Act amendments to Section 301 remains to be seen. In large part, the impact depends upon progress in the ongoing Uruguay Round of Multilateral Trade Negotiations. If the United States succeeds in extending GATT to new areas (such as services, investment, and intellectual property) and substantially improving GATT discipline in traditional areas (such as agriculture and dispute settlement), then the 1988 Trade Act will be less important in the long term. However, in the event that the Uruguay Round does not make sufficient progress in key areas, then the 1988 Trade Act's amendments to Section 301 could be quite significant. Absent improved international trade rules in GATT, the effect of the 1988 amendments could quite well be to ensure more unilateral action by the United States in response to unfair practices abroad.

---

241. *Hearing on S. 1860,* supra n. 3, 64 (statement of Senator Packwood [R-Oregon]).

242. E.g., id., 64 (testimony of Ambassador Clayton Yeutter, U.S. Trade Representative).

243. *March Hearing on S. 490,* supra n. 1, 7 (statement of Senator Moynihan [D-New York]).

CHAPTER 3

U.S. Policy on 301 and Super 301

Geza Feketekuty

The public debate over 301 and Super 301, both inside and outside the United States, is usually posed in simplistic terms: Whether the implementation of the 301 provisions is aggressive enough or too aggressive, and whether it is legitimate or desirable for the United States to violate GATT rules in countering foreign violations of GATT agreements and unfair trade practices not covered by GATT. Legitimate arguments have been put forward on both sides of this political debate, and the Bush administration, in practice, has tried to formulate its policy on the basis of a balanced consideration of arguments that have been put forward.

A discussion of U.S. policy on 301 and Super 301[1] needs to focus on a number of different issues. First, the provisions contained in chapter 1 of Title III need to be examined as the domestic counterpart to the GATT consultation and dispute settlement procedures. Second, these provisions need to be viewed as providing a mechanism for dealing with trade issues that are not covered by current GATT agreements. Third, U.S. implementation of these provisions needs to be analyzed in terms of the trade policy strategy adopted by the Reagan administration to deflect protectionist pressures in Congress. Fourth, the debate over Super 301 in the context of the 1988 trade act needs to be evaluated in terms of the ongoing debate over the extent to which enforcement of U.S. rights under trade agreements should be based on private petitions versus priorities set by the government on the basis of broader policy considerations.

Much of the debate over 301 and Super 301 also revolves around the

---

1. 301 refers to chapter 1 of the Trade and Tariff Act of 1974 (as amended in 1979, 1984, and 1988), which directs the U.S. Trade Representative to enforce U.S. rights under international trade agreements and to take other actions necessary to remove unfair foreign trade practices. The legislation currently in force incorporates amendments included in the 1979, 1984, and 1988 trade acts. The revised version in article 1 of the Omnibus Trade and Competitiveness Act of 1988 covers ten sections, 301 to 310. Super 301 refers to some new provisions included in the 1988 trade act that make it mandatory for the U.S. Trade Representative to identify trade policy priorities with respect to his or her implementation of the provisions contained in chapter 1.

rules of GATT: (1) the failures of the existing dispute settlement process and how the dispute settlement process of GATT needs to be reformed, and (2) the deficiencies or lack of GATT rules in many areas such as agriculture, services, and intellectual property, and rules that should be adopted in these sectors. U.S. policies on 301 have been closely linked to U.S. negotiating objectives in the Uruguay Round, and bilateral consultations and negotiations carried out under 301 and Super 301 were seen as complementing and reinforcing the multilateral negotiations in the Uruguay Round. Moreover, it was intended as a signal to other countries that if they did not address the issues identified by the United States as high-priority negotiating issues in the Uruguay Round, they would have to address them in a bilateral negotiating context under 301. Some foreign countries, on the other hand, have identified Section 301 itself as a negotiating issue. An evaluation of 301 would therefore not be complete without an analysis of its impact on the Uruguay Round.

Domestic Procedures Related to GATT Dispute Settlement Processes

GATT establishes rights and obligations for governments on trade policy issues, including rights and obligations with respect to the settlement of disputes. Individual businesses have no rights, per se, under GATT and they do not have direct access to the procedures of GATT. It goes against the grain of American political philosophy, however, to leave decisions with respect to the exercise of rights and obligations entirely in the hands of the government. Section 301 of U.S. trade legislation is designed, in part, to provide a procedure under which U.S. private actors can get the U.S. government to initiate actions with respect to U.S. rights under international trade agreements, including GATT. In fact, until recently the U.S. government very seldom initiated any actions under international dispute settlement procedures unless requested to do so by a private party.

Section 301 not only offers private actors an opportunity to petition the government to pursue trade issues under the international dispute settlement procedures, but sets out procedures the government must follow in considering such petitions, with predefined time limits for the consideration of such petitions and for the implementation of decisions, public notification, and the opportunity for public comment by other private parties. These due process requirements reflect a deeply held American distrust of governmental action that is not subject to full public scrutiny. Foreigners often complain about the burden imposed by these legal processes in the United States, but they are a critical part of the American system of democratic control.

Legal Authority to Retaliate in Accordance with GATT Rules

Section 301 also contains authority for the U.S. Trade Representative (USTR), subject to the direction of the President, to take specified retaliatory measures when U.S. rights under international agreements are violated. In most other countries, the domestic legal right of the government to retaliate is assumed as part of the inherent powers of a government. In the United States, the assumption is that the executive branch does not have the right to act in the trade policy area unless the Congress has given the executive branch an explicit mandate. Without legislative authority, the president could not, for example, ask the Customs Service to slow down the clearance of a particular country's goods (as France did at Poitiers a few years ago).

Pursuit of Trade-Related Issues not Covered by GATT

Section 301 also serves as a vehicle for dealing with trade-related issues not covered by GATT rules. Section 301 sets out the procedures under which private interests can petition the government to intercede on their behalf with other governments when policy measures not covered by GATT disciplines adversely affect their commercial interests. It also gives the U.S. Trade Representative the right to take retaliatory measures when another government is not prepared to work out a mutually acceptable accommodation in such cases.

For instance, it has been the policy of the U.S. administration since the beginning of the Reagan administration to use Section 301 as an active policy tool in dealing with trade issues in services.[2] Use of 301 was seen as an important element of a coordinated strategy to persuade other countries to agree to multilateral negotiations on trade in services in the GATT. The rationale was threefold. First, the use of bilateral trade channels to address trade issues in services was meant to educate foreign trade officials on trade aspects of services and to establish the precedent for the use of trade channels for resolving international services issues. Second, the use of bilateral channels served the useful purpose of giving domestic services industries an opportunity to familiarize themselves with the approach used by trade officials to resolve trade issues. Third, U.S. trade officials wanted to send the signal that the United States was determined to address trade in services issues, whether bilaterally or multilaterally.

In the same vein, it has been U.S. policy to use bilateral trade channels

2. For a discussion of the policy adopted by the Reagan administration in dealing with trade in services, see USTR 1984, 99–101.

and Section 301 to obtain improved protection of U.S. intellectual property rights in other countries. The competitiveness of U.S. industry is increasingly concentrated in goods and services that have a high intellectual property content, and foreign respect for that intellectual property is an increasingly important condition for achieving access to foreign markets in these goods and services.

Open-Market Oriented Defense Against Protectionist Pressures

In 1985, the large and growing trade deficit led to increasing pressure from the public and the Congress for action by the administration to deal with the trade deficit. Four sets of measures were advocated. First, coordinated steps with other governments to reverse the high value of the dollar. Second, and closely related to the first, a reduction of the budget deficit and easing of monetary policy. Third, the imposition or tightening of restrictions on imports of basic manufactures, which accounted for a large share of the trade deficit. Fourth, adoption of an activist policy to remove foreign unfair trade barriers.

After lengthy internal debate, the administration, on September 23, 1985, announced an export-expanding strategy for correcting the trade deficit.[3] This statement followed by a day a joint announcement of coordinated policy steps by the G-5 group of finance ministers, designed to facilitate a downward adjustment of the dollar. The basic strategy adopted by the administration was to slow the growth of imports through a long-term plan for reducing federal expenditures and to boost exports by persuading major surplus countries to stimulate domestic growth and to reduce import barriers.

The administration recognized that any correction of the trade deficit would require a reduction of the domestic absorption of goods and services in the United States. Administration support for the Gramm-Rudman deficit reduction plan was designed to advance this objective. There was concern, however, that a strategy that would put too much emphasis on the contraction of domestic demand as the solution to the trade deficit would inevitably lead to the parallel adoption of import restrictions by the Congress. Such a course of events would have created a serious risk of restrictive trade policies by other countries and a major global recession, with disastrous consequences for the high debt, developing countries.

---

3. See USTR 1986, appendix B, "Administration Statement on International Trade Policy: September 23, 1985," and appendix C, "Announcement of the Ministers of Finance and Central Bank Governors of France, Germany, Japan, the United Kingdom, and the United States." This report also contains an extensive analysis of the factors behind the U.S. trade deficit in pp. 5–19 and the thinking behind the policies adopted in the fall of 1985 in pp. 65–71 and 97–101.

To deflect political pressures for a "protectionist" solution to the trade deficit, the Administration decided to emphasize the progrowth, export enhancing elements of its package of policy measures, including concerted action by the G-5 to reduce the value of the dollar and policy measures by the surplus countries to expand domestic demand. To reinforce this strategy, the administration also decided to pursue a more active bilateral effort under the provisions of Section 301 to remove foreign trade barriers and unfair trade practices. This was seen as a complementary effort designed to assure that the growth of U.S. exports would not be blocked by high trade barriers.

While most policy analysts, and probably even most members of Congress, agreed that macroeconomic events and policies accounted for the bulk of the deficit, it was also difficult to deny that countries that had been the most successful in expanding their exports to the United States continued to maintain high import barriers that put serious constraints on U.S. exports. If the United States and the world were going to grow out of the large U.S. trade deficit through an expansion of U.S. exports, then it seemed only reasonable to remove external constraints on the growth of U.S. exports. The removal of such barriers could certainly not become a substitute for fundamental adjustments in macroeconomic policies in the United States and elsewhere, but they could be expected to smooth the adjustment path.

The situation faced by the United States in the mid-1980s brought into sharp focus a number of shortcomings in the existing international monetary and trade systems:

First, existing international monetary rules do not establish clear responsibilities for actions to be taken by surplus countries in correcting large trade imbalances. Unless both surplus and deficit countries take steps to correct a major trade imbalance, any effort to correct such an imbalance will have a deflationary bias. This was well recognized in the immediate aftermath of World War II, when the United States and Canada, as the two surplus countries, took steps on both the trade and the financial front to bring about a balanced correction of trade imbalances.

Second, the existing international trade rules do not establish clear graduation guidelines for developing countries that are successful in rapidly expanding their exports. It stands to reason that a developing country that maintained high import barriers to spur the development of its own industries no longer needs those barriers when those industries have developed a capability to penetrate foreign markets. The presumption in support of a liberalization of infant industry barriers is particularly strong if the country involved has developed a large trade surplus.

Third, technological change and the more advanced integration of national economies has created a new situation where policy instruments not currently covered by international trade rules have a significant impact on international trade. Policies affecting trade in services and intellectual property have already been mentioned. One might also mention investment policies, competition policies, and policies affecting the distribution system.

An activist, bilateral trade policy by the United States thus was designed, in part, to compensate for the absence of adequate international monetary and trade rules.

One also needs to recall that in August, 1985, the struggle in GATT over the launching of a new round of multilateral trade negotiations had reached a climax. The United States found itself increasingly frustrated in launching a multilateral negotiation that could deal with shortcomings in the trading system. The decision to make more active use of Section 301, therefore, also was intended to be a clear signal by the United States that it would increasingly rely on its bilateral commercial leverage to remedy shortcomings in the existing trading system if agreement was not reached on launching a new round of multilateral trade negotiations.

Who Should Initiate Policy Actions—Business or Government?

There has been a long-running dispute in the United States over whether enforcement of U.S. trade rights under international trade agreements should be based exclusively on petitions received by the government from private sector interests, or whether the government itself should decide to initiate such actions. Traditionalists, suspicious of the government making arbitrary decisions in areas that could affect private commercial interests, have felt that the government should act only in response to private complaints that another government was violating its commitments under a trade agreement. Others, who favor a more activist role for the government, have argued that the government should not wait for private complaints before initiating actions to seek the removal of foreign violations of trade agreements or other unreasonable or unfair trade actions by foreign governments.

Government trade policy officials have traditionally favored the former point of view for the simple reason that the effort required by a private party to document a foreign violation of a trade agreement was a useful filter for identifying high-priority issues. In a democratic society such as the United States, the success over government policy is measured by the extent to which it satisfies public expectations, and the burden placed on private parties wishing governmental action served to limit legitimate public expectations.

Congressional opinion, as expressed through successive revisions of Section 301, has favored a more activist role by the government in identifying and seeking the removal of foreign violations of trade agreements and major obstacles to U.S. exports. This reflected both an impatience with what many considered an excessively passive U.S. trade policy and a concern that only those economic interests wealthy enough to afford the legal fees could obtain satisfaction under U.S. trade laws.

Congress, in the trade act of 1984, added a new provision to Title III of the Trade and Tariff Act of 1974 (dealing with unfair trade practices) that required the government to identify, on an annual basis, unfair trade practices by foreign governments. This has come to be known as the Trade Estimates Report, which has been published on an annual basis since 1985. The purpose of this provision was to force the government to take a more activist approach with respect to foreign unfair trade barriers and to establish priorities with respect to the barriers that would be addressed in order to achieve the most efficient use of government resources devoted to this activity.

The Super 301 provision of the 1988 trade act needs to be seen, in part, as a Congressional mandate to establish priorities among the list of barriers and unfair trade practices identified in the Trade Estimates Report. In announcing its first set of actions under the Super 301 provisions of the 1988 trade act, the administration clearly indicated that it understood these new ground rules. The USTR announcement of May 25, 1989, on the " 'Super 301' Trade Liberalization Priorities" put a heavy stress on the relationship between the identified practices and U.S. trade liberalization priorities.[4]

The Domestic and International Debate over Super 301

In passing successive versions of the 301 and Super 301 provisions, Congress also intended to direct the executive branch to adopt a more forceful approach in pursuing specific commercial interests. In the immediate period after World War II, trade policy served important foreign policy goals, and this meant that immediate, specific commercial interests were often subordinated to broad, economic, foreign policy and security objectives. The United States, as the key architect and guarantor of the multilateral trading system, used much of its commercial leverage to expand and strengthen market oriented rules, rather than to advance specific U.S. commercial activities in particular countries. This does not mean that U.S. proposals for systemic reforms or for broad, multilateral cuts in tariff and nontariff barriers were not designed to advance broad U.S. commercial interests, but rather that U.S. negotiating objectives were framed primarily in a multilateral, rather than a bilateral, context.

---

4. See USTR 1989b, 1–3.

This multilateral and rule-based approach to trade policy was in part the result of a recognition by the United States, as the most powerful trading country in the world, of its special responsibility for the system. The United States also favored a multilateral, rule-based approach because it was most consistent with its economic philosophy that the government should do nothing more than set the ground rules for markets to operate, and that individual entrepreneurs should make all the commercial decisions. Finally, the United States was highly competitive in most industrial sectors.

Over the years, Congress has repeatedly pressed successive administrations to raise the priority accorded commercial objectives in the policy-making process and to adopt more forceful ways of using the leverage of the large American market to advance U.S. commercial interests. The debate over the revision of Section 301 and the development of the Super 301 provision, in the context of the 1988 trade act, thus needs to be seen as part of a longstanding debate over the use of American commercial power to advance identifiable, specific, concrete American commercial interests.

There are many people in the United States—labor and business leaders, legislators and academics—who believe that U.S. trade relations with other countries are characterized by imbalances in commercial benefits, to the disadvantage of the United States. In support of this assessment, they would point to the greater openness of the U.S. economy as measured by import penetration ratios in key sectors and the proportion of developing country exports that go to the United States. Given this imbalance in market access opportunities, they would argue that the States must be much more forceful in enforcing its commercial rights, in defending its commercial interests, and in establishing more balanced rules of the game. To the extent that the existing international rules are inadequate or ineffective, they would argue that action outside of the system, or even in violation of existing rules, is justifiable and ultimately legitimate.

On the other side there are others, both in the United States and abroad, who argue that you cannot build a viable and credible system of international rules if the largest country in the system violates the rules, or even if the largest country bypasses the multilateral rules and seeks to achieve its objectives by applying bilateral pressure on its trading partners. They would argue that a policy based on an aggressive implementation of Section 301, including Super 301, will undermine the very system the United States has spent so much energy to construct since World War II. Moreover, they would argue that U.S. complaints about unfair trade practices by other countries need to be balanced by a recognition that the United States has not always lived up to its own international obligations, and that the U.S. Congress has often proved most reluctant to bring its laws into compliance with GATT panel rulings.

Both the Reagan administration and the Bush administration have tried to pursue a balanced approach between those who have argued for an aggressive bilateral strategy without restraints and those who have argued for exclusive reliance on the multilateral process, whatever its limitations. The Reagan administration, in the policy measures adopted on September 23, 1985, and the Bush administration, in the policy measures announced on May 25, 1989, in compliance with the Super 301 provisions of the trade act, essentially agreed that a more activist bilateral approach for seeking the removal of unreasonable or unfair obstacles to U.S. exports was warranted under the circumstances. At the same time, both administrations have resisted Congressional and public pressures for a major departure from the traditional free trade policy based on multilateral trade rules.[5]

Super 301 and the Uruguay Round

In implementing the Super 301 provision, the administration established a strong link to the Uruguay Round of Multilateral Trade Negotiations. This seemed a sensible policy, since the objective of both sets of negotiations is to liberalize trade. The objective of the Super 301 provision, Section 1302 of the Trade Act of 1988, is best summarized by its title, "Identification of Trade Liberalization Priorities." The objective of the Uruguay Round is to liberalize trade and reform international trading rules where that is necessary to support the liberalization of trade.

The policy of linking Super 301 to the Uruguay Round was clearly enunciated in the statement issued by the administration on May 25, 1989, announcing the Super 301 priorities for 1989.

Key excerpts from the "Fact Sheet" distributed on May 25, 1989, are as follows: "In implementing Super 301, the United States will aim to eliminate significant trade barriers and trade-distorting practices through multilateral and bilateral negotiations—not simply to increase U.S. exports, but to liberalize trade for the benefit of all nations. . . . the highest trade liberalization priority identified by the USTR is to conclude successfully the Uruguay Round of multilateral trade negotiations by December, 1990. . . . The Uruguay Round directly addresses many of the most significant trade barriers and distortions, and provides the best opportunity to expand and strengthen multilateral rules. It also affords an opportunity to negotiate the elimination of many of the types of barriers enumerated as priority practices under Super 301" (USTR 1989b, 1 and 5).

---

5. For a comprehensive description of the implementation of 301 by the Reagan and Bush administrations see Bradley 1989, as well as Holmer and Bello 1989.

In addition to establishing the Uruguay Round as the top U.S. trade policy priority, the administration listed five categories of trade barriers as areas of priority concern. Within each of these categories, the administration identified a specific country practice that the administration intended to pursue within the Super 301 context. The five categories, and the country practices identified under each category, were: quantitative restrictions (Brazilian balance of payments restrictions); exclusionary government procurement restrictions (Japanese procurement restrictions on supercomputers and satellites); technical barriers to trade (Japanese standards on forest products); trade-related investment measures (trade performance requirements imposed by India on foreign investors); and barriers to trade in services (Indian prohibition on foreign insurance.[6]

The administration also noted that intellectual property issues were of high concern, but were being addressed separately under the so-called Special 301 provision dealing with intellectual property practices. Similarly, the administration made it clear that it assigns a high priority to the elimination of trade-distorting subsidies and agricultural policies, but that these issues were better pursued at this time outside the Super 301 process.

The five categories of barriers identified under Super 301, along with intellectual property, subsidy, and agricultural policy issues, constitute the major U.S. objectives for the Uruguay Round, and the administration announcement noted the consistency between the priorities identified under Super 301 and U.S. objectives in the Uruguay Round.

Super 301 and the GATT Dispute Settlement Process

Much of the controversy surrounding Section 301 and the so-called Super 301 provision of the 1988 Trade Act concerns the threat of potential retaliation by the United States if foreign trade practices considered unfair or unreasonable by the United States were not removed to the satisfaction of the United States. The argument is made that the United States was arrogating to itself the right to decide what was fair or unfair in foreign trade laws or practices. But, as the May 25 "Fact Sheet" pointed out "all we have done unilaterally is to identify our negotiating priorities."

The pursuit of bilateral consultations or negotiations to deal with foreign trade practices is not in itself a violation of either the rules or the spirit of GATT. In fact, the operation of GATT substantially depends on bilateral consultations and negotiations between contracting parties (countries who subscribe to the rules of GATT). GATT only requires that any trade liberalizing measures that result from such consultations be passed on to all contract-

---

6. For a superb analysis of the issues involved, see Ahearn, Cronin, and Storrs 1990.

ing parties. The United States has consistently taken the position that the benefits of any trade liberalization measures taken by other governments pursuant to bilateral consultations with the United States should be extended to all countries. The United States has taken the position even with respect to trade in services and intellectual property, policy areas not currently covered by GATT and therefore not subject to the MFN provisions of GATT.

Another aspect of the implementation of Section 301 concerns the imposition of retaliatory measures if bilateral consultations and other dispute settlement mechanisms fail to bring about a mutually satisfactory resolution of a dispute. The rules of GATT permit such sanctions where a dispute settlement panel and the GATT council finds that a country has violated its GATT commitments, and that country does not eliminate the problem or compensate the injured party.

In the May 25 statement on Super 301, the administration made it clear that it intends to use the dispute settlement procedures of GATT where appropriate. To quote from the "Fact Sheet": "The GATT dispute settlement system, where it covers practices of priority attention, also enables the United States to enforce its rights under GATT and to challenge trade practices that impair benefits we can reasonably expect to receive from GATT rules. Investigations initiated as a result of Super 301 will include the use of GATT dispute settlement where appropriate . . . ".[7]

Neither the use of a bilateral negotiating technique nor the threat of retaliation is thus a departure from longstanding and accepted GATT practice. The real issue ultimately concerns the implementation of the GATT dispute settlement process, where it is relevant, and the method of settling disputes in situations where existing GATT rules do not apply.

The major flaw in the GATT dispute settlement system is that adoption of a panel report by the GATT council requires a consensus in the council, and this allows a country that loses a case to block adoption of the panel report simply by voting against it in the GATT council. Moreover, a country is not subjected to any penalties if it finds a way of blocking the establishment of a dispute settlement panel. In these kinds of situations, where the GATT dispute settlement process is frustrated by a country subject to a GATT complaint, the United States has reserved its rights to retaliate, and has done so on a number of occasions. The United States has felt justified in doing so, because in the absence of such potential retaliation GATT discipline would be meaningless. In fact, such an approach can be considered to be consistent with longstanding GATT concepts such as overall reciprocity and the balance of rights and obligations which underlie GATT.[8]

---

7. Ibid.

8. For a comprehensive legal analysis of the approach adopted by the United States on the use of retaliation in connection with the settlement of trade disputes see Hudec in this volume.

Where a dispute concerns policies not covered by GATT, such as trade in services or intellectual property, GATT dispute settlement procedures, of course, do not apply. To the extent other international procedures do not provide an appropriate and effective mechanism, bilateral consultation and negotiation channels provide the only viable means for resolving the issues. In the absence of a satisfactory settlement of outstanding issues in these areas, the United States reserves the right to take any appropriate retaliatory measures. The issue that has attracted the most controversy in this area is the application of retaliatory measures affecting trade in goods in response to unfair barriers to trade in services or unfair treatment of U.S. intellectual property interests. The United States has taken one such measure in a dispute with Brazil over intellectual property issues related to pharmaceuticals.

U.S international commercial interests in the area of services and intellectual property have grown more rapidly in recent years than U.S. exports of manufactured products, while many foreign countries have succeeded in recent years to substantially increase their exports of manufactured goods to the American market. As a reflection of these trends, business interests with a large stake in services and intellectual property have become an increasing factor in U.S. public support for an open, multilateral trading system. In this situation, the U.S. government has felt compelled and justified in forging a close linkage between trade in goods and trade in services, both in the Uruguay Round of multilateral trade negotiations and in the context of bilateral trade negotiations.

At its core, the controversy about 301 thus centers on the GATT dispute settlement process and the linkage to issues such as services and intellectual property, which are not currently covered by GATT. These are simultaneously key issues under negotiation in the Uruguay Round.

Whatever one's view about the 301 provisions of the 1988 Trade Act, the long-term impact of these provisions on the multilateral trading system are likely to be highly positive. Many countries that viewed past efforts by the United States to strengthen the GATT dispute settlement process as primarily an American effort to restrain their freedom of action now see much more clearly that a strengthened dispute settlement system can also prove useful in restraining American actions. Moreover, foreign concern about potential 301 actions outside of the GATT framework in areas such as services and intellectual property has served to increase the interest of many countries in a successful conclusion of the Uruguay Round negotiations in these areas.

Sources

Ahearn, Raymond J., with Richard Cronin and Larry Storrs. 1990. "Super 301 Action Against Japan, Brazil and India: Rationale, Reaction, and Future Implications." Washington, D.C.: Congressional Research Service.

Bradley, Jane. 1989. "The Super 301 Process." In *Trade Law and Policy Institute,* ed. Harvey M. Applebaum and Judith H. Bello. Washington, D.C.: Practicing Law Institute. September 18–19, 1989.

Holmer, Alan, and Judith Hippler Bello. 1989. "The Promise and Peril of Unilateralism." In *Trade Law and Policy Institute,* ed. Harvey M. Applebaum and Judith H. Bello. Washington, D.C.: Practicing Law Institute.

U.S. Congress. House. Committee on Ways and Means. 1989. *Overview and Compilation of U.S. Trade Statutes.* 1989 ed. Committee Print.

USTR. 1984. *Annual Report of the President of the United States on the Trade Agreements Program: 1983.* Washington, D.C.: Office of the U.S. Trade Representative.

USTR. 1986. *Annual Report of the President of the United States on the Trade Agreements Program: 1984–85.* Washington, D.C.: Office of the U.S. Trade Representative.

USTR. 1988. *Annual Report of the President of the United States on the Trade Agreements Program.* Washington, D.C.: Office of the U.S. Trade Representative.

USTR. 1989a. "The President's Trade Policy Agenda." Washington, D.C.: Office of the U.S. Trade Representative.

USTR. 1989b. "Fact Sheet: Super 301 Trade Liberalization Priorities." Washington, D.C.: Office of the U.S. Trade Representative.

USTR. 1989c. "Fact Sheet: Special 301 on Intellectual Property." Washington, D.C.: Office of the U.S. Trade Representative. May 25, 1989.

Commentary

Claude Barfield, Jr.

Geza Feketekuty's explanation of the passage and implementation of Super 301 represents an able attempt to defend the indefensible. Along the way he rewrites history to a considerable degree.

First, several fundamental facts. Under the provisions of Super 301, the U.S. Trade Representative (USTR) is directed (for 1989 and 1990) to use the *Annual Barriers to Trade Report* as the basis for identifying those trade practices and those nations perpetrating the practices that are having the greatest negative impact on U.S. exports. The president then must enter into negotiations with the countries named to get them to stop the practices within eighteen months; failing this goal, retaliation will occur.

The language seems very direct and straightforward, but the problem is that in other sections of the 1988 law the president is given the discretion not to act on any of this if he deems such action is not in the U.S. economic interest. And therein hangs the source of major disagreement between the administration and outside critics of Super 301.

Critics of the administration, such as the present writer, point out that when the law passed in the summer of 1988 the then–U.S. Trade representative, Clayton Yeutter, assured those who had recommended that the president veto the bill that Super 301 had been defanged—that the final language gave the Reagan administration, and all subsequent administrations, complete discretion *at all points* in the Super 301 exercise. That is, the president did not have to name practices of countries, did not have to enter into negotiations under Super 301, could stop the proceedings at any point, and did not have to retaliate in the end.

Skeptics at the time—again, including the present writer—warned that Congress would challenge this interpretation and this is exactly what happened. From the day the act passed, key members of Congress argued that the next president, in 1989, would be violating the law and breaking faith with Congress if he did not name a number of countries and a number of practices to go after under Super 301.

Allen Meltzer, who served on the staff of the President's Council of Economic Advisers during the waning days of the Reagan administration, has stated that he and others were disturbed by the lack of rebuttal within the administration, but during the election and transition it was just one of the many issues that were left drifting. The same silence continued during the shakedown period of the Bush administration. By the time Bush administration trade officials were in place—most particularly Carla Hills—it had become an article of faith on Capitol Hill that Congress had given the new president an ironclad mandate to name practices and countries.

What ensued between January and May of 1989 was the sordid spectacle of almost every interest in Washington compiling lists of their favorite countries for retaliation. To her credit, Ambassador Carla Hills strongly rebuked a number of congressmen and senators for their overreaching demands, pointing out that Congress itself had established a process by which the most damaging practices (to U.S. exports) would be identified.

Unfortunately, what transpired then was that the administration bowed to congressional pressure and named unfair practices in three countries: Japan, Brazil, and India. These indictments completed the corruption of the 301 process because they were handed down without a pretense of supporting analysis. The *Trade Barriers Report,* upon which such judgments are supposed to be made, consists merely of a compilation of self-serving industry claims and anecdotal hearsay slapped together under one cover to satisfy a congressional mandate dating from 1984. As Robert Lawrence and others have noted, in terms of market-opening results, the Market-Opening, Sector Specific (MOSS) talks with Japan between 1984 and 1988 had been a real success. Japan, more than any other nation, had entered into good faith negotiations with the U.S. Congress, however, demanded that Japan be named and the administration acquiesced. While Brazil and India undoubtedly have major barriers to trade in place, they are no worse than many other countries that could also have been named (and the U.S. trade deficit with these two countries is also quite small when compared with many other nations.)

With regard to Brazil and India, Feketekuty's paper does break new ground. He states flatly what other administration spokesmen have only implied previously—that Brazil and India were chosen because of their resistance to the U.S. administration's multilateral positions on trade issues—and, indeed, exposes once again the 1989 Super 301 process for the procedural and substantially corrupt exercise its critics have maintained it was. Further, it badly undermines the credibility of the administration's repeated claims that its first priority is a successful conclusion of the Geneva talks. Nothing could be more destructive to GATT negotiations than the decisions—openly asserted—to single out for retaliation and retribution the two leading recalcitrant nations.

Finally, the Super 301 episode says a lot about Congress's real sense of the integrity of the constitutional system. During the 1980s, Congress and the Reagan administration repeatedly clashed over Congress's assertions that the executive was flouting its mandate and the laws it had passed—Contras, Irangate, etc. Yet, when the Bush administration openly made no pretense of following the process Congress had established for Super 301, Congress sat back and cheered. Process be damned, so long as Japan was named.

Nineteen-ninety may see a second round of Super 301 citings. And again members of Congress will come forward with numerous candidates for retaliation. In 1989 the Bush administration spokesmen argued that once the president had completed the first year, pressure from Congress would vanish. Just the opposite has occurred. Congress, thinking that the Bush administration will not finally go to the mat on trade issues, is demanding more and more. The situation with Japan is certainly not better than before, and arguably worse. Nations such as South Korea, which made concessions under Super 301 threats cannot again—for international political reasons—trot out a new bag of tricks to dazzle the United States.

Hopefully, the administration has learned a lesson from this experience. At any rate, at least in 1990, it has a perfect rationale for refusing to take action under Super 301. The administration should announce—as it did on telecommunications—that during the final months of Uruguay Round negotiations it will take no actions that might jeopardize those talks, and thus it will choose *not* to name additional practices and nations in 1990.

Commentary

Robert Z. Lawrence

Super 301 and Section 301 are efforts to ensure that competition between the United States and the rest of the world is fair. But what exactly do we mean by "fair"? Frequently, it is argued that U.S. and foreign firms should compete on a level playing field. But the playing field metaphor is inappropriate. The playing field for competition between firms located in different countries will always be sloped in one direction or another because international competition is different from domestic competition. In domestic competition, all firms are subject to identical regulations and taxes and compete in the same product and factor markets. But in international trade, firms are located in different environments. Indeed, economic theory allows us to explain patterns of trade precisely because national economic environments differ. While the field may never be level, however, we can at least obtain agreement over the rules of the game. In a pluralistic world, therefore, what is fair is what countries multilaterally decide is fair.

Yet parts of Super 301, in particular objections to so-called unreasonable practices that do not violate an international agreement, involve the United States in unilaterally imposing its notions of fairness on others. For the purist, therefore, such behavior is unwarranted. But it must be recognized that for the practitioner of trade policy, the rules negotiated multilaterally may simply not suffice. Several genuine problems arise to which solutions must be found. In his chapter, Geza Feketekuty points to some of these and suggests Section 301 and Super 301 may be part of the answer. I will list four of these problems and discuss his responses.

1. What if, despite agreement on rules, we do not like particular trade outcomes?

Increasingly, Americans are calling for a system that guarantees results rather than simply sets rules. Feketekuty explains that Section 301 and Super 301 were, in part, a response to the major imbalances in the trading system, in particular the large U.S. trade deficit. He also suggests, explicitly, that these measures can help reduce the deficit by helping to smooth the adjustment process.

However, the U.S. trade deficit has almost nothing to do with unfair foreign practices, nor will altering the fairness of foreign practices determine the ultimate level of that balance. The increased use of Section 301 and the passage of Super 301 may be explained as a political tactic to divert attention from the real sources of the deficit—our spending patterns. As economists keep repeating, and policy practitioners continue to ignore, a trade deficit must be dealt with through macroeconomic tools that affect savings and investment.

The United States has an interest in removing foreign barriers regardless of the level of the trade balance. Fewer foreign barriers would mean a greater volume of U.S. exports at any given exchange rate level. To be sure, if the United States can persuade other countries to reduce their barriers we would need less of a devaluation to achieve adjustment. But the current level of barriers does not prevent adjustment of the U.S. trade deficit; rather, they make a weaker dollar necessary to achieve it. And unless we change our spending patterns, fewer foreign barriers will mean both more U.S. exports and more imports.

The tendency to confuse arguments about policies designed to improve the U.S. terms of trade (such as Section 301 and Super 301) with policies to reduce the trade deficit is dangerous. An example of this confusion is the SII talks between Japan and the United States. Many of the structural reforms requested of Japan are being made in the name of reducing the U.S.–Japan trade deficit. But without the correct macroeconomic policies, meaningful progress on these issues could be overwhelmed by the effects of exchange rates and spending patterns, causing some to claim the talks were ineffective.

2. What if the government ignores unfavorable outcomes?

Feketekuty begins the history of Super 301 in 1985, but we should actually begin in the early 1980s, when the policies of the Reagan administration in its first term generated immense frustration in the business community by pricing U.S. firms out of world markets through a strong dollar and then ignoring their pleas for assistance.

While the government should have been more attentive to the needs of U.S. traded-goods industries earlier, there is a great danger in the view, expressed by Feketekuty, that we should actually allow private interests to set the priorities of public policies. This is surely a prescription for rent-seeking and capture. In many cases those that scream the loudest do not reflect the broader public interest. A remarkable example of such capture is the semiconductor trade agreement between the United States and Japan which contained a disputed side-letter calling for a 20 percent share of the Japanese market for the products of foreign-owned chipmakers. Thus, chips built by Texas Instruments in Japan qualify for this quota even though they do nothing for the U.S. industrial base or trade balance. Chips built by Fujitsu in the United States would not qualify. We see a corporate, rather than a U.S. national perspective.

3. What if the nations cannot agree about the rules?

This is Feketekuty's strongest case. When areas and practices have not been incorporated in international agreements, does anything go? How can countries be induced to come to an agreement? Feketekuty justifies Super 301 as necessary to bring countries to the GATT bargaining table. Yes, but unfortunately it goes further than that. It includes practices, such as labor rights, that are not being discussed by GATT.

I agree with Feketekuty that the administration has used Super 301 to advance its GATT agenda. I'm not sure the GATT negotiations were what Congress had in mind when it called for "determining priority countries and practices," but defining the GATT negotiations as the major priority of U.S. trade policy was an ingenious adaptation made by the USTR. The paper might be strengthened by a more complete account of the way the countries and practices actually singled out helped contribute to the GATT negotiations. Indeed, contrary to the arguments made by Claude Barfield, I do not think the application of Super 301 has been arbitrary. Brazil and India were deliberately chosen since they are key players in the services issue in Geneva. Singling out Japan reflected more deeply rooted bilateral animosities but the sectors chosen with respect to Japan were also not arbitrary. By choosing supercomputers, forest products, and satellites, the USTR allowed a focus on barriers, since U.S. competitiveness in these areas is unquestionable.

But I believe, from a U.S. standpoint, by relying on bilateral pressures we are paying too high a political and diplomatic price to achieve market opening. Bilateral initiatives should be used as a last resort, not the first line of attack. While it is tempting to use U.S. power bilaterally, it can be counterproductive. If the discussions about the closed nature of Japan were held multilaterally, for example, they would not turn into a debate about the problems of U.S. competitiveness. They would focus on the problem *all* foreigners have in selling in Japan. Moreover, since our goals are more open markets for all foreign products, why should we have to sacrifice our popularity in targeted countries?

4. Finally, what should the United States do when foreigners agree on rules, but do not comply with them?

It is critical to remember that there is a need for agreement on the rules of punishment, not just the rules of the game. Section 301 and Super 301 involve punishment, in some cases, by means that have not been agreed to. It is disingenuous to argue that the United States is simply starting a process of discussion when it invokes Super 301 and places a country on the "hit list." Indeed, if investors are risk averse, the negative impact on a country from being named may actually be greater than the impact from being sanctioned.

When a case is initiated against just one type of Indian product, Indian insurance, for example, it raises the probability that Indian exports will be the subject of retaliation. But since it is unclear which products will be the object of sanctions and how large the sanctions will be, anyone planning to invest in India with the intention of exporting to the United States would have to take this possibility into account. Being named, therefore, casts a shadow on all Indian exports to the United States while being sanctioned will affect only those products actually named.

Let me conclude with a final observation. I think Feketekuty's chapter demonstrates that the USTR has done a heroic job in damage limitation. We are lucky that we have people like Geza Feketekuty, Carla Hills, and Jules Katz interpreting the use of these rules in a sophisticated way, for the most part to advance multilateral objectives. But one could easily imagine how a different set of officials could have placed a different interpretation on these laws with disastrous consequences for the trading system.

Part 2
Evaluations of 301:
Legal, Political, and Economic

CHAPTER 4

Thinking about the New Section 301:
Beyond Good and Evil

Robert E. Hudec

The new Section 301 of the Omnibus Trade and Competitiveness Act of 1988 is probably the most criticized piece of U.S. foreign trade legislation since the Hawley-Smoot Tariff Act of 1930. The new law, a revised and enlarged version of a statute first enacted in 1974, orders the United States government to launch an intensified assault against foreign trade restrictions. Earlier versions of Section 301 had granted the president broad authority to retaliate against foreign restrictions, but the 1988 Congress was not satisfied with the president's use of this authority. The 1988 amendments tightened the law's existing procedures requiring formal investigation of private complaints. In addition, the 1988 amendments created a wholly new set of procedures—the celebrated Super 301 and Special 301—that call upon the Executive Branch to develop its own complaints procedure by (1) making a comprehensive inventory of restrictions in all countries, (2) selecting priority targets from within that inventory, and (3) retaliating if the targeted restrictions are not promptly removed. The total effect of the 1988 amendments is to impose a new and more sweeping set of demands on foreign governments, going well beyond the trade policy rules agreed to in GATT, and backed by a threat of swift trade retaliation, much of which would violate United States legal obligations in GATT.

Foreign governments have been quick to object. They have convened a special GATT meeting to lecture the United States on the evils of uni-

A number of friends and colleagues contributed generously of their time in helping me to prepare this paper. I am particularly indebted to Jagdish Bhagwati who, despite disagreement with some of its conclusions, took a strong interest in the paper from the beginning and, with Hugh Patrick, provided a most distinguished forum in which to present it. I also received good advice from a large number of others who commented on, and often objected to, the several earlier drafts, particularly Robert Kudrle, Daniel Gifford, Carl Auerbach, Gary Horlick, Frieder Roessler, B. L. Das, Michael Finger, Andreas Lowenfeld, David Palmeter, T. N. Srinivasan, Robert Keohane, and William Davey. Finally, thanks to Tom Bayard and the Institute for International Economics for inviting me to test an early version of these ideas before an IIE conference.

lateralism.[1] They have promised to respond to Section 301 retaliation by prompt counterretaliation. They have warned that the new Section 301 procedures may wreck the current Uruguay Round trade negotiations in GATT, and possibly even GATT itself.

Foreign reactions have been sharpened by irritation over the self-righteous tone of the new law. The detailed procedures of the new Section 301 are structured as a series of public investigations and decisions which makes them appear to be "trade crimes" trials. Foreign governments bristle at having their policies "tried" in this manner, and have gone out of their way to ridicule the quasi-judicial appearance of these procedures. Section 301 proceedings, they note, are a totally one-sided affair in which the United States plays both prosecutor and judge, in which the defendants are tried in absentia, and in which Congress has ordained certain guilty verdicts in advance, particularly with regard to Japan.

Within the United States, domestic criticism of the new Section 301 has also reached heights not seen since the days of Smoot-Hawley. In a manner reminiscent of the famous condemnation of Smoot-Hawley by the leading economists of the 1930s, the new Section 301 has been condemned in an April, 1989, statement drafted by Professor Jagdish Bhagwati of Columbia University and signed by forty of the nation's most prominent economists, as well as by its most prominent GATT legal scholar.[2] The statement attacks both Section 301 and a more recent policy initiative calling for "managed trade." With regard to Section 301, the statement condemns both the GATT illegality of 301 retaliation and, on a broader scale, the new law's departure from GATT multilateralism in favor of bilateral initiatives based on bullying smaller trading partners.[3]

The new Section 301 has its supporters, of course. Support begins, naturally enough, with the congressional committees that wrote the new law, and the Executive Branch officials who must administer it. Legislators tend to

---

1. The GATT meeting was held on March 16, 1989. See *GATT Focus*, no. 60 (March-April, 1989): 6.

2. See "Statement of Forty Economists on American Trade Policy," *The World Economy*, 12 (1989): 263–65. The group of forty included four Nobel laureates, four former chairs of the Council of Economic Advisors, and a Who's Who of international economics in the United States.

The Smoot-Hawley statement was issued on May 5, 1930. Signed by 1,028 "economists and teachers of economics," it requested the Congress and President Hoover to withhold approval from the proposed tariff increase. The originators were Professors Paul Douglas of Chicago, Irving Fisher of Yale, Frank Graham of Princeton, and Frank W. Taussig of Harvard. For the text and signatories, see *New York Times*, May 5, 1930.

3. Professor Bhagwati has written a more extended critique, along the same lines, in his paper "United States Trade Policy at the Crossroads," *The World Economy* 12, no. 4 (December, 1989): 439–79.

defend the new Section 301 with the same indignant rhetoric used to justify its enactment, while Executive Branch officials are more inclined to offer behind-the-hand assurances that, like the music of Wagner, Section 301 is not really as bad as it sounds. This official support for 301 is echoed by a fair number of private observers. One influential segment consists of those who support GATT, in general, but who are impatient with the rigidities of the GATT system and feel that it needs a good jolt now and then to do its job. Another more extreme segment includes those who have given up on GATT altogether, as well as those "Power Realists" for whom the existence of power is the only justification needed for its use.

So far, the new Section 301 has not caused any major ruptures in international trade relations. The first annual Super 301 review procedure, conducted in April and May, 1989, induced a surprisingly large number of foreign governments to adopt trade-liberalizing measures in order not to be singled out. As a consequence, the administration's first "hit list" under Super 301 came out smaller and less tendentious than critics had feared.[4] The Special 301 procedure, which deals with protection of intellectual property rights, also managed to circumvent its first potential crisis when, in May, 1989, the U.S. Trade Representative decided that continuing negotiations over intellectual property protection made it inappropriate to initiate formal 301 proceedings against any country. Instead, the USTR merely put the twenty-five most prominent offenders on a "watch list" or "priority watch list." Six months later, three of the countries on the priority watch list were declared improved enough to be moved to the watch list.

The early calm is deceiving, however. Both Super 301 and Special 301 have timetables that require additional determinations and findings in the near future. The strengthened private complaints procedure is also still on the books. Congress may continue to show patience for a while longer, but it is unlikely to ratify the results of the Uruguay Round without a strict accounting of how the new Section 301 has been used. Moreover, in the long run, Congress is unlikely just to leave Section 301 as it is. Most members of Congress view the large number of trade-liberalizing concessions made so far as proof that the basic approach of the new Section 301 is correct. Correct or

---

4. On June 16, 1989, the U.S. Trade Representative identified six barriers to be prosecuted under Super 301, and initiated formal proceedings under Section 301 against them. The complaints were:

Brazil Import Licensing (301-73)
Japan Satellites (301-74)
Japan Supercomputers (301-75)
Japan Forest Products (301-76)
India Investment (301-77)
India Insurance (301-78)

not, any law that produces this many good things for U.S. exporters, without requiring any concessions by the United States in return, is just too good not to be used again.

This chapter examines one dimension of the current controversy over Section 301. It disregards the views of those who argue that Section 301 is good because GATT is dead, or because only power matters. It focuses, instead, upon the debate among those "insiders" who believe that the GATT system, and GATT law in particular, are and will remain the best available medium for conducting the world's trade relations. Among those who share this view, there is considerable disagreement over whether, and to what extent, the new Section 301 is in fact harmful. This chapter examines that question.

The conclusions of the chapter make a distinction between two types of GATT legal violations that are ordered by what might be called Section 301 legal policy. The first is the type of legal violation that tended to occur under earlier versions of Section 301, which were often justified and will probably continue to be justified in the future. The second is the more extreme type of legal violation called for by the 1988 amendments to Section 301, which the chapter concludes are seriously wrong and damaging to GATT. To amplify:

1. The chapter argues that not all disobedience to GATT law is necessarily wrong. It calls attention to instances of U.S. disobedience in the
   recent past in which the disobedience has made a constructive contribution to breaking legal deadlocks and stimulating improvements in
   GATT law. It argues that such disobedience is not only justified, but
   has actually been an important element in the process of GATT legal
   reform over the past decade or so.
2. The chapter also argues that the 1988 version of Section 301, on the
   other hand, has no such claim to justification. The new 301, it argues,
   makes law reform demands that are both excessive and completely
   one-sided. Retaliation in support of such demands cannot be considered legitimate, even under the most tolerant standards.

My primary purpose in this chapter is to introduce the first of these two conclusions, the one about "justified disobedience," into the debate about the new Section 301. I believe it is important to do so for two reasons.

First, I believe that most of the criticism of the new Section 301 has, to date, been rendered ineffective because it fails to deal with the issue of justified disobedience. Most of the critics, foreign and domestic, have rested their case against the new Section 301 simply on the ground that it violates GATT law. That black-and-white argument is proving less and less persuasive among policymakers and observers who have had experience with GATT, and whose experience has taught them that GATT's legal machinery has so many imperfections that it often needs an external jolt to get moving. For many who share this experience, the new Section 301 is a necessary and appropriate response to the imperfections of GATT law. I believe this is a mistaken appraisal of the new Section 301, but I am convinced that the only way to make that mistake clear is to begin by trying to define the case for "justified disobedience." It is only when one understands the conditions under which disobedience might, in fact, be justified that one can evaluate whether the new Section 301 meets that justification.

Second, in the opposite direction, I believe it is also important to call attention to the point about justified disobedience for its own sake. There is a danger of overkill in the current orgy of anti-301 criticism—a too ardent defense of the status quo in GATT, and a too vigorous reaction against any and all forms of extralegal pressure to change it. This, too, would be a mistake. GATT law continues to need major reform if it is to remain credible. In my view, the forces of GATT law reform are weak and halting, and often need the threat of justified disobedience to keep moving forward. The correct response to the new Section 301, therefore, must be more selective. Critics must come down hard on the specific wrongs of the new law itself (some of which are truly outrageous), but they must be prepared to distinguish other types of GATT disobedience that serve a genuinely constructive purpose. In other words, the goal should not be to obliterate the new Section 301 (an unrealistic goal in any event), but rather, to try to redirect some of its reformist energy in support of a more limited and narrowly focused effort to promote real GATT law reform. I will suggest that both these goals—limiting the new 301 and using it positively—should be pursued by turning Section 301's reformist demands back upon the United States itself.

The chapter consists of five sections, followed by two appendixes. The first section contains a nontechnical description of the new Section 301 and a brief analysis of the extent to which it might cause the United States to violate its GATT legal obligations. The second section takes up the case for justified disobedience—the claim that disobedience to GATT law can be justified on occasion as a more constructive alternative than continuing to play by the rules. The third section then tests the notion of justified disobedience by considering the major objections to it. A fourth section attempts to reduce the case for justified disobedience to certain guidelines by which claims of justification can be measured. Finally, the fifth section applies these guidelines to the new Section 301, in an effort to demonstrate why Section 301 cannot be defended in terms of justified obedience, and, in so doing, to identify what is really wrong with the new law, and what should be done about it.

The two appendixes contain, first, a description of the nine cases in which the United States has actually used the power of retaliation in Section

301 cases, and second, a scorecard of the United States's own performance as a defendant in GATT litigation from 1980–89.

What Is the New Section 301, and How Does It Violate GATT?

Section 301 was first enacted in the Trade Act of 1974. Like certain earlier trade law provisions, it granted the Executive Branch broad authority to retaliate against foreign-government trade barriers that violated U.S. rights, or that the executive branch deemed to be unreasonable. The new wrinkle added by Section 301 was a procedure allowing private citizens to file complaints about foreign trade barriers, and requiring the U.S. Trade Representative to investigate them. The law did not actually require the executive branch to retaliate when the investigation found foreign barriers illegal or unreasonable, but the visibility of the law's public procedures was designed to create political pressure to do so.

Since 1974, Section 301 has been amended several times. The amendments have broadened the list of actionable foreign practices. In addition to barriers distorting trade in goods, Section 301 now covers barriers affecting transactions in services, investment transactions, intellectual property rights, and certain internal matters such as workers' rights. While retaliation is still not absolutely mandatory, the amendments have gradually restricted executive branch discretion, increasingly handcuffed by tighter and tighter procedures and deadlines.

The present version of Section 301 can produce trade retaliation in two distinct settings. One is the Section 301 complaint involving a claimed violation of U.S. legal rights in GATT, where the typical procedure is for the United States to file a GATT legal complaint and pursue the enforcement remedies provided by GATT. This is the type of Section 301 proceeding that was most common prior to 1988, and in today's 301 lexicon is sometimes called "Regular 301."

The other setting for Section 301 retaliation is a complaint involving foreign barriers that are not in violation of GATT, but fall within one of the other "wrongs" defined by Section 301. This second category of 301 wrongs includes measures that violate other international agreements, but its major targets are measures like inadequate intellectual property protection which violate no international obligation at all, but which are nonetheless deemed "unreasonable" by the executive branch.[5] Section 301 complaints

5. The Section 301 list of wrongs actually contains two kinds of legal measures—measures that are legal but "unreasonable," and measures that are legal but "discriminatory." The author has always regarded the second category as surplus wording, on the grounds that the term "unreasonable" would certainly cover all the same things. For this reason, and to avoid confusion

about measures in this second category are usually handled bilaterally, because GATT offers no adjudicative procedures to deal with them. Likewise, any Section 301 retaliation that is taken in these cases is taken without GATT authorization. Although proceedings can be initiated by private complaint, Section 301 proceedings against "unreasonable" measures are most likely to arise (and be pursued) in the new Super 301 and Special 301 procedures. Each of these two settings for Section 301 retaliation will have to be considered separately.

GATT-Based Retaliation—Regular 301

The first category of Section 301 actions involves those foreign practices that are claimed to be a breach of GATT obligations and/or a nullification-and-impairment of GATT benefits. Section 301 has always provided that the executive branch may pursue such GATT-based claims by initiating GATT's dispute settlement machinery. In theory, Section 301 allows the U.S. government enough time to follow these procedures. It allows the bare minimum of time needed to process the claim before a GATT panel, and a bit more time to obtain GATT authorization to retaliate if the defendant does not comply with an adverse ruling. It also allows the executive branch to terminate the Section 301 proceeding if the U.S. legal claim is ruled invalid.

The potential for violating GATT law in these cases comes from the fact that the time limits established by the new Section 301 are too tight. The new version of Section 301 requires the executive branch to make a final determination within a month of the GATT ruling. Where the determination is affirmative, the law allows seven months for the offending practice to be corrected, after which time retaliation must be implemented. The law also establishes an outside time limit of twelve or eighteen months from the beginning of the Section 301 investigation, depending on the case.

The GATT dispute settlement procedure will often not be able to meet this timetable. Lots can happen:

> The appointment of a panel can be delayed or blocked.
> The governments can take too long to submit briefs and arguments.
> The panel and/or the governments can fail to find timely meeting dates.
> The panel can take too long to decide the case.
> The panel can fail to decide the case at all.
> The GATT Council can deadlock over approval or disapproval of a panel ruling.

with illegal discrimination, this chapter uses only the term "unreasonable" to describe the legal-but-wrong category of Section 301 offenses.

Follow-up proceedings can get mired down in disputes about what it takes to comply.

Or, finally, the decision to authorize retaliation can get bogged down over what kind, how much, and on what terms. (GATT has authorized retaliation only once in more than forty years, and has only been requested to do so a few times.)

If the past is any guide, one or more delays of this kind will occur in many cases, and the very tight Section 301 timetable will not be met. In those cases, the current procedures of Section 301 could well require the United States to retaliate before GATT authorizes such action. If so, the U.S. retaliation could well be a violation of GATT law. This is the GATT legal problem with the new 1988 version of Regular 301.

Not all unauthorized retaliation will be GATT-illegal. On two occasions prior to 1974, the United States managed to impose Section 301–type retaliation without prior authorization, because the measures complained of happened to be ones for which GATT law automatically authorized compensatory countermeasures. The United States was able to characterize its imposition of new trade barriers as authorized "compensation" under GATT law, while advertising these actions as punitive, 301-type retaliation under domestic law.[6]

In most cases, however, the retaliatory measures will not be pre-authorized, and so will be a violation of GATT unless and until they are authorized by GATT or otherwise excused.[7] Where the delay in GATT proceedings occurs despite good faith on all sides, a United States refusal to wait for completion of GATT procedures would have no excuse, and premature retaliation in such a case would violate GATT law. Such a violation might not bring down the full wrath of GATT if the measure being complained of is clearly GATT-illegal, as is quite often the case. Where the GATT legal status

---

6. Both cases occurred under the predecessor to Section 301, Section 252 of the Trade Expansion Act of 1962. The first was the "Chicken War" dispute with the EC in 1963, where the U.S. withdrawal of GATT tariff concessions was authorized by automatic compensation rights under GATT Article XXVIII:3. For a description, see Abram Chayes, Thomas Ehrlich, and Andreas F. Lowenfeld, *International Legal Process* (Boston and Toronto: Little, Brown, 1968), 249–306. The second was the "Cattle War" dispute with Canada in 1974, when the United States imposed quantitative restrictions by authority of automatic compensation rights under Article XIX:3. See Robert E. Hudec, "Retaliation against 'Unreasonable' Foreign Trade Practices: The New Section 301 and GATT Nullification and Impairment," *Minnesota Law Review* 59 (1975): 461–539.

7. The current favorite for U.S. retaliation is a 100 percent ad valorem tariff applied only to the goods of the offending country. The discriminatory nature of such tariffs invariably violates GATT Article I (the Most Favored Nation [MFN] obligation). The tariff is usually bound at a lower level, so that the 100 percent rate exceeds a tariff binding in violation of GATT Article II. The other standard retaliatory measure is the quantitative restriction, violating GATT Article XI:1, applied discriminatorily in violation of Article XIII.

of the measure is unclear, however, the premature retaliation will be viewed as a quite serious breach of GATT law—an attempt to bypass GATT legal processes by bullying.

The legal consequences of premature retaliation become more difficult to define when retaliation occurs after a genuine breakdown in the GATT legal process. The obligation not to retaliate without GATT authority presumes that GATT will be able to rule on the disputed legal claim, and, later, on the request to retaliate. If GATT is, in fact, unable to rule, the complainant may be free to resort to "self-help" in some circumstances. The legality of such self-help has never been tested in GATT. Where the breakdown is clearly the fault of one side or the other, most GATT members would probably be prepared to treat premature retaliation as either justified or unjustified accordingly. Retaliation in cases where the fault is more evenly (and widely) distributed will most likely produce some kind of legal impasse.[8]

What has been the United States experience so far with regard to retaliation in Regular 301 cases? Appendix 1 contains a description of all Section 301 retaliation from 1975–89, nine instances in all. There have been six instances of retaliation in cases involving GATT-based legal claims.[9] None of the six was authorized by GATT. Only one of the six was clearly GATT-legal, although several others involved general legal breakdowns that would have been difficult to rule on.[10] None of the six actions triggered a legal crisis.

---

8. Where the breakdown is caused by disagreement between groups of countries on both sides, my starting point would be a presumption *against* holding unilateral retaliation to be justified, on the ground that, if the obligation not to use certain trade measures is clear, that obligation should remain binding until an excusing condition (e.g., the claimed breach of a reciprocal obligation) is shown with equal clarity.

On the other hand, it has to be recognized that some obligations are so central to the balance of reciprocity that the inability to resolve disagreement about their meaning may so upset the balance as to deprive other, related obligations of their legitimacy as well. For example, if the key "equitable share" requirement on agricultural export subsidies proves to be unenforceable because of disagreement as to its meaning, do other subrules that happen to prohibit one or another specific type of export subsidy retain their legitimacy?

9. The six cases were:
1. EC Wheat Flour Export Subsidies (301-6).
2. EC Citrus Preferences (301-11). The retaliation was an increased tariff on pasta imports, allowing it to serve as retaliation in another GATT complaint—EC Pasta Export Subsidies (301-25).
3. Japan Leather and Leather Footwear Restrictions (301-13 and 301-36).
4. Japan Semiconductors (301-48).
5. EC Enlargement: Spain and Portugal (301-54).
6. EC Hormones Prohibition (301-62).

10. The retaliation that would have been ruled GATT-legal was that in Japan Leather and Leather Footwear, in which an agreed quantum of increased trade barriers was part of the final settlement.

Retaliation in the EC Wheat Flour case and the EC Citrus-Pasta cases are the clearest examples of the second category.

GATT complaints were filed against three of the six retaliations. Two of the complaints were not pursued to adjudication; the third is being prosecuted, but so far appointment of a panel has been blocked by the United States.[11]

Each of the six 301 retaliations occurred under pre-1988 versions of Section 301, where time limits were not as rigorous. In all but one of the cases, retaliation did not occur until well after 301 time limits had expired.[12]

It is not yet clear whether the 1988 version of Section 301 will actually produce more retaliation sooner. The announced intention of the new statute would seem to require it. But, like its predecessors, the actual text of the 1988 version of Section 301 is an intricate maze of mandatory commands in one place and extremely wide loopholes in the other. One needs a wiring diagram to trace whether mandatory commands given in one part will actually reach their final target without passing through at least one discretionary exit point. Even with the aid of such a diagram, one cannot predict actual outcomes, for this is the sort of statute that only Congress can enforce,[13] and Congress is often a good deal more patient when monitoring such laws than when writing them. If past conduct is any guide, Congress will be prepared to overlook delays as long as, in the end, a minimally sufficient number of heads roll into the basket.

The safest conclusion, therefore, is that this first category of GATT-based 301 cases will continue to produce a steady trickle of premature retaliation, some but not all being GATT-illegal. There will probably not be enough GATT-illegal behavior to trigger a major crisis by itself. On the other hand, the volume will probably be high enough to cause continuing legal friction. The effects of such friction will depend on just how the new Section 301 is actually administered, and particularly on how the United States itself behaves

---

11. A GATT legal complaint in EC Wheat Flour led to the appointment of a panel, but then the complaint was allowed to lapse. A complaint in Japan Semiconductors still appears now and then on the GATT Council agenda (part of the retaliation is still in force), but a panel ruling has never been requested. A complaint in EC Hormones Prohibition is, at this writing, still pending; the EC has been seeking appointment of a panel since February, 1989, and the United States is still blocking the request.

12. The one exception was EC Enlargement (301-54), which was self-initiated by the U.S. administration rather late into the dispute, on March 31, 1986. The United States retaliated, without bringing any formal GATT complaint, as early as May 15, 1986.

13. For articles arguing that some Section 301 criteria should be enforced through judicial review, see Erwin P. Eichman and Gary N. Horlick, "Political Questions in International Trade: Judicial Review of Section 301?" *Michigan Journal of International Law* 10 (1989): 735–64; and Kevin C. Kennedy, "Presidential Authority Under Section 337, Section 301, and the Escape Clause: The Case for Less Discretion," *Cornell International Law Journal* 20 (1987): 127–61.

In the author's view, judicial review would not be granted under the present statute, nor should it be. Statutes of this kind are a form of political bluster in which the Congress overacts for domestic political consumption, counting on the Executive to dilute the reality. Judicial review would require writing a different statute.

when it is on the losing side of GATT legal rulings in other cases. We shall return to this subject in the final section of this chapter.

Retaliation against "Unreasonable" Practices— Super 301 and Special 301

As noted earlier, Section 301 contains a second category of punishable offenses, those that are not GATT wrongs. The main part of this second category consists of measures that violate no legal obligation at all, but that are nonetheless found to be "unreasonable" by the executive branch. In the beginning, the concept of unreasonable measures was limited to restrictive trade and trade-related measures not covered by GATT legal obligations— basically, a mandate ordering the president to fill in the gaps in the GATT legal code. Subsequent amendments, however, have expanded the concept to embrace almost any kind of economic policy measure the U.S. government might want to find offensive. The law itself now gives the executive branch virtually unfettered discretion in identifying unreasonable measures. Congress has also decided to help the executive branch along by enacting a list of specific practices that it *wants* to be treated as unreasonable. After the 1988 amendments to Section 301, the list now includes such nontrade matters as barriers to trade in services, barriers to certain kinds of foreign investment, inadequate protection of intellectual property rights, export targeting, systematic toleration of anticompetitive practices, and denial of workers' rights.

Section 301 does not require the executive branch to retaliate against unreasonable practices, but over the years Congress has progressively tightened the procedural steps that must be followed in handling such claims, in an effort to focus greater and greater political pressure against executive branch decisions not to act. The 1988 amendments to Section 301 added some particularly powerful new procedural requirements. The two most significant are the celebrated Super 301 and Special 301 procedures. Super 301 requires the executive branch to put some teeth into an existing practice of preparing an inventory of barriers to trade and services in all countries: it requires the executive branch to make a decision identifying worst offenders in that inventory; it then sets a deadline for eliminating the worst offenses, after which the executive branch is required to make a public decision whether to retaliate. Special 301 requires a similar inventory of inadequate protection of intellectual property rights around the world, followed by a similar worst-offenders list, a deadline for correction, and a decision to retaliate. Yet another such procedure was enacted for attacking restrictions against trade in telecommunications products, in a separate part of the 1988 law.

Some critics have argued that the mere existence of the rigorous megaprocedures of Super 301 and Special 301 is a GATT violation. Normally,

GATT rejects such arguments, holding to the rule that violations do not occur until trade restrictions are actually put into force. In my view, GATT would almost certainly follow that rule here. As a practical matter, it is just too hard to draw the line between ordinary threats, which occur in every dispute, and the more formalized Super 301–type threats. Moreover, I suspect that governments will find it counterproductive to precipitate legal confrontations over procedures like Super 301 at the point when they merely threaten. Laws like Super 301 are a form of political bluster. The most prudent way of dealing with such legislation is to allow it to blow itself out—standing back when it makes a big splash at the outset, and then trying to broaden, divert, merge, and muddle the subsequent negotiating process into something more equitable and constructive. The last thing GATT should seek is a definitive Right-Wrong confrontation at the outset.

Actual retaliation against unreasonable practices, on the other hand, will by definition be a GATT violation—when, that is, it involves the imposition of new *trade* barriers. By definition, unreasonable practices neither violate GATT, nor "nullify or impair" GATT benefits. Consequently, there can be no excuse in GATT law for imposing GATT-illegal trade barriers in response to them.[14] The executive branch could avoid the GATT problem, of course, by retaliating in a different way—for example, by imposing restrictions on investment transactions or on service industry transactions, instead of raising trade barriers. Section 301 does grant authority to retaliate in these other ways, in any case. Congress has made it clear, however, that for most of the newly identified unreasonable measures it wants to retaliate by closing the U.S. market for goods. It is a safe bet that trade retaliation will be the remedy of choice.

Until recently, there had been little experience with Section 301 proceedings against unreasonable measures. Prior to 1985, most Section 301 cases involved complaints about trade measures in violation of GATT, and were handled under the GATT adjudication procedure.[15] Beginning in 1985, however, Section 301 cases involving practices not covered by GATT law have begun to appear with greater frequency.[16] So far, there has been only one

---

14. The legal status of the usual retaliation measures is explained in n. 7.

15. The only instance of retaliation on nontrade measures during this period was Canada Border Broadcasting (301-15), involving a Canadian tax law that penalized Canadian businesses that advertised on U.S. border television stations. The U.S. retaliation was a mirror image law, the only instance of nontrade retaliation so far under 301.

16. Three celebrated cases were filed in 1985: Brazil Informatics (301-49); Korea Insurance (301-51), and Korea Intellectual Property Rights (301-52). The Brazil Informatics case several times reached the brink of retaliation. In 1987, the Brazil Pharmaceutical case (301-61) was filed, leading to retaliation in 1988. In 1989, five of the six complaints filed in the first round of Super 301 complaints, see n. 4, involved measures that fell into the unreasonable category.

instance of actual trade retaliation against unreasonable practices—a 1988 retaliatory tariff increase in response to perceived inadequacies in Brazil's protection of intellectual property rights for pharmaceutical products.[17] That retaliation was clearly in violation of GATT, and is currently the subject of a GATT legal complaint by Brazil.

Looking ahead, the amount of GATT-illegal retaliation that Super 301 and Special 301 are likely to trigger is again difficult to forecast. If the statements of the legislative authors are taken at face value, the amount will be significant. As noted above, however, Congress is usually more patient in practice, and Congress has the power to relax these demands. Congress will probably grant the executive branch considerable leeway in enforcing these new procedures. In the end, though, it will almost certainly hold the Uruguay Round hostage until satisfied with the ultimate use of these powers. What it will take to satisfy Congress, and what can be done to influence that outcome, are quite open issues at this point. We shall address them in the final section of this chapter.

In sum, we find that Section 301 currently calls for two types of trade retaliation that may be in violation of GATT. One is retaliation in the course of ordinary GATT legal complaints, where the retaliation may be GATT-illegal because somewhat unrealistic deadlines will force it to be taken before the legal process has run its course. The second is trade retaliation against other measures not covered by GATT, particularly those that fall into Section 301's unreasonable category. In this second case, likely to be encountered most frequently under Super 301 and Special 301, trade retaliation will, almost by definition, be GATT-illegal because the measures complained of will give no excuse for it. The new megaprocedures themselves, however, are unlikely to be found GATT-illegal.

So much for the subject matter of the new Section 301, and its potential for causing violations of GATT law. We now turn to the question of whether its GATT-illegal retaliation can ever be considered justified.

The Case for Justified Disobedience

This chapter rejects the easy criticism of Section 301 which simply posits that Section 301 is wrong because it calls for violations of GATT law. The problem with that criticism, in my view, is its assumption that disobedience to GATT law is always wrong. I believe that disobedience to GATT law is not always the more harmful alternative—that in certain situations of legal crisis, disobedience may be less damaging to GATT law than continuing to abide by the rules.

---

17. Brazilian Pharmaceuticals (301-61) is described in appendix 1.

Criticism of Section 301 that ignores the possibility of justified disobe-dience errs in two respects. First, it advocates a legal policy that is simply too rigid for the imperfect world of GATT law. Second, it fails to address the major defense of the new Section 301. Much of the support for the new Section 301 rests on the belief that GATT law needs additional pressures to function effectively, and that Section 301 is an appropriate form of pressure to meet this need. Successful criticism of Section 301 must address the concept of justified disobedience, and be prepared to distinguish the new Section 301 from such disobedience.

The general case for justified disobedience rests on the shortcomings of the GATT legal system. Even though GATT law is rather effective by interna-tional standards, it is still imperfect—indeed, almost primitive—by com-parison with national legal institutions. The substance of GATT law is limited to the area of trade transactions, and even within that area there are huge gaps in its coverage—matters such as variable levies, state trading restrictions, and quota discrimination which in principle ought to be regulated but which in fact are not effectively dealt with in the legal text. Procedurally, GATT is capable of adjudicating most legal claims, but legal rulings can still be blocked by unwilling defendants, and the enforcement of rulings still depends almost entirely on normative pressure.

While it is possible to remedy inadequacies by negotiation, the reform process is often maddeningly slow, and sometimes stalls completely, due to the need for agreement of the nearly one hundred national governments who are GATT's law-making body. Governments tend to support law reform in principle, but when confronted with specific legal reforms that will call upon them to change domestic laws and practices, they encounter strong political pressures to follow the safer course of keeping the status quo. This political caution is not peculiar to GATT; indeed, GATT has probably been more successful in overcoming it than many other international organizations that deal in politically sensitive matters. But it is still strong enough in GATT that law reform is seriously hobbled by it.

GATT's legal imperfections often render it incapable of dealing effec-tively with legal claims made by member governments. The legal impasse created in such situations presents a delicate problem. On the one hand, GATT law is damaged every time member countries respond to such dead-locks by violating the law, for every legal system requires consistent respect if it is to achieve those habits of obedience that constitute the source of legal power. On the other hand, respect for GATT law is also damaged by inaction in the face of such deadlocks, for no legal system can gain respect if it cannot deliver at least part of the protection against legal wrongs that it purports to provide. Domestic interests who supply the political support for GATT will not sit and wait indefinitely for results that never come.

International legal systems rarely, if ever, call for perpetual commitment regardless of outcomes. One possible answer to the dilemma of deadlock is for the dissatisfied government to threaten withdrawal from the agreement if the problem is not corrected. Withdrawal is normally a legally available option in any international agreement. The United States has actually taken that option on a number of occasions during the past decade, most notably in the case of the International Labor Organization and UNESCO. It has even withdrawn from a GATT agreement recently, terminating its membership in the Tokyo Round's International Dairy Arrangement in 1985 in protest over the EC's refusal to abide by minimum price rules.

Withdrawal, of course, is an all-or-nothing type of response, and thus can only be used when approaching total breakdown. Withdrawal might conceivably be a possible answer if certain of the GATT codes neared total breakdown. Withdrawal from GATT as a whole, however, would be too damaging to contemplate in any but the most extreme situation.

In cases where withdrawal is not an appropriate response to a particular legal breakdown, governments sometimes view selective disobedience as a more limited alternative. It sends the same message. Unlike withdrawal from an agreement, of course, selective disobedience is not legally authorized—no sense of obligation could exist if it were. But it may be the only intermediate alternative to doing nothing.[18]

The notion of "justified" disobedience is based on the simple judgment that there are cases where the damage to the legal system caused by inaction in the face of deadlock will exceed the damage caused by some disobedient act trying to force a correction. The best way to illustrate the concept is to describe a few cases in which, rightly or wrongly, the United States claimed the right to practice such disobedience during the past decade or so. Although none of this disobedient action was compelled by the rules of Section 301, all were expressions of the legal policy behind Section 301.

The Wheat Flour Subsidy Case

One example of disobedience claimed to be justified was the United States's resort to retaliatory agricultural export subsidies in the mid-1980s, in response to GATT's failure to discipline EC export subsidies granted under its Common Agricultural Policy (CAP). The United States began by attacking CAP subsidies in several GATT lawsuits. The EC resisted at every step of every

---

18. GATT actually has a procedure for authorizing selective withdrawals of obligations in response to failure of the General Agreement to provide anticipated benefits. Article XXIII:1(c) could be used to authorize rolling back obligations in certain areas if the Contracting Parties found that a deadlocked legal system was causing denial of reasonably anticipated benefits. Ultimately, however, this Article XXIII procedure requires a consensus decision. In the typical case of legal breakdown, governments opposing the deadlocked claim are unlikely to authorize withdrawals against themselves.

lawsuit. In January, 1983, a few months before the panel report in the first case (*Wheat Flour*), the United States signaled its impatience by granting an export subsidy large enough to permit U.S. exporters to seize the entire Egyptian wheat flour market for a year—a subsidy pretty clearly in violation of Subsidy Code rules.[19] Shortly thereafter, the results in the GATT lawsuits confirmed the fears that lay behind U.S. impatience. The basic legal concept of the Subsidies Code—the limitation of subsidized exports to an "equitable share" of world markets—proved to be inoperable in litigation, as did a number of other key rules. The U.S. response to this legal failure was to enact the broad and muscular Export Enhancement Program (EEP) of export subsidies of the 1985 Farm Act, most of which were also in violation of the same Subsidy Code rules.

The case for disobedience here was simply the fact that GATT legal discipline had broken down. There were no effective rules to regulate export subsidies granted by other countries, and there was no evidence of any disposition to negotiate any better rules. Even though retaliatory subsidies turned out not to be a very effective form of pressure, the EC did put its CAP export subsidies on the table in the Uruguay Round. Thus, the U.S. retaliation may have helped open the door to possible legal reforms that may in turn bring these subsidy practices back into GATT legal discipline. If so, the retaliation could well have been more constructive than waiting for such reform to occur by means of persuasion alone. The latter course could well have produced a much larger legal failure as irritation mounted, leading to a larger explosion against GATT law.

The key issue in a case like the export subsidy impasse is whether reform initiatives could have been stimulated, in time, by negotiation within the legal system. The short answer is that we will never know. But experience tells us that persuasion does not always succeed. We also know that even where governments are favorably disposed to reform, external shocks are sometimes needed to provide a domestic political justification for doing so. The demanding government is usually aware of the risks, and has pretty good information about the likely outcomes of continued negotiation.

The Conditional MFN Policy

In 1979, the United States adopted a "conditional MFN" approach to the Tokyo Round Subsidies Code, saying that it would not observe the Code's

---

19. The United States claimed that it was merely taking back some of the world export market that the EC had taken, in excess of its "equitable share," by means of exports subsidies in violation of the Subsidies Code. The means employed, however, were exceptionally low prices that violated the separate obligation of Subsidy Code Article 10:3 against subsidies causing material price undercutting.

new legal obligations toward countries who did not sign commitments to observe the Code.[20] This position violated one of the GATT's most fundamental rules—the "unconditional MFN" obligation requiring that trade advantages given to one country be extended to all other GATT members "immediately and unconditionally."

Although the United States never actually admitted that its conditional MFN policy was a GATT legal violation, it argued that transgressing the unconditional MFN principle was, in any event, justified. It contended that the unconditional MFN obligation, although absolute in form, was in principle premised on at least some minimal degree of participation in the legal community by the other country, and that unconditional MFN treatment never had been, nor politically could it ever be, an obligation that extended indefinitely in favor of nonparticipating members.

At the time, GATT was, in fact, experiencing a rather extensive problem of nonparticipation by developing countries, who were claiming ever larger exemptions from GATT obligations, under the doctrine of "special and differential treatment," while at the same time claiming the right, under the unconditional MFN clause, to receive the benefits of increasing trade liberalization by developed countries. The United States's conditional MFN policy was a warning shot across the bow, advising that this policy could not be sustained. In the background was a domestic political problem in the United States. It was becoming increasingly difficult to muster political support for honoring GATT obligations toward nonparticipating developing countries as their exports to the United States rose.

The actual extent of the United States's legal violation was rather limited, for in response to both legal and political pressure the United States eventually backed down from withholding benefits in the case of most nonsignatories. But the action did communicate a credible threat of further conditional MFN agreements in the future. This threat probably had some immediate impact in expanding developing country participation in the Tokyo Round Codes. Moreover, while the threat was certainly not the only factor, in my view it has also played an important role in persuading developing country governments to participate more actively in all phases of the current Uruguay Round negotiations.

The lesson of the conditional MFN episode is the same as the previous example. If it is true that political support for GATT would not tolerate unlimited free riding, and if simply saying so was not enough to cause devel-

---

20. The same principle was also followed in the Government Procurement Code, where it was applied rather forcefully, but procurement matters are not covered by GATT and thus no GATT obligation was violated. A narrower sort of conditional MFN was applied in the Standards Code; while product standards themselves were expected to be MFN, the legal procedure for filling complaints about U.S. standards was open only to Code signatories.

oping countries to reconsider, the extralegal nudge of the Tokyo Round conditional MFN policy could well have saved the MFN principle from much greater damage later on.

The "New Issues" Problem

The final example of disobedience is the U.S. response to the so-called new issues problem. In the early 1980s, the United States argued that a major defect in GATT was its limitation to trade in goods. GATT law did not protect other markets in which the evolving comparative advantage of the United States was becoming most heavily concentrated—markets for services, intellectual property rights, and other high technology information. That sectoral imbalance, the United States claimed, was creating a political problem for GATT in the United States. Support for GATT was declining on the part of many U.S. goods producers whose comparative advantage was slipping, and there was no compensating increase in political support from those service and technology industries who stood to gain from larger international markets, because the GATT legal system was not offering any protection at all to them.

The United States sought to correct the perceived sectoral imbalance by legal reform. At the 1982 GATT Ministerial meeting, it proposed negotiating an extension of GATT legal disciplines to cover international transactions in services, intellectual property rights, and certain other nontrade spheres. The proposal was both overbroad and one-sided, but the 1982 Ministerial meeting bypassed those problems and rejected the whole idea. Resistance continued for another four years. Gradually, the United States tried to increase the pressure by threatening to pursue its objectives bilaterally (a sort of de facto withdrawal from GATT), and also threatening, and in one case actually imposing, GATT-illegal trade retaliation in response to barriers in these nontrade areas. The message was that the United States would not regard itself bound to honor existing GATT obligations on trade unless GATT law incorporated similar obligations on these new nontrade issues. The main outline of the U.S. proposal was finally adopted in late 1986, as part of the agenda for a new Uruguay Round of trade negotiations.

This final example of U.S. disobedience was often pursued in a fairly arrogant manner, but before condemning the entire operation it is worth asking a few of the same questions asked above: How long would it have taken to persuade governments to accept the proposed Uruguay Round agenda? Indeed, what would happen to the Uruguay Round today if the threat of bilateral retaliation were removed entirely? Was there, and is there, any point at which the dangers of failing to move on these inadequacies would be greater that the dangers of disobedient behavior?

The term *civil disobedience* would be a misnomer for the kind of illegal behavior being discussed in these examples. Civil disobedience is usually reserved for cases involving a moral duty to disobey morally wrong laws. The concept presupposes a mature legal system with power to enforce its laws, and it contemplates a moral act by individual persons who will actually suffer the full legal consequences of disobedience. By contrast, the examples of GATT disobedience given above involve disobedience within an imperfect legal order, with little enforcement power, by governments rather than individuals, and which, however well-intentioned, can in no sense be considered moral acts.

The type of disobedience being discussed here has a more pragmatic justification. It is merely a disagreeable necessity, a "lesser evil" chosen to prevent a more damaging outcome. It is justified only in those situations where continuing to play by the rules threatens to produce a legal impasse or other legal failure that carries a still greater risk of damage to the legal system.

The trick, of course, is to identify those cases in practice—to define more specific guidelines as to *when* disobedience might be appropriate, and *how* such action should be taken. We shall turn to that task in the section after the next. First, however, having sketched the general case for justified disobedience, it is time to entertain some rather obvious general objections to it.

Objections to the Case for Justified Disobedience

First Objection: Legal reform cannot be brought about by threats of disobedience. Governments will not be willing to accept new legal commitments in exchange for new legal rights if they cannot rely on existing legal rights being enforced. The conduct of the disobedient government impairs the law's reliability. It indicates that the disobedient government will consider itself free to disobey the new obligations too, when it is no longer satisfied with its bargain.

Answer: It is undoubtedly true that disobedience will impair the reliability of a legal system if it reaches a sufficient level of frequency. It is not true, however, that reliability requires absolute obedience.

Government leaders, like experienced business executives, are far less shocked by instances of disobedience than observers might assume. Both in government and in business, it is understood that, no matter how firmly a promise is made, the promising party's ability to perform always depends to some degree on subsequent circumstances, including events that affect the fairness of the final outcome. Parties understand that contracts sometimes have to be adjusted because of such unexpected changes, and they routinely consent to such adjustments even though the changes reduce the net advantage of the contract. They will not tolerate an excessive number of such demands, nor will they want to do business again if the demands are not in good faith.

But they are prepared to live with some degree of unpredictability. These are human institutions; there is no other choice.

Tolerance of uncertainty is even greater in agreements between governments than it is for private contracts. Governments are the most clumsy and unpredictable of all contracting parties. Their capacity to perform is always subject to the vicissitudes of their own internal politics. Because government policy can always be changed, agreements like GATT can never be viewed as stone monuments representing some full and final answer of the domestic decision-making process. Rather, they are usually a moment of agreement captured in writing, the performance of which must then be worked for, over and over again during a never-ending process of decision making. Governments understand that compliance is never certain and, thus, understand the possibility that compliance may sometimes fall short when new situations arise.

At the risk of being misunderstood, one could point out that every member of GATT is legally free to terminate all of its GATT obligations on sixty days notice.[21] It would not be correct to suggest that governments are actually free to exercise this legal right; most governments are enmeshed in political commitments and economic constraints that make that course of action all but unthinkable. But the termination clause does make it clear that it is not the legal bond per se that holds GATT law together. It is, rather, the convergence between what GATT law does and what governments need. The viability of the GATT legal system ultimately rests on maintaining that convergence. Perpetual convergence, of course, is extremely rare. So is perfect compliance.

As in most things, the answer to this objection ultimately comes down to a question of degree. Reliability of legal obligations is essential, but not to the exclusion of those pressures for change that are necessary to maintain viability.

Second Objection: The risk of legal failure is a risk that both sides of a dispute can appreciate. The country or countries resisting a particular demand also have an interest in maintaining GATT's credibility in the other country. They, too, can measure the risk of damage, for they have embassies there and can read the *New York Times.* If the risk of damage to GATT is a serious one, it will be in their interest to resolve the deadlock, and they can be counted upon to act. This is the better way of resolving the problem.

Answer: The assertion that other governments will recognize the risk is probably correct, but the assertion that they will be willing and able to act in time does not conform to my own experience. Retreat from positions is the most

---

21. GATT, Protocol of Provisional Application, paragraph 5 in GATT, *Basic Instruments and Selected Documents,* (Geneva: GATT, 1969), 4:77.

difficult maneuver governments make. Retreat is almost invariably attacked by political opponents who charge that strength of purpose would have prevailed, a charge that can never be disproved. There is a tremendous pressure to temporize, to wait for some better or clearer political excuse. A legal policy that counts upon other governments to retreat in time runs a very high risk.

In addition, it is not necessarily wise to wait until the very brink of disaster before acting. The greater the impatience and frustration back home, the more violent a government's response may have to be. Neither side is the ideal judge of the right time. The demanding government will probably have a tendency to strike too early, while the target government will tend to defer action too long.

In many cases, retaliation will actually be a necessary part of the retreat from crisis-producing deadlocks. The target government may see the need to compromise, but be unable to do so without the excuse of external compulsion.

Third Objection: Disobedience can never be limited to the proper cases. Once the possibility of disobedience is granted, governments will inevitably abuse and overuse such powers. One need look no further than Section 301 itself to see how a plausible case for some limited degree of disobedience has grown into widespread bullying in favor of special interests. This being so, any attempt to recognize a justification for disobedience will do more long-term damage to the legal order than will a policy of always insisting on playing by the rules.

Answer: I cannot prove this third objection wrong, but I believe it errs in two respects. First, while tolerance of disobedience clearly does increase the risk of ordinary bullying, the risk is not a certain outcome. As bad as Section 301 looks, the rhetoric of this statute will not be the last word as to what actually happens. Earlier versions of Section 301 also called for a great deal of bullying, and yet, so far, the United States has managed to confine the actual use of those powers to something a good deal less than system-threatening coercion. This is due, I believe, to very substantial pressures for restraint that are encountered when governments—especially well-off governments—actually try to use economic force. These pressures have a sobering influence not only on officials in the field, but also on their legislative overseers. These forces of moderation continue to exist. The new Section 301 looks a lot worse than previous versions, but it, too, has already been softened quite a bit in its first year of administration.

Second, while it is true that even a mere risk of losing control should be avoided unless there is a very good reason for taking it, I believe the objection errs for failing to appreciate that such a reason does exist. GATT law is still a pretty defective product. Consequently, it is like that famous bicycle that trade policy experts always refer to when describing trade liberalization—it must keep moving forward or it will fall over. GATT law must likewise continue to show improvement, or it will fall into disuse. The last decade or two of GATT law reform does not give much encouragement about the pace of reform that can be expected from within the GATT legal system itself. To keep reform moving, there does seem to be a need, from time to time, for the stronger kind of law reform pressures that disobedience can generate.

In sum, while there is a risk of losing control, that risk is not as great as the surface appearance of the new Section 301 might suggest. Equally important, there is an countervailing risk of legal stagnation. Once again, the answer really comes down to the problem of balancing the risks.

Fourth Objection: The option of resorting to disobedience is open to only the few large countries. Small countries have to think twice before trying these tactics against big countries.

Answer: Probably so, although the imbalance in power is not unique to the issue of disobedience. The GATT's leading superpowers, primarily the United States and the EC, have always played a disproportionately important role in all aspects of GATT law. GATT was created due to their initiative; all subsequent GATT negotiations and legal reforms were largely their doing; their continued adherence to GATT is a sine qua non of GATT's viability. To be sure, bullying would not be a responsible use of this natural power. But neither would allowing GATT to atrophy so that it loses the domestic political support that sustains U.S. and EC participation.

It should not be assumed that limited access to the weapon of disobedience must necessarily produce one-sided results. It depends on how one defines justified disobedience. Not all large country objectives are injurious to small country interests. In my view, the key to any claim of justification must be a requirement that the objective of the disobedient behavior be consistent with the general objectives of the community, and, moreover, that the objective be a negotiated legal reform of a general character. These requirements are developed in the next section, where guidelines for justified disobedience are discussed.

None of the above is meant to say that the result is as fair as it should be. Smaller countries have more to complain about than the major powers. GATT law has always contained a number of serious inadequacies for them, particularly for those who export temperate agricultural products, and those who export textiles and other labor-intensive products. The fact that these countries do not have the same power to demand attention to legal shortcomings is not fair. I do not believe, however, that suppressing all large country disobedience would make things any fairer.

Fifth Objection: Only the United States appears to believe that the need for GATT legal reform is urgent enough to require the additional pressure of threatened disobedience. The other major powers, Europe and Japan in particular, seem not to share this sense of urgency. Left to themselves, they seem willing, and able, to support the GATT legal system as it is. This suggests that the United States's call for GATT legal reform does not rest on objective factors, but rather, on the aberrant needs of United States domestic politics.

Answer: The short answer is: Yes, but so what? The United States may be an erratic player, but it is clearly the most important player. If obtaining support for GATT in U.S. domestic politics really does require adopting a major law reform agenda, then, peculiar or not, the importance of maintaining U.S. participation in GATT is certainly worth it. Legal reform is not, after all, an evil objective.

A longer and better answer would run as follows: It is true that neither Europe nor Japan has been particularly interested in GATT law reform for its own sake. As best one can tell, both have supported legal reform only because, and to the extent that, it is useful in containing protectionist pressures in the United States. In my view, however, this passive stance masks a fundamental similarity of interest with the United States. Trade policy in both Europe and Japan does, in fact, rely heavily on the existence of a credible GATT legal system. In Europe, the Treaty of Rome was carefully aligned to GATT requirements, the EC Commission has used GATT negotiations to establish its power, and GATT pressures are constantly used to justify adoption of specific EC policies, such as a subsidy policy or the harmonization of government procurement practices. Japan, meanwhile, has justified innumerable trade policy measures as GATT-required, most recently a string of fundamental agricultural trade liberalizations based on GATT dispute settlement rulings.

As has long been true in the United States, the more that GATT law is used to justify trade liberalization at home, the greater will be the pressure from domestic interests to have GATT law bind trading partners as well. This reaction is already well under way. After two decades of sometimes bitter opposition to GATT dispute settlement procedures, the EC has now become one of GATT's most frequent plaintiffs. Even Japan, perhaps the least litigious country in GATT, has finally found it necessary to pursue a full-blown GATT legal complaint—a 1989 action against EC antidumping rules for "screwdriver assembly" products.

So far, the EC and Japan still appear to believe they can manage a middle position on GATT legal reform—allowing the United States to take the lead, contributing enough support to maintain GATT law at minimal credibility, and yet still keeping GATT law tame enough to allow as much freedom of action as possible. In my view, however, their own trade policies have already become far more dependent on GATT law than they realize, and their freedom of action is already giving way in larger and larger chunks. Consider, for example, the extent to which both these superpowers have swallowed unpleasant legal rulings in the past year or two, because they felt it necessary to maintain the momentum toward stronger dispute settlement. This trend will continue. The pressures of protectionism are growing in all countries. Countries wishing to maintain a liberal world trading environment are going to need increasingly more GATT law to keep their own policies in line. They will probably not need to engage in all the legal table pounding that U.S. trade politics seems to require, but they will need a law that works.

Some Possible Guidelines for Justified Disobedience

Earlier, a pragmatic definition of justified disobedience was offered. It was suggested that it be defined in terms of lesser evil. That is, disobedience would be justified only in those situations where it involved a lesser risk of damage to the legal system than continuing to play by the rules. We turn now to attempting to define those guidelines with a bit more specificity.

To put the bad news first, it is clear that one cannot, in fact, prescribe criteria that will actually measure comparative risks. Being realistic, one has to recognize that this balancing-of-risks approach can cover some fairly extreme situations. The more angry and irresponsible the political environment—in other words, the greater the political disposition to reject GATT—the more risks one may have to take in order to escape the destructive tendencies of such attitudes. The judgment about justification, therefore, has to be a judgment made on the spot after weighing all the factors of each particular case—the nature and importance of the issues at stake, the history of the particular impasse, the positions and the political dynamics of the major parties, and the general state of the surrounding legal and political environment.

It should be possible, however, to define certain outer limits beyond which disobedience will generally be unproductive. By "unproductive" I mean something narrower than unjustified. I mean to identify those situations in which disobedience has a reasonable chance of making a constructive contribution to the legal system in question. The term *safe harbor* comes to mind, although one must hasten to add that no act of disobedience is ever really "safe."

Defining such a set of safe harbor criteria should probably be done separately for every country. The following guidelines are written with the U.S. system of government in mind. They are offered with the usual reservations.

Structural Guidelines

At present, I can think of only one guideline describing how the decision to disobey should be made. It emerges from the preceding discussion about the case-by-case nature of the problem. It is simply this: if critics cannot define in advance the circumstances in which it is permissible to disobey GATT law, neither can governments. Governments should not, therefore, adopt legally binding rules defining when GATT-violating powers *must* be used.

The earlier versions of Section 301 generally observed this guideline, giving the executive branch considerable discretion to decide whether to use such powers on a case-by-case basis. The new Section 301 declares an intent to be far more directive.

Substantive Guidelines

The following five substantive guidelines may be suggested:

i) The objective of the disobedient act must be to secure recognition of a legal change that is consistent with the general objectives of the Agreement. This is not as rigorous a condition as it might seem, for general objectives are usually rather broad and can be served in many ways. But this first criterion will help to exclude those demands clearly at odds with the enterprise—for example, "managed trade." It will also require the disobeying country to accept application of the same principle to its own behavior.

ii) Disobedience undertaken in support of a claim must be preceded by a good faith effort to achieve the desired legal change by negotiation. This is a minimum condition of necessity.

iii) Disobedience must be accompanied by an offer to continue to negotiate in good faith, with a pledge to terminate the disobedient action upon satisfactory completion of such negotiations. Negotiated outcomes are the key to the legitimacy of any such disobedience. Negotiation requires consent, and consent requires, indirectly, that the legal objective be balanced enough to obtain the approval of most participants. Disobedience focused only on obtaining legal changes advantageous to the disobedient country cannot claim legitimacy.

iv) The extent of the disobedience must be limited to that which is necessary to achieve a negotiated legal reform of the kind needed to solve the problem. Obviously, there can be no quantitative measures of such necessity. Recognition of this principle is important, however, for the issue of the appropriate quantum is always a subject of serious debate within the retaliating government.

v) Finally, governments acting out of a concern to improve GATT law must necessarily respect that law as fully as possible, even when disobeying it. Accordingly, they must accept the power of the legal process to judge their disobedient behavior, and must accept the consequences imposed by law. In plain terms, the disobedient government must accept a panel proceeding promptly, cooperate in a prompt decision, abstain from blocking the decision, and accept a fair measure of retaliation without trying to punish the plaintiff.

A further word of explanation should be added about the final two guidelines—(iv) limiting of the quantum of retaliation, and (v) accepting the legal consequences of the disobedient behavior, including retaliation. It might be objected that, taken together, these two guidelines miss the whole point of retaliation. How can retaliation be effective if the retaliating government has to limit the amount of economic pain it inflicts, and then, on top of that, has to accept an equal amount of economic pain in return?

These guidelines are based on a view that government-to-government trade retaliation is not the pain-inflicting sort of exercise it appears to be. Generally speaking, retaliation inflicts nearly as much pain upon one's own importers and users as it does on exporter interests on the other side. The greater the quantum, the greater the pain visited on one's own citizens.

Retaliation is primarily a symbolic act, a way of making clear the seriousness of the government's objection to whatever it is retaliating about. To be an effective symbol, it does require some degree of eye-for-eye proportionality. Once the minimal level of proportionality is reached, however, the symbolic value of retaliation does not increase when the quantum is increased further. Governments understand this, and when actually faced with retaliating will usually look for a way to limit the quantum to the least amount consistent with an effective message.[22]

The notion that a retaliating government should have to accept counter-retaliation (also mainly symbolic in purpose) is likewise not as self-defeating as it may look. The purpose of the initial retaliation—sending a message—will have been served. Having to accept counterretaliation is obviously something the retaliating government would prefer to avoid, but it is not fatal. Indeed, GATT's recent experience seems to be that once each side has bloodied the other's nose a bit, both sides generally seem better able to sit down and work out agreed solutions. Legislators might have some difficulty saying this in public, but those who understand the realities of international trade policy should have no difficulty understanding it.

Applying the Guidelines to the New Section 301

GATT-Based Retaliation—Regular 301

GATT's need for effective dispute settlement is growing. Dissatisfaction with the effectiveness of GATT law is particularly acute in the United States, but it

---

22. Neither the present nor earlier versions of Section 301 limit the discretion of the executive branch in choosing the amount of retaliation. As a practical matter, discretion is limited

is also growing in other countries as governments who comply with GATT legal rulings face growing demands that foreign governments be made to comply as well. If forward momentum toward meeting these expectations cannot be maintained, domestic pressures will force governments to turn to other ways of resolving problems, and the use of GATT law will drop even more sharply than it has risen over the past decade.

The United States and some other GATT members have been pressing for reform of the GATT dispute settlement procedure since the early days of the Tokyo Round. At the time these efforts began, GATT adjudication procedures were in a state of atrophy due to a long period of inactivity. To date, these reform efforts have made considerable progress toward restoring a working procedure. By the end of the 1980s, the volume of GATT litigation had grown to its highest level ever, and for most cases the procedure was working as well or better than ever before.

Nonetheless, a number of serious structural defects remain. Earlier, we presented a list of factors that can cause delay and deadlock in GATT legal proceedings. There are, in fact, countless ways for the losing party to drag out or block the process. GATT has experienced a vivid reminder of these defects during the past two years. Despite the growing number of successful adjudications, there has also been a sharp increase in the number of deadlocked legal disputes.

Reform efforts continue, but the resistance to further strengthening GATT's legal powers has been, and remains, considerable. Despite the considerable attention given to dispute settlement reform in the Uruguay Round, the results so far do not promise any major breakthroughs in the near future. Many countries, including some of the most powerful ones, are less than enthusiastic about making GATT law any stronger.[23]

Continuing to press for negotiated legal reforms is obviously the policy that must be followed in this situation. As has always been true, however, negotiations alone may not be able to produce the improvements needed. Governments will remain reluctant to accept legal change, particularly when

---

by the expectation of proportionality, but within that framework there is considerable room to choose among varying estimates of trade damage, and to choose the duration of the measure, and the reasons for relaxing or eliminating it.

23. One of the minor surprises of the early Uruguay Round negotiations has been the breadth of the opposition to major change. Various proposals were made to limit the power that losing parties now enjoy under the consensus principle. The proposals received virtually no support apart from the United States. The developing countries, who should above all have wanted a stronger law, did not trust the process to work even-handedly (and probably were concerned about defending their own legal shortcomings). Even the greatest champions of GATT law—the Nordics, the Swiss, and the Commonwealth countries—thought that GATT adjudication should remain consensual, arguing that it is not productive to force governments into proceedings or rulings that they are not prepared to accept voluntarily. Negotiations are continuing, however.

they have to face up to the prospect of having to change their own wrong policies. Waiting for negotiations to resolve the problem, therefore, is not a risk-free policy. There could be a point when continuing to rely on negotiations will be riskier than trying to force the issue by means of some disobedient act.

A deadlock in the dispute settlement negotiations is the sort of situation in which disobedience could well be justified:

i) The objective—making GATT dispute settlement more effective—has repeatedly been endorsed by all members of GATT.
ii) There has certainly been a serious effort to negotiate that objective, for almost two decades.
iii) Any disobedient action would take place, one may presume, in the context of continued efforts to achieve a negotiated solution in the Uruguay Round.

In my view, therefore, criticism of the new Regular 301 that argues against the use of any and all GATT-illegal measures in dispute settlement deadlocks is wrong. Some disobedience on behalf of further legal reform could well prove to be justified. Besides being wrong, such criticism will also be ineffective, because many of those who have experience with GATT reform negotiations will be very reluctant to accept a standard that requires total dependence on the present procedures, and/or the present reform negotiations.

The real problem with the 1988 version of Regular 301 has to be more narrowly defined. The real problem is twofold. First, as a structural matter, the new law tries to remove most of the executive branch discretion over when to retaliate, and to control retaliation by means of preestablished procedures that operate automatically. The complex network of required steps and deadlines looks like something that an absentee landlord might write when attempting to run a farm by mail. And it has about as much chance of getting it right. Like farming, the kind of judgments needed for justified retaliation cannot be programmed in advance.

The second and more important problem with the new Regular 301 is that its substantive standards cannot be regarded as a legitimate law reform objective—not, at least, as they are presently being treated by the U.S. government. The new law imposes deadlines on GATT adjudication and compliance that are more demanding than ever before. By themselves, these standards are probably excessive, it being unlikely that any GATT government could meet them on a regular basis. The fundamental problem with these standards, however, is that the United States seems to have no intention of complying with them itself. It has never complied with them in the past, nor is it doing so now in the several GATT legal proceedings currently pending against it. This is fatal. There can be no conceivable justification for disobedience when the objective is legal reforms that apply only to others.

The one-sidedness of the new Regular 301 is quite blatant. At the very time the U.S. Congress was writing these severe deadlines and penalties for other governments, Congress was simultaneously declining to act on legislation needed to comply with two GATT legal rulings then outstanding against the United States—legal rulings on which action was already long overdue according to the new Regular 301 deadlines. In one case, a ruling against the so-called Superfund tax, the Congress did not enact compliance legislation until late November, 1989, after the ruling had been outstanding almost thirty months. In the other case, a ruling against a new Customs User Fee, Congress has still not enacted compliance legislation at this writing, when the ruling has been outstanding for twenty-five months. Regular 301 allows only eight months before requiring retaliation.[24]

The United States has recently reaffirmed its disregard of the new 301 time limits in no less than four other pending cases. It has announced that one other adverse GATT ruling will not be complied with until after the Uruguay Round—some two, three, or more years after the ruling—when the United States can see the negotiating concessions made by other governments.[25] In two other cases not yet decided, the United States has already violated Regular 301 deadlines by blocking appointment of a panel for eleven months in one case and thirteen months in another.[26] The United States will almost certainly violate the Regular 301 deadlines in yet a third pending case, where it has already taken nine months just to compose a panel.[27]

---

24. The cases also violated the 301 deadline measured from time of initiation. Both cases were filed in GATT in October, 1986. Under Section 301 standards, retaliation would have been called for no later that eighteen months after initiation. By November, 1989, each case had been on the GATT agenda thirty-six months without correction.

The Superfund example was a particularly egregious example of delay, for there was not the slightest doubt, from the moment it was enacted, that the Superfund tax was a GATT-illegal measure.

25. The case was a February, 1989, ruling on an EC complaint against the U.S. Section 337 law. Although the Uruguay Round is scheduled to conclude at the end of 1990, no one really expects that deadline to be met. Even if it were, it would take Congress at least six to nine months more to enact the "fast track" approval legislation, assuming that is how compliance occurs.

26. The two cases were an EC complaint about Section 22 agricultural restrictions on sugar and other products, and another EC complaint about U.S. retaliation in the Hormones dispute. In May, 1989, the United States finally agreed to establish a panel in the former case; the latter still remained blocked (albeit also engaged in settlement negotiations) at the end of 1989.

27. The case is the Brazilian complaint against U.S. retaliation in the Pharmaceuticals dispute. The U.S. retaliation is clearly in violation of GATT. Even though the United States is treating this as a case of justified disobedience where retaliation will not be withdrawn until the problem is solved, one could still expect compliance with Regular 301 standards in getting the

In all, that makes six cases in which the United States has violated the new Section 301 deadlines in the past two years. Only one case has been found during this period where the United States complied with its 301 deadlines—a case in which the panel ruled that the United States was not in violation.[28] (Appendix 2 contains background data on U.S. participation in GATT litigation for the past decade, including its compliance record as compared to other defendant countries.)

The serious discrepancy between the standards of Regular 301 and the actual legal behavior of the United States would justify informing the United States that it has no business telling others what to do until it gets its own house in order. To stop there, however, would be to consign GATT dispute settlement to its lowest common denominator. GATT law reform needs more pressure than that. In responding to Regular 301, therefore, equal emphasis must be given to raising the standard of U.S. behavior—if possible, by using Section 301 standards against the United States itself.

The heart of the problem is the tendency of Congress to regard itself as immune from the rules it writes for others. If one asks how this happens, the answer is that Congress does this everywhere and all the time. It is just another instance of the traditional separation in most Congressional legislation between (1) spending to buy things for constituents and (2) taxing to pay for them. There has always been a tendency to make this separation in trade legislation, dividing (1) the demands for good things from other countries from (2) the "payment" in trade concessions that the United States will have to make to get them.[29] The root cause of this general tendency, I suppose, is

---

case decided. After the nine months spent already, Regular 301 allows only nine more months for a ruling.

One other pending case, a September, 1988, complaint by Sweden under the Antidumping Code, did not produce a ruling before the end of 1989, but sources close to the case indicate that a ruling could come soon. If the ruling is adverse, however, there will be almost no time left before Section 301's overall deadline of eighteen months expires.

28. The case was an August, 1988, Brazilian complaint against the United States under the Subsidies Code; a panel ruling was made before the end of 1989. The fact that Brazil's case looked like a sure loser from the outset may have had something to do with U.S. cooperation in a speedy procedure.

29. I recall my first exposure to the phenomenon back in 1963 when I first read the House Report on the Trade Expansion Act of 1962—the law that granted the President authority for the 1963–67 Kennedy Round negotiations (House Report 1818, 87th Cong., 2d Sess.). According to the report, the United States would gain "several hundred thousand" jobs per year from increased exports due to the Kennedy Round, while losing at most 18,000 jobs per year from increased imports (10). Likewise, the report contained the assurance that the U.S. trade balance, already in surplus with "almost every country in the world," would produce an even larger surplus after the negotiations (7). Negotiators for foreign governments during the Kennedy Round had fun teasing the U.S. negotiators over these statements, saying that their governments were going to have to think twice about agreeing to a deal that was as bad (for them) as the one described by the House of Representatives.

nothing more than that legislators derive significant political benefit from it. Constituents respond favorably to laws that claim to accomplish good things at no cost.

The Congress's tendency to concoct such no-cost illusions seems to have gotten much worse over the past decade or so. Worse or not, it has certainly become a more serious problem in the trade policy area, because Congress is now playing an increasingly directive role in trade policy. In contrast to past trade laws that merely set general goals, current trade laws attempt to assert control over daily operations of U.S. trade policy, and thus tend to enshrine all these one-sided demands as operative legal requirements. Section 301 is such a law.

What can be done to contain the excessive demands for GATT dispute settlement that arise from this one-sided view of the world? The short answer is that Congress must somehow be confronted with a two-sided world.

The first step must be to bring home the truth about the United States's own legal performance—the fact that, in GATT dispute settlement, the United States is guilty of worse sins than the ones it complains about in others. General statements of mutual culpability are ineffective. There has to be an inventory of specific sins, the inventory has to be credible, and it has to be brought home from as many quarters as possible.

The EC has for some years been publishing such an inventory at a broader level, responding to U.S. "unfair trade restrictions" lists with its own list detailing unfair and illegal U.S. trade restrictions.[30] This is the right idea, but the task needs a more credible and objective accuser. There is good work for academics here. One promising agenda would be a conference in Washington reviewing all U.S. trade behavior, including dispute settlement behavior, under the standards of Section 301.

In addition, other governments must be prepared to inflict parallel treatment of U.S. sins. The demonstration that U.S. exporters will be treated according to the same standards is generally one of the most effective ways to bring moderation to demands being made by Congress. For example, several U.S. administrations have succeeded in justifying narrow interpretations of the U.S. countervailing duty law by submitting specific examples of how U.S. exporters would be adversely affected if other countries adopted the broader interpretations being proposed. The same thing has to happen here. I find it hard to see any relaxation in the awesome self-righteousness of Section 301 policy until U.S. policymakers are forced to recognize that real U.S. exporters (who vote) are going to be affected by the standards they set.

Won't mirror-image retaliation be dangerous? Won't this just further

---

30. See "E.C. Releases 1989 Report on U.S. Trade Barriers," *European Community News*, no. 12/89 (Washington, D.C.: EC Office of Press and Public Affairs).

weaken GATT law by setting another bad example? Won't this run the risk of a trade war?

I don't think so. The EC has, in fact, followed such a policy on two occasions in the mid-1980s, responding to U.S. Section 301 retaliation with counterretaliation within 24 hours.[31] (It also threatened the same result several other times when the United States was considering retaliation.) In both those cases, the United States passed up the opportunity to strike back with counter-counterretaliation. Having sent its message once (the real purpose of the retaliation), the United States was prepared to focus on settling the case after that. In the end, I think we can count on governments to contain such tit-for-tat retaliations before they become dangerous.

Indeed, the main danger is the reverse—the possibility that other GATT governments will hesitate too long and too hard before retaliating at all. The United States has already started using more precipitous 301 retaliation, against Japan, Brazil, and the EC. Japan, the EC, and several other GATT countries have already shown themselves hesitant to retaliate in kind—both in cases involving illegal U.S. retaliation and in other cases where rulings on other U.S. legal violations have been pending in GATT so long that they are over-ripe for retaliation. The reason for the hesitation, I am afraid, is not so much the danger that retaliation will get out of hand, but rather, the danger that enforcement may get out of hand—that retaliation may set precedents that will one day be used against them. One must hope that governments will eventually see that they are courting a greater danger of even more one-sided demands by waiting.

Retaliation against "Unreasonable" Measures— Super 301 and Special 301

The greatest threat of GATT-illegal retaliation is posed by the new Super 301 and Special 301 procedures, particularly their expanded emphasis on securing the removal of "unreasonable" government practices that are not in violation of any GATT rule. Trade retaliation in response to such measures would clearly violate GATT law. The U.S. Congress obviously believes it is justified in disregarding the GATT obligations of the United States to the extent necessary to accomplish this result.

In my view, this more infamous branch of the new Section 301 has the same two characteristics as the new Regular 301 provisions discussed in the previous section. That is:

---

31. The two cases were the EC Citrus case (301-11) and the EC Enlargement case (301-54). The EC was prepared to do the same thing in response to U.S. retaliation in the recent Hormones case (301-62) but postponed the counterretaliation at the last moment.

1. There is a plausible case for some degree of justified disobedience here—for some pressure to overcome the inertia toward needed reforms of the GATT system.
2. The new Section 301 procedures, however, direct the United States to employ disobedience for excessive objectives that cannot be justified, objectives that reflect an even more one-sided view of who must do the reforming.

The case for some disobedience lies in the need for reform of the overall substance of GATT law. As described briefly in the first section of this chapter, in the early 1980s the United States began to pursue a broad set of negotiating demands seeking to expand the substantive coverage of GATT law to include both better disciplines on trade policy measures within the traditional confines of GATT law, and new legal disciplines on the so-called new issues, such as services and intellectual property, that lay outside traditional GATT boundaries. The U.S. agenda was first considered, and rejected, at a GATT Ministerial meeting in 1982. Pressed forward during the mid-1980s, the U.S. agenda slowly acquired broader and broader support, but the agenda remained blocked by developing countries who demanded correction of many standing problems first. The agenda was finally accepted in September, 1986, as the negotiating agenda for the Uruguay Round trade negotiations. As this is written at the end of 1989, the outcome of the negotiations is still to be determined.

Viewed overall, the objectives of the U.S. reform agenda did conform to the guidelines for justified disobedience.

While the U.S. agenda was far from a balanced one,[32] the type of distortive policies attacked by the United States were policies that most observers would classify as being in conflict with the prevailing norms of international economic relations. With regard to improvements in the existing law of GATT, it is no secret that present GATT law fails to cover a large number of market-distorting practices that most governments would not defend on policy grounds. Critics sometimes forget just how many gaps there are. Setting aside the complete breakdown in sectors like agriculture and textiles, the basic legal structure of GATT has enormous conceptual gaps—on subsidies, on voluntary restraint agreements, on variable levies, on discriminatory quantitative restrictions, on safeguards, and on state trading.

There is likewise broad agreement, I believe, about the soundness and economic rationality of employing GATT-type policies in dealing with government restrictions in most of the new issues areas—particularly in services,

---

32. For example, the United States vision of international trade in services initially excluded all labor-intensive services, and especially those that involved movement of laborers into the receiving country. While opening negotiating positions typically tilt the table, the effort to define the new field of activities to exclude uncomfortable issues was hardly justifiable.

trade-related investment measures, and intellectual property rights. Governments are aware that the growing volume of international transactions in these
areas cannot be sustained without a parallel development of the international
legal order. There is also general agreement, I believe, that the direction of
that development must be toward the same type of open economy sought by
GATT. One must be more careful about assuming agreement over the specific
content of proposed norms, for there are still sharp disagreements about the
balance of interests in areas such as intellectual property rights. But even here
there is usually a fair degree of common ground on basic principles—e.g.,
that creators of inventions or artistic works deserve meaningful international
protection of their work. (Those who were surprised by the flood of concessions made in April-May, 1989, in response to the first round of the Super 301
procedure—including the author—were probably guilty of underestimating
the aura of "bad policy" that had already attached itself to most of the
restrictive measures the United States was complaining about. Many of these
measures already had quite strong opposition at home.)

The U.S. objectives in this area have consistently been a new set of
negotiated obligations. The United States did spend several years seeking
agreement to such negotiations. The resort to additional pressures began
sometime in the mid-1980s. The first pressures were vague and not necessarily GATT-illegal, such as the frequent threat to negotiate bilaterally if
GATT-wide negotiations were not possible.[33] Later, there came a stepped-up
series of bilateral 301 demands on services and intellectual property issues,
threatening trade retaliation that would have been GATT-illegal. It was not
until 1988 that the United States actually imposed GATT-illegal trade retaliation on a non-GATT matter—the Brazil Pharmaceuticals case.[34]

Had the situation become urgent enough to justify using GATT-illegal
pressures to induce negotiations? The U.S. administration obviously believed
so. It was concerned about a growing protectionist surge in Congress; it found
the traditional base of GATT political support was eroding, and believed that
successful defense of GATT required expanding the coalition to include those
economic sectors that would benefit from stronger legal protection on new
issues subjects. U.S. officials would probably have conceded that collapse
was not imminent, but would have argued that negotiations had stalled and
that extralegal pressure at this point, instead of waiting for a full-blown crisis
to develop, was really the more moderate response.

Was the disobedience accompanied by an offer to negotiate a general
solution? Prior to the 1988 law, I believe the answer was yes. The ultimate

---

33. The most visible threats of this kind involved proposed free-trade areas, which are
GATT-legal.

34. See appendix 2.

focus of the U.S. disobedience was the new round of GATT negotiations. Even though specific bilateral demands were obviously pressed for their own sake, it was always made clear that bilateral solutions were not the preferred mode of operation. (As will be seen shortly, one of the major changes wrought by the 1988 Act was its apparent rejection of negotiated solutions.)

It is not necessary to make the case that the actual conduct of the United States in this area conformed to these guidelines. Compliance with at least one key guideline—respect for GATT law—has yet to be determined.[35] The main point is that the possibility of justified disobedience continues to exist. The law reform objectives of the Uruguay Round agenda remain consistent with GATT objectives, and their achievement remains an issue of critical importance to future political support of GATT. GATT's ability to attain those objectives by negotiation remains anything but certain. Accordingly, there may well be a reasonable case for justified disobedience in the event these negotiations reach the brink of failure.

For this reason, it is neither correct nor persuasive to criticize the new Super 301 and Special 301 simply on the ground that they call for violations of GATT law. There may well have to be GATT disobedience of some kind. Once again, the real problem with these new procedures is something that has to be more narrowly defined. The problem lies in their failure to conform to most of the guidelines needed to justify this sort of disobedient behavior. The failures are many.

Structurally, even though retaliation is not legally mandatory under Super 301 and Special 301, the time-locked procedures they establish are designed to force decisions into a rigid framework that cannot take account of actual circumstances. Unless the relevant congressional committees are prepared to back down substantially, the retaliation program of the new 301 violates the cardinal condition that retaliation not be locked-in in advance.

As for its substantive demands, the wrongs defined by the new Section 301 fail to conform to the guidelines in two major respects. First, however worthy they may be as an abstract matter, many of the objectives of the new 301 would have difficulty fitting within the scope of accepted international

---

35. The one U.S. act of retaliation in this campaign, in the Brazil Pharmaceuticals dispute, is clearly illegal. The United States agreed to submit Brazil's GATT legal claim to a dispute settlement panel, but at the same time has been responsible for delaying the proceedings substantially. The United States seems poised between taking its medicine and not doing so. Delay and obstruction may prove the compromise position.

If allowed to rule, the panel will almost certainly declare the United States in violation. Then the issue will be whether the United States blocks adoption of that ruling, and/or blocks a subsequent request by Brazil to retaliate. On two occasions in 1988, the United States did block requests by the EC for authority to retaliate over its failure to comply with the Superfund ruling; in 1989, the United States resisted a Canadian effort to retaliate in the same case.

policy objectives. The insistence on "fair and equitable access" for intellectual property products would be one example. This provision demands unilateral reduction of ordinary trade restrictions explicitly authorized by GATT law, without any justification other than political pressure from the industry that would benefit. The "workers' rights" provisions of 301 have similar problems. Although most governments would support the principle of workers' rights, the idea of using trade policy to create international discipline over such matters has generally been regarded as improper, because it usually ends in demands for trade restrictions against "pauper labor."

Second, and more important, the new Section 301 contains no evidence that the U.S. Congress is prepared to accept a negotiated solution to any of these demands—the essential condition for any justification of disobedience. Both the text and the rhetoric of the new law are devoid of any commitment to submit U.S. behavior to the "reasonableness" standards of Section 301, much less to negotiate a balanced reform in which the United States would agree to give equal consideration to the problems of concern to other countries.

As was true of Regular 301's excessive deadlines for GATT dispute settlement proceedings, the root problem here is the law's one-sided perspective. But in the case of Super 301 and Special 301, the law's one-sidedness involves something more than the traditional spend-now-pay-later approach to trade legislation discussed in the previous section. This part of the new Section 301 rests on an explicit policy of one-sidedness. The basic idea is that the U.S. market is more open than the markets of its trading partners (particularly Japan), and that this imbalance is something that other governments are obliged to correct, unilaterally, by granting the United States greater access to their markets.

The perception of greater openness has existed throughout the postwar years. It probably has some basis in fact. In the past, however, policymakers have recognized that such claims of openness would not support demands for unilateral trade concessions from other countries. Judgments as to the relative openness of markets are extremely difficult to verify, and, even if they could be verified objectively, other governments could not bear the political cost of conducting one-sided negotiations based on that premise. Consequently, the response in the past was simply to shake a congressional finger at the executive branch for allowing others to get away with giving less, and to direct the executive branch to try to achieve a better balance in the next round of reciprocal trade negotiations. This solution was generally looked upon as tolerable, because the gains from this imperfect bargaining process, in terms of the very substantial trade liberalization achieved in all key countries, far outweighed the "loss" of having contributed a bit more liberalization than others.

By 1988, the perception of imbalance had evolved into a firm conviction, and with this new certainty came a new sense of urgency, proclaiming that the imbalance was becoming so serious that immediate, one-sided concessions were needed to rectify it. Three factors seemed responsible for the new assertiveness. First, despite unanimous professional opinion to the contrary, congressional and constituent opinion seized upon the current U.S. trade deficit as compelling proof that there was, in fact, a serious imbalance in market access under the present system.[36] Various explanations have been offered to explain why Congress became so attached to dealing with the wrong cause of the trade deficit, the most persuasive being that Congress was unwilling to deal with the right cause—the budget deficit—and found foreign trade barriers a most satisfying scapegoat. In any event, once the trade deficit became attached to this longstanding perception of greater market openness, that perception was transformed into a hard fact measurable in numbers.

Second, association with the trade deficit also turned the problem of relative market openness into something that was totally one-sided. In the past, observers might agree that U.S. trade policy had a slight edge in virtue among sinners—the United States sinning, say, 30 percent of the time while others sinned 40 percent of the time or more. The trade deficit image, however, makes the problem look like one of foreign behavior alone—namely, the foreign restrictions that prevent the United States from earning the additional $150 billion needed to balance its deficit. The fact that the United States has similar restrictions becomes irrelevant; indeed, such restrictions have to be considered beneficial because they keep the trade deficit from getting worse.

The third new element in the picture was the growing tendency of legislators and other U.S. officials to think of trade policy in terms of "unfairness." While the unfairness concept goes back to the original 1974 version of Section 301, it has become a far more pervasive and popular idea during the past decade. It is manifestly easier to approach trade liberalization as a process of demanding the removal of unfair trade restrictions abroad (no payment required), rather than negotiating away trade barriers by offering reciprocal

---

36. Stated in its simplest terms, the explanation of the U.S. trade deficit accepted by most economists is simply that the United States is consuming more than it produces—in 1986 numbers, producing $4.5 trillion while consuming about $4.65 trillion. Given that the U.S. economy has been producing at full capacity during this period, the difference between what we produce and what we consume has to be financed by borrowing or selling assets, and shows up as a trade deficit—$150 billion on these numbers. So long as U.S. consumption remains in excess of U.S. current production capacity, increasing access to foreign markets will change nothing. If the United States had exported another $150 billion of goods to Japan in 1986, those exports would not have changed the trade deficit, because, so long as U.S. consumption remained the same, those exports, drawn initially from the domestic stock of goods, would have had to be replaced by $150 billion in goods from somewhere else—either in the form of more imports from somewhere else, or in the form of reduced exports to somewhere else. In either case, the trade deficit at the end of the year would have been the same.

U.S. concessions in return. Quite naturally, the new perception of imbalance fell right into this groove. The imbalance created when foreign governments impose an extra $150 billion worth of trade restrictions on U.S. exports is obviously unfair—so unfair, indeed, that it would be almost immoral to think of paying anything to have it removed.

Most of 301's excess demands and one-sidedness could be smoothed away (or smothered) if its various objectives could be merged into the exchange of concessions that will take place in the Uruguay Round negotiations. The distinctions between paid-for and not-paid-for concessions will inevitably be blurred in the large end-of-the-day package that is presented for approval. For this to happen, certain parts of the legal timetables for Super 301 and Special 301 have to be slowed down a bit, but this is possible. Congress and the administration can agree to stretch that time frame about as much as they wish. The key will be whether Congress will allow the rigid one-sided perspective of the new Section 301 to be pushed aside in practice, and accept the practical need to make reciprocal concessions.

The tenor of certain trade policy pronouncements since passage of the 1988 legislation indicates that there may be some chance of Congress accepting such an outcome. When pressed on the issue of U.S. compliance with recent GATT legal rulings, U.S. officials now routinely explain that, while Congress is unable to pay the political cost of passing such GATT-compliance laws by themselves, Congress would be willing to consider compliance legislation, and other troublesome policy changes, if they are packaged together with all the other concessions the United States will be making for benefits received in the Uruguay Round, and if they are buried in nonamendable "fast-track" legislation that immunizes legislators from special interest groups.

This tentative, highly fragile ray of hope is usually presented without any appreciation of the ludicrous comparison it presents with Section 301 itself. Here we see Congress asking other governments for patient understanding of its own political impotence, while a few doors down the hall Congress is slamming its fist on the table, demanding that those same governments enact liberalizing legislation without any quid pro quo at all, within six, twelve, or eighteen months of being ordered to do so by the United States. Ludicrous or not, however, this cautious U.S. scenario does present at least the possibility that these two inconsistent strands of U.S. trade policy can be brought together, in a positive way, at the end of the day.

The chances that Congress might be persuaded to accept an end-of-the-day negotiated solution obviously need some improving. The one-sided rhetoric of Section 301 has by no means been silenced. Indeed, it is still the dominant pose being struck.

The first step in breaking down this self-righteous posture must once again be to develop a persuasive inventory of parallel U.S. sins. The objective should not be to disprove the perception of imbalance as such. There is no objective way to measure and compare relative market openness, and even if there were, it would probably show that the U.S. market is relatively more open than many others. Rather, the objective must be to chip away at the absolute one-sidedness of the U.S. position. The true picture of U.S. performance is the picture of the 30 percent sinner (probably 40 percent after the Reagan years). Even if others are 50 percent sinners, it should be possible to establish that this is not a ball game in which only the United States is entitled to bat.

The EC list of unfair U.S. trade practices, mentioned earlier, is the sort of thing needed, but once again a more credible accuser is needed. Also a more credible list. This will be more difficult than it seems. "Unreasonable" happens to be a very slippery concept—basically, it's the nasty little things you do that I don't do. To develop a credible inventory of such measures, one must first draw the normative standards out of the U.S. claims under Section 301, and then go on to identify the *parallel, analogous,* or in some other way *equivalent* U.S. measures that would be covered by those standards. That is a process in which academics should be able to make a significant contribution. As suggested earlier, one might think of a conference on judging U.S. trade behavior according to its own Section 301 standards—applying all the statutory criteria under the definition of "unreasonable" as well as the implicit criteria of any other claims the United States has actually made.

Once again, some show of force will probably be necessary to get across the message that the rest of the world really does not accept the U.S. view of its own rectitude. Countries should be prepared to retaliate in kind whenever the United States retaliates against unreasonable practices. Trading retaliation with the United States is not risk-free, of course, particularly on such broad and unverifiable normative terrain. Oddly enough, a good inventory of parallel U.S. sins will probably help to legitimate such action and thus help to keep it from getting out of hand.

Conclusion

Fifteen years ago, I wrote that the original 1974 version of Section 301 was "a highly dangerous piece of international brinksmanship."[37] Since then, I have come to the conclusion that there are worse things than breaking the law. One is to do nothing while a legal system destroys itself because it cannot cure its own weaknesses. Although the GATT legal system has achieved much, it remains very much exposed to the dangers of self-destruction. Governments

---

37. Hudec, "Retaliation against 'Unreasonable' Foreign Trade Practices," 463.

talk a good game, but they find it very difficult to pay the price of legal reform when it comes to their own performance. As this paper has shown, the United States itself is a leading example of the gap between rhetoric and willingness to pay. I believe the very strong natural resistance to legal reform can be overcome if key governments exercise leadership, pulling their own performance along in the vacuum created by their demands. A realistic GATT legal policy, however, must leave some room for extralegal behavior in times when impasse threatens, as it surely will.

The 1988 version of Section 301 is a bad law. But its evil is not that it authorizes violation of GATT law in pursuit of law reform objectives. Some such authority should be part of any government's arsenal of legal policy options.

What is wrong with the new Section 301 is that it seeks to employ such authority for law reform objectives that, in their present form, do not have the remotest claim to legitimacy. The heart of the problem is that the law is based on an outrageous premise—namely, that the commands of Section 301 do not apply to the United States. The new Section 301 is a law for the rest of the world only. Besides being wrong in itself, the one-sided premise has also corrupted the substantive content of the new Section 301, leading Congress to include many substantive standards that are wholly unreasonable on any terms.

For all its wrongheadedness, however, Section 301 shines a bright light on the many gaps and inadequacies of the present GATT legal order. Moreover, the impatience it expresses is a vivid and timely warning that patience is limited—that a flourishing, wall-to-wall international economy cannot tolerate for very long a legal order that covers only a part of its surface, and covers even that part pretty poorly. The message of the new Section 301, and the energy behind it, is worth preserving if that is possible.

This chapter has suggested that the proper answer to the new Section 301 is to begin by attacking U.S. legal performance under the standards of its own Section 301. Such an attack should have the kind of double effect that is needed. On the one hand, it should have a moderating effect on the substance of U.S. demands, forcing reconsideration of the unrealistic or unworthy requirements Congress was willing to impose on others. On the other hand, turning the moral ardor of 301 back upon the United States should also have the effect of helping to raise the level of U.S. legal performance, and thus help to preserve its ability to continue leading the law reform effort.

Will the legal behavior of the United States respond to such pressures? There is no assurance. Few countries equal the United States's sense of its own rectitude, and (same thing) its ability to ignore the facts of its own behavior. Still, if anything can work, the towering self-righteousness of the new Section

301 has the best chance. A government cannot generate this much moral heat without burning holes in its own armor.

Things would be a lot easier if one could turn the clock back to 1988 and write a more reasonable, "justifiable" Section 301. This will not happen, however. In the end, the best result one can hope for is that the Executive Branch will find it possible to use Section 301 powers no more frequently nor unreasonably than before, the political goals of Section 301 will be declared achieved in the form of meaningful legal reforms that occur both in the Uruguay Round and outside it, and that the legal reforms will include, as a first condition, a meaningful reform of U.S. legal performance.

APPENDIX 1. U.S. RETALIATION IN SECTION 301 CASES

This appendix presents a summary description of the instances in which the United States has retaliated in Section 301 cases, including both retaliation based on the legal authority of Section 301 itself, and, as sometimes happened, retaliation based on other legal authority at hand. The appendix covers all Section 301 cases, spanning the period January, 1975, to the end of 1989.

1. EC Wheat Flour Export Subsidies (301-6). The United States filed a Subsidies Code complaint against the EC subsidy. Prior to the actual ruling, the United States, partly out of irritation with EC obstruction of the case and partly out of a simple political need to respond, granted a countersubsidy on wheat flour exports that took away from EC exporters the entire Egyptian market for a year. The EC filed a legal complaint against the U.S. subsidy, but allowed it to lapse. The U.S. subsidy ended after one year.

   The Subsidies Code panel was *unable* to reach a decision on whether the EC export subsidy exceeded the key "equitable share" standard of Article 10. After some delay and a further impasse over subsidy policy, in 1985 the United States responded by enacting a very broad Export Enhancement Program (EEP) export subsidy program targeted against EC export markets. The program was still in force at this writing.

2. EC Citrus Preferences (301-11). A GATT panel found that EC tariff preferences on citrus, granted to Mediterranean suppliers, constituted nonviolation nullification and impairment of benefits accruing to the United States under GATT. The EC blocked adoption of the report, supported by a fairly broad coalition of other countries. The United States then imposed a retaliatory tariff increase, raising rates on EC pasta products to 25 and 40 percent ad valorem, as compensation for the EC's impairment of its citrus exports. The EC claimed the U.S. action violated GATT, and responded immediately with counterrestrictions on walnuts and lemons to punish the U.S. violation. The case was settled when both sides concluded an agreement involving a series of

trade concessions on both sides, on both the products in dispute and on other products.

The Citrus retaliation on pasta imports served a double purpose, for it also enforced a separate U.S. complaint, EC Pasta Export Subsidies (301-25). Deadlock occurred when the U.S. obtained a 4 to 1 panel ruling that the EC's pasta subsidy violated the Subsidy Code, but the EC and several other countries blocked acceptance of the majority ruling. The Pasta case was also settled as part of the larger Citrus settlement, with, inter alia, a reduction of the EC export subsidies on pasta.

3. Canada Border Broadcasting (301-15). The complaint involved an "unreasonable" Canadian practice of denying tax deductions to Canadian businesses for television advertisements on U.S. border stations received in Canada. The United States responded by enacting a mirror-image tax law denying deductions for advertising on Canadian border stations. This is the only instance of nontrade retaliation in a Section 301 case. GATT was not involved.

4. Argentina Export Restrictions on Hides (301-24). The complaint charged that Argentina had failed to observe a bilateral trade agreement obliging Argentina to liberalize hides exports in exchange for U.S. tariff concessions. In response to Argentina's failure to honor its obligations, the U.S. terminated the bilateral agreement and the tariff concessions made under it. No GATT rights, or GATT proceedings, were involved.

5. Japan Leather and Leather Footwear (301-13 and 301-36). The United States received a favorable ruling in two GATT complaints about Japanese quantitative restrictions (QRs). The case was then settled with a substantial, but not complete, liberalization by Japan. Japan agreed to accept retaliation in the form of increased tariffs on about $24 million worth of trade as compensation for barriers not removed.

6. Japan Semiconductors (301-48). The parties reached a bilateral settlement of a U.S dumping proceeding; Japan undertook to cease dumping semiconductors and to remove barriers to semiconductor imports into Japan. Later, the United States claimed Japan had failed to carry out both obligations, and imposed a retaliatory tariff increase. The quantum of retaliation was reduced when the United States was satisfied that Japan was observing the dumping undertakings, but the retaliation for allegedly violating the market access commitment has continued. Japan filed a GATT legal complaint protesting the retaliation, but has not prosecuted it.

7. EC Enlargement: Spain and Portugal (301-54). At the time of the accession of Spain and Portugal to the EC, the United States requested a delay in the implementation of certain agricultural arrangements pending a GATT examination of their legality. The EC declined. The United States claimed that implementation of the measures without GATT review was a violation of its GATT legal rights. The United States imposed retaliatory QRs in response to certain new restrictions on Portuguese imports; the initial quota limits were increased when it was determined that the EC measures were less damaging than expected, and the U.S. QRs had little or no effect. In response to import levies on Spanish imports, the United States imposed a 200 percent ad val-

orem tariff on various EC agricultural products. No GATT legal proceedings were initiated.

The EC again promptly counterretaliated with similar QRs and tariffs. The case was settled bilaterally with EC assurances that certain levels of imports would be maintained, and with EC tariff concessions as compensation for the increase in Spanish and Portuguese border restrictions.

8. Brazil Pharmaceuticals (301-61). The United States complained that Brazilian patent law did not give adequate protection to intellectual property rights on pharmaceutical products. Failing agreement, the United States imposed a discriminatory 100 percent ad valorem tariff on certain imports from Brazil. Brazil filed a GATT complaint, and a panel was created in February, 1989. The panel has not yet ruled.

9. EC Hormones Prohibition (301-62). The United States sought to invoke the Standards Code dispute settlement procedure for a technical ruling on the scientific basis of the EC Hormones ban. The EC countered by proposing to submit the case to a legal panel for a ruling on the relevance of the technical issues; the United States refused. During this impasse, the EC implemented the prohibition, and the United States imposed a retaliatory tariff increase in response. The EC drafted counterretaliation measures but then postponed them. The parties settled some aspects of the dispute, but the larger part of the retaliatory tariffs remain in effect.

The EC filed a GATT complaint concerning the U.S. retaliation in November, 1988, but the United States has blocked creation of a panel, citing the EC's refusal to submit the case for a technical ruling as a justification. Concurrently, the parties have continued to engage in extensive bilateral settlement efforts.

In a few other Section 301 cases, retaliation proceedings were commenced after complaints had become mired in lengthy proceedings without any results. Retaliation was then cut off at the last minute when signs of progress justified more delay.

1. Brazil Informatics Restrictions (301-49). The complaint involved trade, investment, and intellectual property restrictions. After trade issues had been removed from the case, the United States responded to a deadlock on the other issues by preparing a retaliation order restricting imports of Brazilian informatics industry products. The order was then suspended pending further negotiations, which eventually resolved the dispute.

2. Canada Fish Export Restrictions (301-55). The United States obtained a panel ruling in February, 1988, holding that Canada's export restrictions violated GATT. After negotiating about implementation of the ruling for over a year, the United States commenced retaliation procedures in April, 1989, in response to new Canadian measures that replaced the export restriction. The retaliation proceedings were then deferred in favor of a second dispute settlement proceeding, this time under the U.S.–Canada Free Trade Agreement, to rule on whether Canada's new measures complied with GATT (the GATT rules having been incorporated into the FTA). In October, 1989, the FTA

panel ruled that Canada's new measures were not in compliance. At the end of 1989, the parties were still unable to agree on what compliance with this new panel ruling required, and a somewhat diminished threat of Section 301 retaliation still hung over the case.

3. Taiwan Beer, Wine, and Tobacco (301-57). The complaint involved violation of GATT-type obligations under a bilateral trade agreement (Taiwan is not a GATT member). President Reagan ordered retaliation to begin, but implementation of the order was suspended when Taiwan corrected its practices.

4. Korea Beef Restrictions (301-65). The United States won a GATT panel ruling in May, 1989, finding Korean restrictions in violation of GATT. In September, 1989, in response to Korea's refusal to accept the report by that time (i.e., after four months), the USTR made a determination calling for a retaliatory suspension of tariff concessions, but then suspended the retaliation procedure until mid-November to give Korea more time. Korea accepted the GATT legal ruling in November.

APPENDIX 2. U.S. PERFORMANCE IN GATT DISPUTE SETTLEMENT, 1980–89[38]

This appendix presents some background data describing where the United States stands in terms of its overall performance in GATT dispute settlement proceedings in recent years. A convenient period for measuring current U.S. behavior is the decade since the end of the Tokyo Round. Because the legal complaints filed in 1989 have not, as a group, progressed far enough to be classified, the sample studied here consists of the 103 GATT complaints *initiated* in the nine-year period from January, 1980, to December, 1988. Classification is based on events that occurred up to the end of 1989.

Of 103 legal complaints filed in GATT during the 1980–88 period,

36 were against the United States (35 percent),
30 were against the EC,
14 were against Japan,
9 were against Canada, and
14 were against "other."

Of the 56 complaints during this period that were pursued to the point of appointing a GATT panel,

19 were against the United States (33 percent),
14 were against the EC,
8 were against Japan,

---

38. The data in this appendix is taken from as yet unpublished research by the author. A full report and analysis on this data, covering GATT dispute settlement from the origins of GATT in 1947–48, will appear in print in a book to be published in 1991 by Butterworths (USA).

6 were against Canada, and
10 were against "other."

As of July 1, 1989, there were 34 adverse legal rulings issued in those 56 panel proceedings. Of these, the EC had the lead with 9, the United States having 8:

9 against the EC (7 violations, 2 nonviolation nullification and impairment),
8 against the U.S. (all violations),
6 against Canada (all violations),
4 against Japan (all violations), and
7 against "others" (all violations).

What about compliance with those adverse legal rulings? I've scored the compliance of each of the leading countries, using as my standard whether in my judgment the Senate Finance Committee would consider the result a vindication of United States rights if the United States had been the plaintiff. The results:

Japan: out of 4 adverse rulings, substantial compliance in all 4,
Canada: out of 6 adverse rulings, compliance in 4, noncompliance in 1, and 1 too recent to call,
EC: out of 9 adverse rulings, 3 compliance, 3 where adoption of the ruling was blocked but the case was eventually settled with a compromise, and 3 too recent to call, and
United States: out of 8 adverse rulings, there were 3 cases where compliance occurred, and 5 cases where it did not—although in 3 of the 5 noncompliance cases the United States has formally indicated an intention to comply, eventually. (N.B. If one were to add the Domestic International Sales Corporation (DISC) case, decided in the 1970s but not resolved until 1984, the United States would add another case of noncompliance, making its compliance record 3 out of 9.)

It is appropriate to explain my judgments on the U.S. compliance record more fully.

The 3 cases in which the United States *complied* were:

1. The 1984 ruling against the Manufacturing Clause. The United States complied because the law had been reenacted for only four years, and Congress allowed it to expire in July, 1986. (Good result, but compliance occurred twenty-six months after the ruling, a great deal longer than Section 301 time limits.)
2. The 1986 ruling against the Wine Equity Law. The United States complied because the law was a special addition to CVD law that had been enacted for only two years, and the law expired without hurting anyone. The compliance was more or less accidental, because the U.S. International Trade Commission did apply the law as written, denying relief on the ground that the economic condition of the industry did not meet the law's "injury" requirement.

3. The 1987 ruling against the Superfund Tax, where Congress actually enacted new legislation to change the noncomplying law. The legislation was enacted thirty months after the panel ruling, again far beyond 301 deadlines.

The 2 *noncompliance* cases that are final were both punitive retaliation cases:

1. The 1981 ruling against a U.S. embargo against Canadian tuna exports in response to a dispute over fishing waters. The United States did withdraw the embargo when Canada capitulated, but the law requiring retaliation remains in force and would have the same GATT-illegal result if the same facts occurred again. (On whether this should be scored as compliance, consider: If the United States had been in Canada's position as plaintiff, would you want the job of explaining to the Senate Finance Committee how you had "won" the case?)

2. The 1984 ruling against a discriminatory QR on sugar exports from Nicaragua, where the United States said it would not observe GATT when political relations deteriorated this far. On compliance: The violation was later merged into a total embargo, and the embargo was successfully defended as an Article XXI national security measure. In my view, the Article XXI defense could not have been used on the sugar quota action alone. Granted that the only limit on the Article XXI defense is that a government must be able to claim it with a straight face, I cannot imagine a U.S. administration being able or willing to utter the "national security" words in describing a reduction of a sugar quota. Never underestimate the legal force of being laughed at.

The three *pending noncompliance* cases are:

1. A February, 1988, ruling against the U.S. Customs User Fee. A bill claiming to comply with the ruling was nearly enacted before the 1989 session of Congress expired, and will be resubmitted in 1990. On why it is taking so long, observers cite concerns about revenue, due to the budget deficit, plus the difficulty of constructing a fee structure that satisfies dozens of interests and interest groups. (Whether the bill finally enacted will actually comply with the GATT ruling will be another issue; many alternatives considered so far would not be considered compliance.)

2. A February, 1989, ruling against Section 337, that the administration has said will not be corrected until the results of the Uruguay Round are known— probably as a part of the Uruguay Round "fast-track" legislation, if at all.

3. A June, 1989, panel decision finding the U.S. sugar restrictions in violation of GATT. The United States has accepted the ruling, and has said it will try to comply before the end of the Uruguay Round.

With regard to the judgment that the 1984 U.S. legislation enacted in response to the DISC ruling should also be classified as *noncompliance,* that judgment is argued at length in my article "Reforming GATT Adjudication Procedures: The Lessons of the

DISC Case," *Minnesota Law Review* 72 (1988): 1443–1509. In essence, the argument is that the law that replaced DISC, called FSC, contained essentially the same GATT legal flaw as DISC. FSC purported to grant a tax exemption limited to foreign-source income only (the GATT requirement), but its definition of foreign-source income was so generous that it reduced that limitation to a sham.

Commentary

David Palmeter

In our system of government, we need Section 301 or something like it. Congress has constitutional power over foreign trade and, without legislative authorization, the executive branch cannot even act to enforce undisputed U.S. rights under trade agreements. Thus, a statute conferring that power on the executive is needed. This Section 301 does.

However, Section 301 confers this power not only on the executive, but effectively on private parties as well, who are given legal tools by which they can all but compel governmental action. Thus, in my view, the problem with Section 301 is not the power that it confers on the executive, but the essential privatization of that power.

The evolution of Section 301, as Robert Hudec has described, is ominously like what occurred in antidumping law and countervailing duty law in the 1960s and 1970s. These laws—particularly the countervailing duty law—became progressively "legalized" over the years as policy considerations increasingly were made irrelevant. Similarly, each legislative "strengthening" of Section 301—in 1979, in 1984, and especially in 1988—has pushed the law in the direction of a private remedy.

We seem to be adopting a system of "privatization of retaliation." Private grievances increasingly are being given a legal remedy, thereby permitting private interests to drive trade policy. If Section 301 becomes so "legalized" that it resembles the antidumping and countervailing laws, we can wonder whether the 301 toothpaste ever can be put back in the tube, regardless of what international reforms eventually are achieved.

Section 301 developments seem to result not only from pressures applied by strong industries to key members of Congress, but also from the widespread belief that the transgressions of the United States against "fairness" in international trade are trivial when compared to those of others. The belief seems to be that no one else adheres to GATT to the degree that we do, so why should we worry about GATT?

Hudec takes seriously the question, "Why should we worry about GATT?" He takes seriously the argument that the world trading system is far from perfect, that many of those imperfections adversely affect the United States, and that few, if any, of our trading partners are very interested in doing much about it. He makes the consequent case for "civil disobedience" of GATT better than do Section 301's advocates themselves.

There is a place for civil disobedience in any legal system, including the legal system that applies to international trade. But, as Hudec very effectively and very eloquently points out, to say this is not to say that, with Section 301, the United States is acting in the tradition of Thoreau, Gandhi, or Martin Luther King. Far from it. Hudec demonstrates quite convincingly that Section 301 falls far short of meeting whatever standards might justify GATT disobedience. If there is a case for considered, deliberate GATT disobedience, Section 301 does not make it.

A very serious question concerns the extent to which the perception in Washington—particularly in Congress—that GATT needs this extralegal pressure reflects ignorance, dismissal of GATT, denial of the facts, or just plain cynicism. Appendix 2 to chapter 4 makes a convincing case that, in many ways, the United States can be described accurately as the "Bad Boy of GATT." Certainly the U.S. record that would justify this description needs to be made known to a wider public than so far has been the case. That record, in Hudec's words, "is certainly not a record that places the United States in a position to dictate rules to others."

Here Hudec reaches his key remedy for this unsatisfactory situation, and in a democracy it is always the best remedy: information. "Congress must somehow be confronted with a two-sided world." Information is crucial. Congress—and the public—need to be aware of the specific sins of the United States as they are aware of the specific sins of others if we are to have any hope of overcoming what Hudec calls "the awesome self-righteousness of Section 301 policy."

And with that word—self-righteousness—Hudec hits the key to what really is dangerous about 301 policy: the awesome—the unmitigated—self-righteousness of it all; the unquestioned assumption that we are right and the world is wrong—worse, that the world is unfair; the threat to take our toys and go home if the world will not play the game our way.

In the process of this 301 tantrum, we turn traditional virtues into vices. Consider the Structural Impediments Initiative discussions with Japan. While not formally part of Section 301, they grow out of the political dialogue that led to the present version of Section 301, and are part of the overall "fairness" allegations that are made against Japan—and will, perhaps, be made next against Korea and other East Asian exporters. The gist of these complaints against the Japanese is that they study too long and too well, that they work too hard, that they consume too little, and that they save too much. These odd complaints are made with a straight face.

A frequent defense of Section 301 is that it is merely an internal legal mechanism. Others have no right to complain, so the argument goes, until they are affected by action actually taken under 301, until 301 "crosses the border." The argument is akin to saying that when a country makes bellicose and threatening statements about its neighbor, issues ultimatums, mobilizes its forces and fires up its tanks, the neighbor has no cause to complain because no one has crossed its border yet.

Section 301, in fact, has enormous impact even before it "crosses the border." The climate it fosters is not a good climate: it fosters resentment, it contributes to xenophobia, and, in general, it poisons the atmosphere.

Hudec has challenged the academic community to get at the "root problem" of Section 301; its one-sided perspective. This would be a welcome endeavor. We need chapter and verse not only of U.S. programs that are unjustifiable, or illegal, by 301's standards (such as Section 337 and customs user fees) but also of those that are "unreasonable" by 301's standards.

How about agriculture? How reasonable is it that the United States is permitted to maintain extensive quotas on sugar, cheese, wheat, cotton, and peanuts because of a special 1955 waiver of our GATT legal obligation for agricultural products? Or might not a developing country contend that our system of patent protection—a legal monopoly—gives an "unreasonable" advantage to technologically oriented industries? Fair and unfair, reasonable and unreasonable, are judgments on which people of goodwill legitimately may differ. People of not so goodwill, with an economic interest in the outcome, may differ even more.

Section 301 tells the world that, in the view of the United States, these are decisions that nations are entitled to make unilaterally. To claim the right of unilateral judgment for ourselves is to concede that right to others. It is a dangerous claim.

Hudec most effectively has made the case against Section 301 largely by making—in good lawyerly fashion—the case for it as well. When he is done, he shows that there is no case for Section 301 in its present form. The challenge is to make this known to the lawmakers and the policymakers.

CHAPTER 5

The Political Economy of U.S. Trade Policy: A Study of the Super 301 Provision

Helen Milner

I. Introduction

American trade policy has begun to move in a different direction, as reflected in its new trade laws. For the past sixty years, trade in this country has followed a principle of broadly balanced reciprocity based on the practice of unconditional MFN status.[1] Unconditional MFN guaranteed the diffusion of the benefits of trade liberalization to all states practicing this principle; it encouraged seeking a broad balance of concessions overall. It helped reduce the striking of bilateral trade agreements and other discriminatory practices, all of which promoted the politicization of trade. This form of reciprocity provided the basis for the post–World War II international trading system; it is one of GATT's central norms. It has been an extremely effective practice; with its use, global trade has flourished.

Despite (or perhaps because of) this success, U.S. trade law seems to be turning away from unconditional MFN. In particular, the adoption of the so-called Super 301 provision in the Omnibus Trade and Competitiveness Act of 1988 signals this change. Super 301 violates (at least) three norms associated with the current international trade regime. First, it is inherently discriminatory since it singles out particular countries for their unfair trade practices. Second, it calls for unilateral action, since the United States is the sole judge and jury in a foreign nation's case. Finally, it operates on an aggressive,

I would like to thank Michael Aho, David Baldwin, Jagdish Bhagwati, Hugh Patrick, Douglas Nelson, Paula Stern, and the participants at the Conference on Super 301 held at Columbia University, December 1–2, 1989, for their generous help on this project.

1. J. Bhagwati, *Protectionism* (Cambridge, Mass.: MIT Press, 1988), 35–36. Prior to the 1920s, the United States employed conditional reciprocity as its trading norm. This narrow form of reciprocity may resemble what America is now turning toward in its policies. Such reciprocity, then and now, has been related to American economic weakness. See William Kelly, "Antecedents of Present Commercial Policy," in *Studies in United States Commercial Policy*, ed. William Kelly (Chapel Hill, N.C.: University of North Carolina Press, 1963).

narrow, and perhaps unbalanced conception of reciprocity. If particular practices in a foreign country are not altered, then the United States will shut equivalent parts of its market for that nation. Worse yet, some have called for evaluating foreign compliance with this law in a "results-oriented" fashion, meaning that the opening of the foreign market would be judged by the increase in the U.S. share of exports to it, not by the world's share of exports.[2] Growth in the American share would then be reciprocated by continued openness of the U.S. market to that country's exports. This results-oriented approach is not formally part of Super 301, but it may, de facto, come to be the standard for evaluating foreign compliance with it. This practice would in all likelihood be a forerunner to a system of "managed trade." In contrast, a "process-oriented" standard for evaluating compliance—i.e., seeing that the "unfair" foreign practice was altered but not looking at its consequences for U.S. trade—would imply less discrimination for the new law.

While all of the ramifications of the new Super 301 provision are not yet understood, it is important to examine how Super 301 was designed and adopted and what problems it was intended to address. This chapter thus looks at three issues. It asks whether U.S. trade law is changing by examining the evolution of the unfair trade practices provision (Section 301) in U.S. law. Next it looks at what forces prompted this evolution. The domestic politics of the U.S. trade deficits are the focus of the second section. Finally, the international dimensions of Super 301 are probed: what international problems was it designed to deal with and what are the consequences of using this provision for international relations? This chapter argues that while initiated as a response to international problems, the Super 301 provision actually provides a solution to certain domestic problems and will probably exacerbate international tensions.

II. The Evolution of the Unfair Trade Practices' (301) Provision

Reciprocity and retaliation have long been components of U.S. trade law and practice. Well before the 1980s, these principles were incorporated in American trade law. In particular, the Super 301 provision can be traced at least back to 1962. In the Trade Expansion Act of 1962, the president was granted the ability to retaliate against foreign practices that discriminated against U.S. exports. According to Section 252 of the Act, if "unreasonable" or "unjustifiable" foreign import restrictions were found in the case of manufactured goods, the president could withhold trade agreement concessions from that

---

2. *New York Times*, April 14, 1989, sec. D; *National Journal*, March 12, 1988, 658.

country. For agricultural goods, the president could go even further; in response to these unfair trade practices, duties or other import restrictions could be imposed.[3] Stiffer retaliatory measures were given to agriculture since it had been excluded from the GATT negotiations. The United States, however, was more constrained in the case of industrial goods since they were the key parts of GATT's trade liberalization process. Concern over violation of GATT principles then limited the retaliatory scope open to the United States.

This precursor of Super 301 was incorporated into the Trade Expansion Act of 1962 to deal with the fears raised by European economic integration. The start of the Common Market in 1958 raised concerns in the United States that American goods would be shut out of the EC market. These concerns were heightened, when in response to the EC, the British and Scandinavians created the European Free Trade Area (EFTA), which also had the potential for discrimination against U.S. goods. While GATT allowed customs unions and free trade areas as exceptions to its antidiscrimination norms, the United States felt the need for a lever to ensure that integration in Europe did not exclude the United States. To a large extent, this seems to have been the motivation behind Section 252.[4] Wielding the threat of retaliation, the United States could credibly press the Europeans to keep their markets open.

In the early 1970s, Section 252 was revised by giving the president expanded latitude in the attempt to combat unfair trade practices abroad. In the 1974 trade bill, giving the president authority to negotiate in the Tokyo Round of GATT talks, Section 301 enabled the president to take a wide range of retaliatory actions against any country that has "unjustifiable" or "unreasonable" import restrictions or any export subsidies that reduce the sales of U.S. good abroad.[5] This section broadened both the definition of unfair trade practices and the types of retaliatory measures that could be invoked. As with Section 252, however, the statute left much discretion to the president. When the section was used, how foreign countries were dealt with, and when and how retaliation was employed were all left to the president to decide. Not only did this section give the United States great leverage in forcing other countries' markets open, but it also, in the eyes of one expert on U.S. trade policy, constituted the United States' "most flexible import restraining weapon."[6]

Although potentially powerful, Section 301 (as well as Section 252) was

---

3. William Kelly, ed., *Studies in U.S. Commercial Policy* (Chapel Hill: University of North Carolina Press, 1963), 118; I. M. Destler, *Making Foreign Economic Policy* (Washington, D.C.: Brookings Institution, 1980), 146 ff.; I. M. Destler, *American Trade Policy* (Washington, D.C.: Institute for International Economics, 1986), 117ff.

4. Kelly, ed., *Studies in U.S. Commercial Policy*, 233.

5. Destler, *Making Foreign Economic Policy*, 159–60, 181.

6. Destler, *American Trade Policy*, 135.

hardly ever used. Between 1975 and 1979, only eighteen petitions for Section 301 were filed; on none of them did the president take retaliatory action.[7] After minor revisions in the 1979 trade bill, Section 301 was invoked more frequently: 35 times between 1980 and 1985. But here again, the successful removal of the trade barriers and/or retaliation did not occur.[8] This contrast between the great potential utility of Section 301 and its actual use was one of the key reasons for its revision in the 1988 trade bill. Congressional frustration with the president's unwillingness to use Section 301 as it was intended impelled Congress to revise the statute.[9]

Between 1980 and 1985, the Reagan administration conducted U.S. foreign economic policy according to the principle of benign neglect. (Conducted, here, may be too strong a word, and benign is certainly what the administration wanted everyone to believe it was.) Basically, the priority was to fight inflation domestically; exchange rates and trade policies were neglected. The outcome of this was malign: by mid-1985, the United States had run up vast trade and budget deficits, while the dollar remained substantially and persistently overvalued. By this point, the United States had seen its exports decline by a third, as its imports rose even faster.[10] Bringing with it plant closures and high unemployment, this worsening of America's international position created much pressure at home for protectionism. Benign neglect had failed.

In 1985, then, as a result of concerns over the huge U.S. trade deficits and mounting protectionist pressures, Congress began action on a new trade bill. Presidential inaction in the face of growing trade imbalances created anger in Congress, for the representatives bore the brunt of these domestic pressures. Many in Congress felt that strong action needed to be taken to reduce the trade deficit. It was felt that countries running large and persistent surpluses with the United States were acting unfairly and should be forced to reduce these surpluses. In particular, wrath was expressed against Japan, whose trade surplus accounted for about a third of the U.S. deficit. In the wake of failing bilateral negotiations to open the Japanese market for particular products, Congress initiated a bill to declare Japan an "unfair trader" and retaliate by imposing across-the-board import duties on its products.[11] In late

7. Ibid., 120.

8. *National Journal,* March 28, 1987, 772.

9. William Cline, "Reciprocity: A New Approach to World Trade Policy?", in *Trade Policy in the 1980s,* ed. William Cline (Washington, D.C.: Institute for International Economics, 1983), 136.

10. Helen Milner, *Resisting Protectionism,* (Princeton, N.J.: Princeton University Press, 1988), 300.

11. See, for example, *New York Times,* March 27, 1985, sec. D; *New York Times,* March 29, 1985, sec. D.

1985, as these Congressional pressures grew, the Reagan administration changed course. In the fall, the administration launched a host of unfair trade practices cases as part of its new, aggressive trade policy stance. Responding to domestic pressures, the administration announced its support for "fair trade," not just free trade. Combined with international coordination to reduce the dollar's value, these moves were intended to forestall a trade bill aimed against Japan and other surplus countries. [12] The administration also pledged to work with Congress in writing a new trade bill that would deal specifically with unfair trade practices. Much of the administration's action was designed to appease Congress.

In 1986, Congress began drafting this new bill. Activity on all parts of U.S. trade law was planned, but two events forced attention to the retaliatory unfair trade practices section. First, the slow reaction of the trade balance to the changes in the dollar's value made domestic groups and Congress less sanguine about an exchange rate solution to the deficits. Moreover, if exchange rates did not work, then it was surmised that this was due to market barriers abroad. Even in the wake of the dollar's fall in value, U.S. exports were slow to respond because of unfair trade practices abroad. At least this was the conclusion many reached.

Second, the presidential campaign intervened. The Democrats began using trade policy as a central issue in their campaigns. The policies they promoted were ones with a "get tough" aura to them. Retaliation for unfair trade practices abroad was a favorite, and it had wide appeal for parts of the Democrats' traditional constituencies: farmers (who had lost exports), blue-collar workers (who had lost jobs), and organized labor. The Democrat who raised the unfair trade issue most forcefully was Richard Gephardt (D-Missouri). His now-famous Gephardt amendment, which proposed mandatory and equivalent retaliation against countries who failed to reduce their surpluses, was the centerpiece of his campaign and of the trade legislation debate throughout 1987. Gephardt's amendment to Section 301 focused critical attention on the issues of retaliation and unfair trade and pushed for a results-oriented approach. [13]

The slow reductions in the trade deficit after the large fall in the dollar's value, the failure of various sector-specific trade negotiations, and the Gephardt amendment's high visibility pushed Congress to seek remedies by rewriting U.S. trade laws, especially Section 301. Specifically, many in Congress wanted to make this statute a more fearsome weapon with which to

---

12. See *New York Times,* September 21, 1985, sec. A; *New York Times,* September 24, 1985, sec. D.

13. *New York Times,* April 9, 1987, sec. D. For discussion of the Gephardt amendment's specific terms, see *New York Times,* April 30, 1987, secs. A and D.

negotiate trade barrier reductions. Many also wanted to expand the definition of unfair trade practices, so that it would include export subsidies and targeting and "unfair" labor practices abroad. Democrats also desired to restrict the president's discretion by imposing deadlines and making retaliation mandatory. They also hoped to reduce the executive's autonomy by moving the responsibilities for initiation, negotiation, and implementation from the President to the U.S. Special Trade Representative (USTR), who was more responsive to Congress. The legislation also sought to name entire countries as violators rather than focusing on specific products. While the early revisions targeted "surplus" countries in particular, the final bill states that countries with "consistent patterns of unjustifiable or unreasonable" trade practices must be named. This modification itself revealed a consistent pattern: all of the early proposals to revise Section 301 were far more protectionist and limiting of the president's discretion than was the language in the bill actually adopted.

Super 301 was born in late 1988 as part of the Omnibus Trade and Competitiveness Act after over three years of congressional activity. Super 301 orders a National Trade Estimate, showing foreign barriers to U.S. trade and their costs. On the basis of this, the USTR is required to investigate countries with "consistent patterns" of unfair trade practices. If these practices are found to be "unjustifiable" or "unreasonable," the USTR must try to get the countries to halt them within a certain period of time. If the practices continue, then the president must retaliate against an equivalent value of the foreign country's goods. The president can decide not to retaliate under two conditions: when the adverse impact of retaliation for the U.S. economy would be extreme or when retaliation would cause "serious harm" to U.S. national security. If he chooses not to retaliate, he must explain in detail his reasons to Congress. Super 301 is thus targeted against whole countries, not particular products; it limits presidential discretion through stricter provisions, tight deadlines, and use of the USTR; and, finally, it mandates retaliation unless the president can show, on specific grounds, that this would hurt the United States. Section 301 now has more "teeth" than before, but again this is only a potential, since the executive still has much discretion in its use.

III. The Domestic Sources of Aggressive Reciprocity

Societal Groups

Where did the interest in revising Section 301 come from? Its provisions can be identified with either market-opening or market-closing intentions. Those wishing for open markets at home and abroad may see it as necessary to pressure foreign countries to open their markets and thus to reduce demands for protection back home. If "unfair" trade practices abroad are eliminated, then the problems of U.S. firms in penetrating those markets or in maintaining their market share at home are due to the firms' own lack of competitiveness, and *not* to activities by the other country. On the other hand, those wanting protection at home may use the law as a legal camouflage for justifying closure at home, assuming the other country will not change its practices. Even if it does agree to change, however, Super 301 can be a formula for "managed trade," in which the other country accepts a specific percentage of American goods in return for maintaining certain import levels in the United States. Super 301 then may have supporters among groups favoring either greater free trade or protectionism.

The type of reciprocity in Super 301 is theoretically less likely to appeal to groups interested in open markets. Large exporters and multinational firms, especially those with substantial global intrafirm trade networks, are (in addition to consumers) likely to be supporters of freer trade.[14] These groups should desire more broadly balanced, multilateral reciprocity. Aggressive, sectoral reciprocity may not resolve their problems and may aggravate them. If country A agrees to open up its market to more exports from industry Y in country B, this may not at all affect industry Y's (in country B) total exports. Firms in industry Y may ship more to country A, but they are likely to lose exports in third markets either as country A ships its excess domestic production abroad or as third suppliers forced out of A's market compete elsewhere, including in B's own home market. Increasing bilateral trade for an industry has no necessary effect on the global trade balance of the industry in one country.[15] Why firms would pay the costs of lobbying for (or even negotiating) such increased bilateral access given the very limited gains (not to mention, low probability of success) is not self-evident. A more broadly balanced, multilateral reciprocity agreement, however, makes more sense from their perspective. If, as in the GATT system, a number of countries who control the majority of trade in an industry agree to further open their markets, then the chances for an improvement in the global trade balance of an internationally oriented industry in any one country would be greater. This suggests that

14. Milner, *Resisting Protectionism;* I. M. Destler and John Odell, *Antiprotection* (Washington, D.C.: Institute for International Economics, 1987); Bhagwati, *Protectionism*.

15. It is even possible to imagine a situation in which the bilateral increase leads to a decrease in global trade for the industry. If an industry is operating at full employment, then attempting to increase exports to another country (without reducing domestic production or third country exports) may increase costs of production, leading to price rises that undermine the good's competitiveness at home and/or abroad. The U.S. semiconductor industry seems to fit this pattern in the 1980s. After the agreements with Japan to increase U.S. access, U.S. producers may have actually lost global market share as they tried to increase exports to Japan when they were operating at nearly full-capacity levels.

many large exporters and multinational firms may prefer broader reciprocity over more narrow forms; they should be more interested in a new GATT round that would liberalize trade multilaterally than in a law forcing sectoral reciprocity on a bilateral basis.

The above scenario has assumed a favorable outcome: that is, that the country threatened (A) agrees to open its markets to B. A more likely outcome is that it does not agree, and country B is forced to retaliate. In this case, internationally oriented firms will bear significant costs. The high probability that aggressive reciprocity will lead to mutual retaliation and the high costs of this outcome for internationally oriented firms, especially relative to the low potential gains from successful reciprocity in a bilateral situation, should lead these firms *not* to prefer such aggressive, bilateral reciprocity, as in Super 301.

Not all exporters and multinationals may fit this model, however. The new strategic trade policy literature suggests conditions under which some internationally oriented firms will prefer narrow, bilateral reciprocity. In a two-firm, two-country duopoly where scale economies, R&D expenses and/or learning effects are very significant, aggressive reciprocity to force open foreign markets may be the optimal solution.[16] Under these conditions letting one country keep its market closed while the other remains open can lead to a sizable and irreversible cost advantage for the former country's firm, which may then be able to drive the other out of business. Aggressive reciprocity should be preferred by firms in this situation.[17] They still, however, face the risk that the worst possible outcome will result: mutual retaliation.

Did American firms with large exports and/or multinational production and trade support the aggressive reciprocity legislation proposed in amending Section 301? Substantial evidence indicates that these types of firms were split, as our two models would predict. Most opposed the early legislation targeting Japan specifically.[18] Fears of retaliation that engendered this opposition also made internationally oriented firms oppose the sweeping, mandatory retaliation against "surplus" countries contained in the early trade law revisions, as well as in the Gephardt amendment.[19] The "tough" retaliatory proposals that eliminated the president's discretion in "unfair" trade cases did not appeal to large exporters and multinationals.[20] They feared retaliation. A

---

16. Paul Krugman, ed., *Strategic Trade Policy and the New International Economics* (Cambridge, Mass.: MIT Press, 1986).

17. For an argument and evidence on this, see Helen Milner and David Yoffie, "Strategic Trade Policy and Corporate Trade Demands," *International Organization* 43, no. 2 (Spring 1989): 322–56.

18. See, for example, *New York Times*, February 1, 1985, sec D.

19. *New York Times*, June 21, 1987, sec. D; *National Journal*, April 18, 1987, 927–31; *New York Times*, April 9, 1987, sec. D, *New York Times*, April 30, 1987, sec. D.

20. *National Journal*, April 16, 1988, 1021.

spokesman for one multinational firm stressed that the Gephardt amendment would only "invite retaliation." He stressed that "our [U.S.] companies are the ones expanding in Europe and Asia. If a trade war starts, they are the ones that will be taken hostage."[21] In addition, firms realized that even filing a 301 case could be extremely costly. As one analyst noted, if a firm initiates an unfair trade practices case, it risks losing all future sales in that country, no matter how the case is decided.[22]

Not all internationally oriented firms opposed Super 301, however. In fact, an important group supported it. Global high technology firms seemed to split with other international industries in their preferences. For high technology industries the presence of large scale economies, heavy R&D requirements, and steep learning effects means that access to markets abroad is critical to their survival, as strategic trade theory notes. Unequal access, where an industry in one country has access to the market of another country but keeps its own closed, spells disaster for the other country's industry. For firms in these situations, the risks imposed by threats to pry open foreign markets are probably less than the costs of living with such unequal access. It is not surprising then that firms in the telecommunications, aircraft, and semiconductor industries have turned to favor a more aggressive U.S. approach. As one report noted, "In the business community, . . . a 'third force' has emerged, since the late 1970s, of global corporations in high technology sectors who are not sympathetic to old-fashioned defensive import protectionism but are not unequivocal antiprotectionists either. Their chief concern is to open foreign markets, especially in sectors where dynamic economies of scale or learning by doing are essential if rapidly growing R&D costs are to be sustained."[23] Through the U.S. industry advisory committee to the Uruguay Round negotiations, these firms communicated their desire for a tougher U.S. policy to the executive. Global firms still tend to favor free trade, but an increasing split in how to promote this goal has become evident. Interest in a broadly balanced, multilateral approach through GATT is favored by a number of global industries in the United States; for example, those firms interested in new issues such as services, investment, and intellectual property rights are still strong supporters of multilateral efforts in the Uruguay Round.[24] But a growing "third force" has helped push for a more aggressive approach, as embodied in Super 301. Most internationally oriented firms, however, have remained more committed to multilateralism and the next

---

21. *New York Times,* April 9, 1987, sec. D. Fear of retaliation was pervasive; *New York Times,* May 13, 1987, sec. A.

22. *National Journal,* August 13, 1988, 2,126, as Boeing has feared in its protests against Airbus.

23. Sylvia Ostry, *The Political Economy of Policy-Making: Trade and Innovation Policies in the Triad* (New York: Council on Foreign Relations, 1989), chap. 2, 6.

24. Ibid., chap. 2, 7.

GATT Round than have other firms or labor organizations in the United States.

While some global firms lent their support to toughening U.S. trade law, the main supporters of aggressive bilateral reciprocity in the mid-1980s were organized labor and domestically oriented industries.[25] Indeed, organized labor and its political coalition partner, the Democratic party, proposed the toughest new trade law revisions. Organized labor was also the most enthusiastic supporter of the Gephardt amendment. Retaliation against countries running large surpluses with the United States was an idea initially proposed by the AFL-CIO and domestically oriented industries besieged by imports.[26] Given these actors' likely preferences for protection in the home market, aggressive reciprocity made sense, since it had the distinct possibility of leading to such closure. These groups saw the potential for increasing protectionism in Super 301, in contrast to the "third force" of high technology firms who saw its trade liberalizing potential. The growing pressures of these domestic groups on Congress, combined with the new interests of global high technology firms as communicated to the executive, help explain why Super 301 was created.

Congress and Its Relationship with the Executive

To understand the forces leading to the Super 301 provision, it is necessary to examine congressional-executive relations. Congressional interest in aggressive reciprocity arose because of the growing import pressures placed on labor and manufacturing in domestically oriented industries and the loss of export capacity affecting high technology industries. Pressures from important constituents prompted the Democrats in Congress to initiate trade law reform. Targeting large "surplus" countries for retaliation seemed one way to attack these problems. The Democrats were playing for electoral advantage.[27] But they were also playing another game; this one entailed their relationship with the executive branch.

While jurisdiction over most issues is de jure allocated between the

---

25. *National Journal*, April 18, 1987, 927–31; *New York Times*, June 21, 1987, sec. D; *New York Times*, April 30, 1987, sec. D.

26. *National Journal*, April 18, 1987, 927–31; *New York Times*, June 21, 1987, sec. D.

27. While some argue that support for Super 301 was bipartisan, voting data in Congress suggest it was more partisan. While some Republicans (for example, Heinz and Danforth) joined the chorus for a tougher policy, the lopsided votes suggest the majority of Republicans were wary of this strategy. See *New York Times*, April 22, 1988, sec. D. Votes in the House for trade bill: 244 Democrats and 68 Republicans; votes against: 2 Democrats and 105 Republicans. *New York Times*, April 28, 1988, sec. A, Senate votes for bill: 52 Democrats and 11 Republicans; votes against: 1 Democrat and 35 Republicans.

legislature and the executive in the Constitution, in actual practice this juris-diction is quite flexible. Trade policy is a case in point. Prior to 1934, trade policy (mainly the setting of tariffs) was the province of Congress; with the Reciprocal Trade Agreements Act (RTAA) of 1934, Congress relinquished control over duty levels to the president. Some have claimed that this act gave jurisdiction to the executive and "insulated" Congress from societal pressures on trade issues, thereby making trade policy less susceptible to the entreaties of rent-seeking groups.[28] Trade, they imply, became the province of the executive and thus could be guided by larger American foreign policy goals. This interpretation appears too simple.

Rather than viewing the 1934 Trade Act as a one-time transfer of author-ity over trade to the executive, it is more appropriate to view the issue of jurisdiction as part of an ongoing negotiation between the two branches. It is not so much that Congress gave up control over trade or took itself out of the business of trade policy-making in 1934, but more that about every five years or so Congress and the president renegotiate control over the issue. In this renegotiation, Congress has two conflicting goals, as does the president. Congress wants to satisfy the demands of its constituents, but it also wants to avoid blame for policies that, driven by unlimited and conflicting constituent demands, may lead to massive failures.[29] In other words, it needs to satisfy important constituent demands for protection, while avoiding another Smoot-Hawley trade bill. The executive may also face conflicting pressures. On the one hand, the president may desire control over trade so he can use it to pursue general foreign policy goals. On the other hand, he cannot neglect domestic pressures since this is likely to result in Congress reappropriating the issue, as a result of domestic complaints. But these pressures are likely to conflict with the executive's international goals.

These cross-pressures on both groups tend to result in an unstable situa-tion in which authority has to be constantly renegotiated. Thus, over the postwar period, each time the president has wanted to renew his negotiating authority to pursue a larger foreign policy goal—that is, ensuring the continu-ance of a liberal multilateral trading system—he has had to renegotiate U.S. trade law. To obtain negotiating authority, the president has had to relinquish control over some other aspect of trade policy. As one commentator noted, "over the years, Congress has never granted an administration what it wanted on trade without exacting a price".[30] Congress has usually demanded greater

28. See, for example, Stephan Haggard, "The Institutional Foundations of Hegemony," *International Organization* 42, no. 1 (Winter 1988): 33–58; Destler, *American Trade Policy.*
29. On "blame avoidance," see R. Kent Weaver, "The Politics of Blame Avoidance," *Journal of Public Policy* 6 (October-December, 1986): 371–98.
30. *National Journal,* June 28, 1986, 1,590.

control over areas where domestic constituents have pressured it to make changes or be more responsive. In the domestic negotiations over trade in the early 1950s, Congress added the "peril point" statute and made the escape clause easier to use in order to appease domestic interests; in exchange, the president received authority for liberalizing trade through multilateral negotiations. In the early 1960s, Congress made the price for its delegation of authority the acceptance of a Special Trade Representative that would be more responsive to congressional needs. In the 1970s, the exchange involved altering antidumping and countervailing duty laws so they were easier to apply in return for granting negotiating authority. In the 1988 bill, aggressive reciprocity in the form of Super 301 became the price for presidential negotiating authority. Each trade bill has been "part of the long tug-of-war between the legislative and executive branches over who is to make foreign policy."[31] While some have seen the period from the late 1970s on as a time of declining presidential control over trade, it seems more appropriate to view this period as one more episode in the recurring struggle between the two branches—each wanting control, but each realizing (for different reasons) that too much responsibility may also be undesirable.[32]

The 1988 trade bill can be seen as part of this recurrent domestic negotiation process. Facing the termination of negotiating authority in 1988 and the initiation of the Uruguay Round at the same time, the president needed new authority to sustain certain foreign policy goals. The executive branch did not want a trade bill considered in 1985 or 1986 since these were years of strong protectionist sentiment concomitant with the largest U.S. trade deficits ever. Any deal struck with Congress at this time would extract too high a price for presidential negotiating authority. As the deficit figures improved and U.S. exports soared after 1986, a better deal could be struck. So by delaying, the president could obtain the negotiating authority he needed at a lower price. Congress needed to satisfy its constituents—especially important Democratic supporters, such as organized labor. Revising the trade laws, in particular Section 301, could help do this. But by delegating authority for the administration of Super 301 to the USTR and leaving much executive discretion, Congress also avoided blame for any mutually undesired retaliation that might occur. Congress thus sent a signal to the president that he should be more responsive to domestic pressures, and Congress signaled its constituents that it was interested in protecting their interests. By accepting the bill, the executive branch signaled its concern for domestic interests without giving up its ability to pursue broader foreign policy goals. Super 301 was then the crux of the negotiated settlement between Congress and the president.

---

31. *New York Times,* October 6, 1987, sec. D.
32. See Destler, *American Trade Policy.*

IV. The International Dimensions of Super 301

As I have argued, Super 301 provided a solution to the *domestic* problems associated with the huge trade imbalances of the 1980s.[33] The *international* ramifications of Super 301 will be more problematic. If strictly enforced, it will, in all probability, have a detrimental effect on foreign relations. Although reciprocity via tit-for-tat strategies can produce cooperation in theory, in the trade area such strategies are more likely to produce "feuds," or spirals of mutual retaliation.[34] Some have suggested that retaliatory policies could provide the basis for a "self-enforcing" system of liberal trade, but the reciprocity provisions of Super 301 are not likely to constitute such a basis.[35] The application of Super 301 entails both costs and benefits; its supporters believe the benefits outweigh the costs, while its opponents view the costs as too high. I argue that the costs will probably exceed any benefits.

Those who favor aggressive reciprocity as embodied in Super 301 see it as having three related advantages. First, the creation of Super 301 sends a signal to other countries. It makes U.S. distress over unfair trade practices abroad evident and its shows U.S. intolerance of these practices. The discussions leading to Super 301 also suggest to other countries that the United States will not tolerate vast trade deficits and the trampling of its industries by foreigners who are protected by their governments. It is intended as a sign that things must change. This signaling function was apparent during consideration of the Gephardt amendment. Although a majority disapproved of it, the House of Representatives voted by the slimmest margin to accept the amendment in early 1987, during the visit of the Japanese Prime Minister to the United States.[36] This was a signal to the Japanese of how bad things could get unless changes were made. As one analyst of trade policy remarked, the 1988 trade bill "would likely have little direct influence on American commerce, [but] it is psychologically important for the signals it sends to world markets."[37]

Some see its benefits less in this psychological dimension than in Super 301's ability to improve the U.S. negotiating position. The statute constitutes a "significant club" that, looming in the background, will help the United States negotiate away trade barriers with other countries.[38] By increasing the

---

33. As in the past, this solution will prove unstable in time. As international conditions and domestic pressures change, Congress and the executive will be forced to renegotiate the trade "deal" in a new trade bill.

34. R. Axelrod, *The Evolution of Cooperation* (New York; Basic Books, 1984).

35. C. Michael Aho and Marc Levinson, *After Reagan: Confronting the Changed World Economy* (New York: Council on Foreign Relations, 1988), 100.

36. *New York Times*, April 30, 1987, sec. A.

37. *National Journal*, April 9, 1988, 952.

38. *New York Times*, May 21, 1989, sec. C.

president's powers to retaliate, it should "strengthen the hand of American negotiators".[39] In this view, retaliation will not be necessary; the key is to create a credible threat to retaliate, which Super 301 supposedly provides. The provision then is intended to "scare other countries into opening their markets wider to American goods but . . . not [to be] so threatening as to provoke a retaliation and downward spiral in world trade."[40]

Finally, the Super 301 provision is not only designed to signal and scare others, it is also meant to protect the United States against unfair trade practices. If countries refuse to change these practices, then the United States will defend itself by protecting its industries.[41] Super 301 provides the legal means to do this. In this view, the actual use of retaliation is beneficial since it will defend important American interests. The implicit national security metaphor is not unintended. Reflecting a growing belief within and outside the government, one industry spokesman pointed out that American "economic interests . . . have become strategic interests."[42] An increasing emphasis on deterrence and retaliation in U.S. trade policy is thus justified, since it is how Americans have successfully conducted their national security policy in the postwar world.[43]

These potential benefits from Super 301 must be considered relative to its likely costs. Those fearing the high costs of such aggressive reciprocity note, first, that ending all unfair trade practices against the United States will do little to help reduce U.S. trade deficits. The elimination of these practices may cut U.S. trade deficits by, at most, 10 percent—about $12 billion of the total U.S. trade deficit of $120 billion, and maybe $6 billion of the total U.S. deficit with Japan of $50 billion.[44] Unfair trade practices are not the central cause of American trade deficits; countries' foreign trade practices were "the same or worse when America ran big trade surpluses" with them.[45] These small material benefits from ending unfair practices must be assessed relative to the high costs that Super 301 may impose.

Two central problems stand out. First, Super 301 implies a unilateral judgment about what is fair and unfair internationally. It makes the United States the judge and jury assessing a foreign country. This unilateralism will cause problems. Countries simply will not let another nation cast judgment on, and try to force change in, their laws, policies, and practices. It is an infringement on their sovereignty and will provoke resistance. Moreover, the

39. *New York Times*, August 4, 1988, sec. D.
40. *New York Times*, March 27, 1987, sec. D.
41. *New York Times*, May 2, 1988, sec. D.
42. *New York Times*, January 29, 1989, sec. C.
43. Aho and Levinson, *After Reagan*, 98.
44. *New York Times*, May 27, 1989, sec. A; *New York Times*, May 28, 1989, sec. D.
45. *New York Times*, February 14, 1987, sec. A.

United States will be judging its own case; it is an interested, not a neutral, judge. No fair way exists for one country to evaluate its own case in a dispute with another. Judgment by the United States, then, is likely to be seen as unfair and hence to provoke retaliation.[46] Unilateralism will bring destructive spirals of mutual retaliation with each country viewing the other as acting unfairly. Ronald Reagan proposed an interesting test of Super 301: he suggested that Americans "don't pass any trade law that we wouldn't want another country to pass in just the same form."[47] In terms of this Kantian imperative, it seems unlikely that the United States would tolerate being named publicly as an unfair trader and forced under threat of retaliation to change its domestic practices; it would probably refuse to negotiate and would retaliate if retaliated against.

This unilateralism leads to a second problem. Aggressive, bilateral reciprocity violates central tenets of the postwar international trading system. GATT upholds the principles of multilateralism, nondiscrimination, and neutral dispute settlement. Super 301 may encroach upon all of these. It implies bilateralism, may lead to discriminatory trade agreements that favor American commerce, and constitutes unilateral dispute settlement. Super 301 will bypass GATT, and it will violate its central principles. Its legality under international trade law is debatable.[48] The United States thus may be violating international law as well as undermining GATT. Both actions will be costly. Violations of international law by leading powers will induce other states to violate those laws as respect for them declines. Disregarding GATT norms will bring the entire system into question and may lead to its breakdown, as U.S. actions did to the Bretton Woods monetary regime in the early 1970s. Since GATT has helped provide a stable, prosperous trading environment for forty years, ending it should not be done lightly. Moving from a system of multilateral negotiation and dispute settlement to a bilateral one will increase the costs of negotiating trade liberalization and will greatly politicize the process.[49] Undermining the GATT system in exchange for marginal improvements in the U.S. trade balance does not seem to be a rational strategy.

These different costs and benefits are already evident in the international response to Super 301. Passed in mid-1988, the trade bill required that the

---

46. *New York Times*, June 27, 1987, sec. A.

47. *New York Times*, March 12, 1988, sec. A.

48. *New York Times*, May 27, 1989, sec. A; Cline, "Reciprocity," in Cline, ed., *Trade Policies in the 1980s*, 131 and 136.

49. Moving from an anarchic position (with no rules) to a system of aggressive reciprocity (bilateral tit-for-tat) may indeed lead to increased cooperation, as Axelrod has argued. But shifting from a system of multilateralism and broad reciprocity to one of narrow reciprocity is likely to produce less cooperation and more conflict. Where one starts from makes a difference for the type of effect that bilateral tit-for-tat strategies will have.

USTR name its first group of unfair trading countries within a year. The USTR then had a set amount of time to "consult" with these countries to obtain the elimination of these practices. If no agreement to do so emerged, then retaliation was required. The adoption of Super 301 thus set in motion a number of actions that reveal both the costs and benefits of this measure. As its supporters predicted, the provision did send a signal to other countries. It also seemed to "scare" some into opening their markets. To avoid the onus of being named an unfair trader, South Korea, Taiwan, and Japan all began negotiating with the United States to reduce their trade surpluses.[50] The first two also agreed to liberalize certain sectors, to import more U.S. goods, and/or to "freeze" their surplus levels with the United States. In return for these concessions, the United States did not name them under Section 301.[51] These countries "blinked." But a number of others, including Japan, did not.

The European Community reacted as opponents of Super 301 predicted. It announced that Super 301 was a violation of international trade law and that it would challenge it legally. Further, the EC said it was unilateralism at its worst and that it would not accept any judgments made under Section 301. If named, it would refuse to negotiate with the United States, and if the United States sanctioned it, the EC would retaliate in full force.[52] The EC thus issued a challenge to the United States, forcing it to either back down or start a trade war. Since many in Congress felt the EC had to be named, the president was caught in a difficult position. He ended up "blinking" and not naming the EC, much to Congress's and other domestic groups' dismay.

In late May, 1989, the USTR announced the list of unfair traders under Section 301. It cited Japan for procurement practice in supercomputers and satellites and technical barriers in lumber, India for barriers to foreign investment and in insurance, and Brazil for its import licensing restrictions.[53] Japan immediately reacted as the EC had. It refused to negotiate and condemned the United States action as unfair, unilateral, and a violation of international law. Japan resented the action and claimed it would be "counterproductive" since the publicity would make Japan more "inflexible."[54] In this case, congressional pressure forced the president to name Japan. But the executive branch did this in only a minimal way, again acquiescing to Japanese pressure as it had done for the Europeans. The USTR adopted a narrow interpretation of Super 301. Instead of condemning the entire domestic distribution process in

---

50. *New York Times*, May 13, 1989, sec. A; *National Journal*, June 17, 1989, 1,564–65.

51. *National Journal*, June 17, 1989, 1,564–65; *New York Times*, April 18, 1989, sec. A; *National Journal*, June 24, 1989, 1,685.

52. *New York Times*, May 20, 1989, sec. A; *National Journal*, June 17, 1989, 1,564–65.

53. *New York Times*, May 26, 1989, secs. A and D.

54. *New York Times*, May 16, 1989, sec. D; *New York Times*, May 26, 1989, sec. D; *New York Times*, May 27, 1989, sec. A.

Japan, as many wanted to do, it named only a few sectoral problems. These were sectors where the USTR estimated change could be most easily wrought. In the wake of Japanese refusals to negotiate under 301, the USTR also initiated a set of talks *outside* the 301 framework. These structural impediments talks addressed the issues that were originally intended to be negotiated under Super 301. But "the Super 301 framework was [found to be] excessively rigid and confrontational", so the USTR tried a new approach.[55] The minimal use of 301 combined with the structural impediments talks seems so far to have satisfied Congress. In the case of Japan then, the United States was forced once again to back down in the face of Japanese resistance. While the structural impediments talks may prove fruitful, they have cost the United States dearly in terms of ill will with the Japanese and a loss of face abroad.

The Brazilians have also reacted negatively. And in today's interdependent world they were able to issue their own veiled threat against the United States. Brazil reminded the United States that it could not repay its international debts (held mainly by the United States) if it could not export.[56] The United States has not yet taken any action against Brazil. So far, Super 301 does not seem to be proving very useful. The marginal benefits it may extract in the future may not make up for the ill will, conflict, and challenge to international trade law that it has evoked.

V. Conclusions

Super 301 marks a change in the character of U.S. trade policy. It implies a move from a system of broadly balanced reciprocity to one of aggressive, sectoral reciprocity. It signals U.S. suspicions of unfair practices abroad and American intolerance of these practices and continued trade deficits. Whether Super 301 means an actual change in the practice of U.S. trade policy depends on how the president employs it and on the U.S. economic situation. As shown, Super 301 can be interpreted in many ways; the president still retains much discretion over its use. If he decides to use it minimally, as he has so far, then the law may not presage much change in the substance of U.S. policy. If pressures arise that force its strict interpretation, the president may well lead a dramatic change in U.S. policy.

As this chapter has suggested, the pressures leading to such a change are tied to economic conditions.[57] Rapidly rising import competition, a domestic

55. *National Journal,* June 3, 1989, 1,367; *National Journal,* June 17, 1989, 1,562–66; *New York Times,* May 27, 1989, sec. A.

56. *New York Times,* May 27, 1989, sec. A.

57. Such aggressive, narrow reciprocity has also been associated with the decline of U.S. power internationally. The loss of American hegemony may induce it to give up its free trade stance in favor of a narrower conception of its role in the international trading system. See, for

recession, and falling export levels all set protectionist forces in motion, while weakening the coalition supporting a liberal, multilateral trading order. These domestic forces bring pressure to bear on Congress for change, and Congress in turn looks to the executive for action. The recurrent renegotiations about authority over trade issues between Congress and the executive reflect this process. In the 1980s, Super 301 was the compromise that resulted from this renegotiation. Should the economic situation deteriorate in the future, a new negotiation will probably occur in which presidential discretion over Super 301 is further reduced.

Super 301 has not yet made its impact on international relations fully apparent. Its advantages as a signaling device, a credible threat (compellent or deterrent), and a means of protecting U.S. industry against unfair practices may turn out to be important. But its costs appear high. Angering friendly nations, like the EC and Japan, with its unilateralism and undermining the GATT system, which has provided stability and prosperity, are not helpful for improving trading relations, especially in the midst of a new GATT negotiating round. The potential for aggressive reciprocity imposed unilaterally to trigger a trade war that damages everyone involved is also great.[58] Super 301 may turn out not to be all that super. It may temporarily resolve certain domestic tensions, but it is likely to create more international ones.

---

example, Robert Gilpin, *The Political Economy of International Relations* (Princeton, N.J.: Princeton University Press, 1987).

58. Some suggest that to achieve cooperation the United States must run the risk of a trade war, as it does in its national security policies. The United States must credibly threaten to start a war in order to prevent others from doing certain things. This analogy to the national security area does not seem appropriate. Super 301 is like using the threat of nuclear war to force the Soviets to negotiate a change in their economic system. It is provocative, inviting a fight.

Commentary

I. M. Destler

I must look briefly backward before I look forward. I will look backward not at changes on the world scene but at specific patterns of trade policy-making in the United States. Our nation did, in fact, accomplish something rather impressive in the postwar period—it led itself, and the world, toward more liberal trade. Like Helen Milner, I ask how this was accomplished politically, although I answer the question somewhat differently. And my answer is linked to our present plight, for I believe that one of our primary means for managing our domestic trade politics has led naturally and logically, if not very happily, to Super 301.

An earlier panelist suggested that the United States ought to be "totally committed to liberal trade." That would be nice, but it is not the real world: it never has been for the United States, or for any other country. The most one can hope for is trade policy that leans in the liberal direction, and the only way to achieve this is to manage and mute and limit the pressures that work in the opposite direction. Since the Reciprocal Trade Agreements Act of 1934 (a watershed event, as Douglas Nelson rightly notes), the United States has been quite successful in accomplishing this. And one central means—the genius of the 1934 act—has been to shift the locus of U.S. political action, to some degree, from American to foreign markets, from our trade barriers to theirs, from the import to the export arena. We would reduce our trade barriers, but only as part of a process that brought other nations to reduce theirs.

This approach brought U.S. export interests into the political game; not as strongly as import-impacted interests, but enough so that officials could call on them and use them to counter the protectionists. This gave more running room to determined, purposive, liberal-minded executive leadership. We used bilateral negotiations to reduce U.S. tariff barriers in the 1930s, and we used multilateral negotiations from the 1940s onward. In the Tokyo Round of the 1970s, we applied a similar approach to nontariff barriers. And as bilateral trade conflicts have grown, the emphasis has continued. During Robert Strauss's tenure as special trade representative, for example, the people who came to him on Japanese trade issues were the steel people or the color TV people—interests seeking to curb imports. But he shifted the emphasis, when he could, to products he was not hearing a lot of noise about—beef, citrus, telecommunications—because they offered export-expanding opportunities.

By pushing on the export side, Strauss could appear tough to domestic constituencies while working to make trade grow. Like his predecessors and his successors, he could nurture support from, and engagement of, internationalist interests. President Lyndon Johnson, according to reliable authority, virtually invented an organization called the Emergency Committee for American Trade (the now-famous ECAT) in 1967. Johnson was worried about the protectionist backlash that followed the Kennedy Round, so he called up David Rockefeller and others and urged them to "put something together" to counter it.

There was political courage in this emphasis on export markets. As Bob Baldwin points out, the smoother short-term course is compromise on the import side, to manage trade. When we press to open export markets on sensitive products, we risk controversy and political damage—as Makoto Kuroda notes. The path of least resistance in both the United States and its trading partners is to limit sensitive imports, to negotiate voluntary restraint agreements. U.S. officials have done this from time to time, of course, most egregiously on textiles. But where they have had leeway, they have tended to tilt to the export side. And members of Congress have tolerated—sometimes even encouraged—this emphasis, even as they were making protectionist noises.

A central political means of tilting U.S. policy toward liberal trade, therefore, has been shifting the locus of action from import politics to export politics. As long as this led to the reduction of trade barriers on a most favored nation basis, liberal economists and GATT true believers could all cheer: it might produce some trade distortion along the way, but the overall effect was clearly trade creating and welfare enhancing.

But this approach depended upon the continued support of export interests. They might or might not be initiators of action, but they had to back it. And for them to back it, for this approach to be credible to them, and to members of Congress, it needed to produce—or appear to produce—significant gains for their trade. They needed to be doing decently on world markets.

Unfortunately, how well they did—and hence how successful U.S. export bargaining appeared to be—depended importantly on broader trends. And in fact, the credibility of moderate, MFN-style export bargaining was undercut by two major developments of the 1980s. One was the U.S. trade imbalance—whose increase early in the decade ballooned the number of trade losers in the U.S. economy while keeping exports stagnant, and whose persistence thereafter has reinforced the perception that something is wrong with the U.S. trade situation and liberal trade policies. The second development was the rise in the relative position of competing economies, Japan above all, and of leading industries in those economies.

In this altered economic and political climate, U.S. export interests—high tech industries in particular—grew more demanding in pressing their interests. As Geza Feketekuty pointed out, the Reagan administration had to respond, to seize the initiative on trade, to act more aggressively on the export side; the alternative was to lose all credibility and political capacity in Washington trade policy. When an internationalist industry like semiconductors pushed for action that included managed trade, at least as a fallback, it was difficult for the administration to resist.

So the combination of the macroeconomic imbalance and the relative decline of the United States forced even greater reliance on the politics of export expansion. What was, for Cordell Hull and his successors, a politically astute means of expanding two-way trade and managing and limiting protectionist inroads, risked becoming, in the environment of the 1980s, aggressive unilateralism: "either we get access to your market or we withhold access to ours." The meaning of reciprocity shifted, from emphasis on the balance on concessions in a specific negotiation, to the balance of market conditions in a particular sector, as viewed through American lenses.

With apologies for this very quick summary of the last fifty-five years or so of American trade and political history, what do we find when we look ahead? Will U.S. superaggressiveness on exports prove transitory? Is it simply the product of a trade deficit that will recede with that deficit, when we finally tackle the budget and the savings-investment imbalance that remains its root cause? Are the provisions in U.S. trade law that bolster it—Super 301 above all—something that can be softened, defanged, as part of the Uruguay Round negotiations? Or does Super 301 signal a transition to a very different sort of U.S. trade policy?

I don't know the answers to these questions. I do think we know something about some of the things that will shape the answers.

One factor will be whether or not our trading partners give priority to Section 301 in the Uruguay Round. I hope very much that they do: that they move "beyond good and evil" to practical efforts to influence it. They should not be hung up on legalistic arguments about whether it is appropriate GATT business, or on the related notion that because 301 is a unilaterally adopted U.S. trade statute it should be unilaterally removed. In practice, the only plausible route I see to getting it amended, refined, cut down to size—Super 301 in particular—is through a multilateral negotiation, with the results submitted to Congress under the fast-track, no-amendment approval procedure.

Other nations may want to press the United States very hard on this set of issues, particularly the one-sided aspect of 301 that Bob Hudec rightly condemns. But it would be naive and self-defeating for others to say they will not bargain on 301 because it is an outrage and up to the Americans to correct; unless, of course, these nations in fact want the negotiations to fail and are looking for something to blame. As Henry Nau has argued here, they should press the issue in the Uruguay Round, since this offers their best hope of modifying U.S. law and U.S. practice.

Suppose we have a relatively successful Uruguay Round, and suppose Congress approves the results. Will aggressive American unilateralism continue? To some degree, yes. We are not going to see a return to the 1950s or early 1960s. But U.S. aggressiveness might recede somewhat—to levels the international system finds easier to live with. How much it recedes will depend importantly, in the short run, on our capacity to improve on our shameful fiscal performance of recent years. I cannot bring from Washington any great new hope for action on these matters, but sometimes in our politics the dark is greatest before the dawn.

Suppose we do address this issue with some effectiveness in the coming years, and suppose we emerge from our current trade imbalance. What happens to U.S. trade policy in the longer run? Much depends on our response to two major geopolitical shifts: the longstanding movement toward equalization of power among the centers of the noncommunist world that Bob Baldwin points to,[1] and the sudden, rapid disintegration of the Warsaw Pact (and the security threat to the West) that David Baldwin points to.[2]

Logically, there is no reason the United States cannot live within, and do very well within, the world we are moving into. Constructively adjusting to large changes is difficult politically, but the potential gains from multilateral trade should continue to increase with the rise of other strong economies, and the decline of communism is something we have long hoped for. The trade numbers do not suggest that the world is moving toward regional trade blocs: the EC does trade more within than without its borders, but North America and East Asia do not—they trade globally. There is, to be sure, growing concern in the United States about Japanese economic strength and financial power, but there is also a growing number of interests in building interdependence with the Japanese.

We do need to hold our own in such a world, however. Our capacity to maintain a decent relative economic position, and adequate political support for open trade policies, will depend on demonstrating anew that the American economy can compete. Our overall performance in the 1980s was not so bad

---

1. At the conference.
2. At the conference.

as some critics suggest. But it was certainly uneven—we need to give much greater priority to savings and investment and enhancing productivity. Only if Americans see their own world position holding up, their advanced industries doing well in global markets, will our political leadership be likely to continue pushing for opening others' markets rather than closing our own.

Commentary

Douglas Nelson

Helen Milner's chapter provides an excellent place to begin a discussion of the political economy of U.S. trade law generally and the new Section 301 in particular. Milner describes one approach to linking economic and political factors in a unified account of the evolution of Section 301 and related issues. Milner's account of this relationship is developed primarily in terms of the political preferences of various economic actors. Given the explicit assumption that the institutional environment of this political action has not undergone substantive change in this century, the focus on preferences makes perfect sense. I would like to argue, however, that the institutional environment has undergone change so fundamental that to ignore it risks missing the importance of the politics surrounding the 1988 Trade Act and Section 301 in particular.

It seems to me that, simplifying only slightly, the analytical core of Milner's chapter can be represented as follows:

1. Exogenous change in the macroeconomic environment redistributes income among firms.
2. This systematically alters firm preferences with regard to trade policy.
3. Firms change their lobbying behavior, causing politicians to change their voting behavior and the orientation of their constituent service on trade issues.
4. This process leads to marginal change in the trade law.

While this sort of analysis seems to capture one important aspect of the politics of trade policy, it would seem to have a hard time addressing two of the most fundamental questions raised by recent developments in the politics of U.S. trade law in general and the new Section 301 in particular:

First, why do firms respond to a deterioration in their competitiveness via trade policy lobbying? and

Second, how do we identify and account for system transformation, as opposed to marginal change within the system?

Both of these questions require explicit attention to institutional structure of a sort that is lacking in Milner's analysis.[1]

Consider the first question. Although Milner's positive analysis proceeds from the presumption that macroeconomic change induces political action by (presumably rational) firms, in the normative analysis that closes the chapter she recognizes that trade policy response will have little effect on the source of the problem. If the root of U.S. balance of payments and competitiveness problems is to be found in nearly a decade of irresponsible macroeconomic policy (as most economists would agree), why do firms not directly attack the real problem; or, at a minimum, pursue industry-level policy goals with a more direct impact on their interests?[2] There would seem to be two ways to go on this: ignorance or irrationality on the part of firms; and/or perverse institutional incentives. I think most of us will agree that the first approach is unlikely to be fruitful.

The analysis of the institutional structure of incentives to political action is still very much in its infancy. Virtually all of the systematic work on the politics of trade policy proceeds under the assumption that trade policy is separable from other political issues and that it can be represented as one-dimensional (i.e., that trade policy choice can be represented as picking a point on a dimension running from protection to liberalization). These institutional assumptions effectively assume away the sort of question we have just raised. If, instead, we start from the presumption that firm/industry political action is a response to generic adjustment or competitiveness problems and that the political system offers a menu of possible responses with varying costs and effectiveness, it is clear that, as rational political-economic actors, firms will seek the most efficient form of political response. In this more general context we can ask not only about the structure of incentives that results in the use of trade policy mechanisms, but we can also evaluate the implications of changing the incentive structure.

While the first question is of general interest and importance, the second (system transformation) is of more direct interest here. In understanding and explaining the importance of the 1988 Trade Act, especially Section 301, it is

---

1. There is, in fact, a peculiar implicit institutional assumption: change in the law (e.g., change in Section 301) constrains political behavior, but change in the political structure does not (or is of second-order importance).

2. One might argue that some kind of "free rider" problem undermines systematic collaboration among firms/industries on macroeconomic policy issues, but this still does not explain why firms seek *trade policy* intervention from the government.

absolutely fundamental to understand the institutional context. That is, contrary to Milner's assertion that the Act represents just one in a long series of more-or-less marginal adjustments between the executive and the legislature over trade, the widespread concern it triggered reflects a more general concern about the collapse of the political arrangements whose construction began with the Reciprocal Trade Agreements Act of 1934 (RTAA) (Nelson 1989a). For the present purposes, the most significant aspect of the institutional transformation that began with the RTAA was a shift in the locus of trade policy activism from the legislative to the executive branch. That is, Congress ceded to the executive the power to define the trade issue and to set the agenda for governmental action on trade. Congress retained only the power to check executive action.[3] From Roosevelt through Carter (with a near lapse under Eisenhower), while the executive used its agenda-setting power to promote liberalization as a foreign policy issue, protectionist pressure was deflected into the various administered protection mechanisms established to insure that the liberalization program resulted in "no serious injury" to U.S. industry.

These administered protection mechanisms are fundamental to the operation of the trade policy management system as well as to fears about its collapse. It is now fairly well understood that (in addition to acting as a political pressure release on the trade policy issue), by focusing the legislative politics of protection on the details of administered protection, the new system tended to reduce protectionist pressure more generally.[4] As long as the executive was actively promoting liberalization, administered protection continued to serve its protection-management function. What we often forget, however, is that administered protection was only one part of a broader trade management system, and when that system began to break down, the administered protection mechanisms became vehicles for congressional trade activism.

Many parts of the story of this system's collapse are well understood.[5] One part of the story is the regrettable lack of executive leadership on trade policy in the 1980s, but perhaps the most important element was the deterioration of the institutional structure within Congress that managed international trade issues. Like all legislative issues before Congress, trade policy is man-

---

3. It should be clearly noted that this refers to a de facto cession of authority. Congress, of course, retained de jure control over tariffs granted it in the Constitution.

4. The basic logic behind this conclusion is that the switch from a system under which Congress directly legislated a tariff schedule ("legislated protection") to one in which it legislated the rules under which administrative mechanisms provided protection ("administered protection") made the output of the political process more like a public good, with the implication that collective action problems of the usual sort would tend to undermine effective political action on the issue. See Nelson 1989a for more on this and Hall and Nelson 1989 for a more precise formulation of the logic.

5. Destler 1986 is an admirable presentation and analysis of the facts relating to the sources of change in the trade policy system.

aged by a well-institutionalized division of labor embodied in the committee system. Until recently, the main lines of trade policy were managed by the Ways and Means Committee of the House of Representatives and the Senate Finance Committee. For most of three decades, the Democratic leadership of these committees (especially Ways and Means) used this division of labor to protect the executive's agenda-setting power and to promote liberalization. In the early 1970s, however, the reform of the committee system resulted in dramatically reduced power of committee chairs and increased power of sub-committee chairs, with the effect that opportunities for political entrepreneurship by relatively junior members were greatly increased. One form such entrepreneurship was to take was that members on other committees (especially Energy and Commerce, and Agriculture) were able to claim jurisdiction over the trade issue. The importance of this was concealed for a while by continued executive commitment to trade policy, but clearly emerged with the Reagan and Bush administrations' neglect of the issue.

This suggests a rather different linkage between macroeconomic problems and trade policy. Politicians (especially upwardly mobile politicians) are always looking for issues. With fiscal responsibility seen fairly widely as a political loser, the emergence of a large trade deficit made "international things" highly visible. That made trade policy attractive to political entrepreneurs, while the collapse of the trade issue regime in Congress reduced the entry costs for new entrepreneurs. Once the trade issue was reopened, the relative costs of participation for firms and citizen-agents were also reduced, thus inducing an increase in political action.[6] That is, institutional change resulted in a change in the incentives to public political action.

The emergence of Section 301 is a particularly revealing aspect of the new politics of protection. Prior to the 1988 Trade Act, the antidumping, countervailing duties, and escape clause mechanisms had been the overwhelmingly dominant administered protection mechanisms—both in terms of case load and time spent legislating on trade. The problem with these mechanisms as entrepreneurial platforms is that they are fundamentally reactive and fundamentally domestic. This is fine as a basis for constituency service, but it

---

6. Once we have identified the institutional change inducing increased political action, the more traditional analysis of preferences for political outcomes and the distribution of capacity for effective pursuit of those preferences is made much more useful.

While my commentary on Milner's chapter has emphasized the importance of institutional factors on final outcomes in the political economy of trade policy, I hope I am not taken to be denying the significance of other changes. In particular, as Bhagwati (1988), Destler and Odell (1987), and Milner (1988) have all observed, the dramatic growth of international trade and investment following World War II should have increased the numbers of antiprotectionists. However, as I argue in my review of the latter two works (Nelson 1989b), it would be wrong to conclude that an increase in antiprotectionist activity necessarily implies a fundamental change in the organizational and institutional asymmetries favoring protection seekers.

does considerably less well as a basis for public position taking. The attraction of Section 301 is precisely that it permits a policy orientation that is both activist and international. The difference from the post-1934 regime could not be more stark: under the old system trade policy was insider politics, revolving around marginal changes in the structure of a well-established legislative and bureaucratic system, and the manipulation of that system as part of normal constituency service; the emerging system returns trade policy to the public agenda of Congress.

The implications of this for the future are both clear and distressing. If the domestic regime regulating the trade issue has broken down (or is showing signs of breaking down), we may expect a discontinuous change in both the domestic (protection) and international (liberalization) aspects of U.S. trade policy. I believe it is this aspect of the recent U.S. trade policy process that should concern both academics and practitioners.

REFERENCES

Bhagwati, Jagdish. 1988. *Protectionism*. Cambridge, Mass.: MIT Press.
Destler, I. M. 1986. *American Trade Politics: System Under Stress*. Washington, D.C.: Institute for International Economics.
Destler, I. M., and John Odell. 1987. *Anti-Protection: Changing Forces in U.S. Trade Politics*. Washington, D.C.: Institute for International Economics.
Hall, H. Keith, and Douglas Nelson. 1989. "Institutional Structure in the Political Economy of Protection: Administered versus Legislated Protection." Department of Economics, Syracuse University. Unpublished paper.
Milner, Helen. 1988. *Resisting Protectionism: Global Industries and the Politics of International Trade*. Princeton, N.J.: Princeton University Press.
Nelson, Douglas. 1989a. "Domestic Political Preconditions of U.S. Trade Policy: Liberal Structure and Protectionist Dynamics." *Journal of Public Policy*, 9, no. 1: 83–108.
Nelson, Douglas. 1989b. "The Political Economy of Trade Policy." *Economics and Politics* 1, no. 3: 301–14.

Commentary

Paula Stern

The Omnibus Trade and Competitiveness Act of 1988, and especially Section 301 of the Act, which is a major new element of U.S. trade policy, are best understood in a historical context.

The 1988 Act and its 301 functions are the latest in a line of changes in U.S. trade legislation over two decades through which Congress has increasingly reasserted its constitutional prerogative to regulate foreign commerce.[1] Section 301, when viewed in this manner, represents continuity in a political process in which Congress and the executive branch vie (within limits) over who regulates foreign commerce (Congress) and who negotiates for the United States of America (the president).

Section 301 also has distinctive features growing out of the special circumstances of the 1980s. New forces were operating in America as it was created. The country had reached a turning point in its economic history. Starting in 1983, it found itself experiencing record-breaking trade deficits year after year. These were stimulated by the combined effects of the super-dollar in the early 1980s, and a deterioration in competitiveness relative to U.S. trading partners dating from the 1970s, and in the case of key manufacturing industries like autos and steel, from an even earlier time.

The Omnibus Trade and Competitiveness Act was passed in the summer of 1988 by a bipartisan majority of legislators who held four basic beliefs. These beliefs find numerous expressions throughout the Act, most particularly in Section 301. The first was that unfair trade is a major cause of the U.S. trade deficit and the problems of its industrial sector. The second was that presidents tend to subordinate U.S. economic interests to foreign policy concerns. The third was that the Reagan administration, during its eight years in

---

1. In the early to mid 1970s, Congress passed a series of measures to assert itself over the president in the foreign policy arena, including the Trade Reform Act, the War Powers Act, the Jackson-Vanik amendment, the Nelson amendment, and the Arms Export and Control Act. In this same period, Congress passed the Budget and Impoundment Act. For further historical background regarding its actions, see Paula Stern, *Water's Edge: Domestic Policy and the Making of American Foreign Policy* (Westport, Conn.: Greenwood Press, 1979), 203–8.

office, had neither adequately nor consistently administered the trade laws mandated by Congress in previous trade bills. And fourth was the belief that America's dominance in a more competitive world economy had slipped and the time had come to focus on opening markets for U.S. exports.[2]

I. Unfair Trade as a Factor in the U.S. Trade Deficit

On theme one, the impact of "unfairness," Congress probably miscalculated and continues to do so. Diverse factors—including relative rates of economic growth; fiscal and monetary choices at home and abroad; tax, savings, investment, and exchange rate policies made individually or collectively around the world; and the domestic cultures of important U.S. industries—have a far greater impact on the trade deficit than does direct microeconomic regulation of trade itself.

Even though many members recognized that macroeconomic factors were key, they nevertheless tended to emphasize "unfair trade" as the source of the U.S. trade deficit.[3] For those members interested in drafting a market opening–oriented bill, the existence of barriers to U.S. exports abroad grabbed their attention and captured their legislative energies. Much of the energy, however, eventually was channeled into changes in the rules for restricting imports or in limiting the president's discretion not to retaliate in Section 301 cases.

Congress had a tendency to exaggerate the impact of legislative slings and arrows aimed at other nations' trade practices. While Congress debated these trade restricting measures, petitions under the existing rules mounted. U.S. trade laws targeted at foreign unfair practices were invoked very frequently during the Reagan administration's era of record-breaking trade deficits. But despite hundreds of complaints, less than 1 percent of total U.S. imports were actually challenged as unfair under U.S. trade laws.[4] The volume of U.S. imports affected by antidumping and countervailing duty investi-

---

2. Critics of the Democratic Congress might argue that the four reasons for congressional action cited above are in reality only justifications for politics being the primary motivator for congressional action. The Democrats and their allies in organized labor, such critics would argue, needed an issue to pick against the president and the trade deficit numbers were the only negative numbers in the economy, and so trade became the target for politically motivated and unjustifiable attacks on the president. This interpretation, however, ignores the strong push for a trade bill that came from the Republican side of the aisle, most prominently from Senator John Heinz (R-Pennsylvania) and Senator John Danforth (R-Missouri) both of whom were outspoken in their criticism of their fellow Republican, President Reagan.

3. Commentators note that foreign barriers were falling in the 1980s while the U.S. deficit soared.

4. Paula Stern, "The Trade Deficit: Ways to Spell Relief," paper presented at the National Economists Club Trade Policy Forum (November 12, 1985), Washington, D.C.

gations as a percentage of total imports amounted to only 0.2 percent in 1987, 0.4 percent in 1988, and 0.2 percent during the first half of 1989. Even in the cases where the U.S. International Trade Commission (ITC) and Department of Commerce (DOC) made affirmative determinations, the average dumping duty applied in 1987 on dumped or subsidized goods was 1.2 percent. In 1988, the average was 3.7 percent; in the first half of 1989, the figure was 1.4 percent.

These figures somewhat understate the importance of unfair foreign practices in causing the U.S. trade deficit, but they do suggest orders of magnitude. For example, foreign unfair trade practices are rarely, if ever, cited as causes of the U.S. trade deficit in autos and consumer electronics, yet these two items account for 60 percent to 70 percent of our deficit with Japan and are huge factors in the deficit with the world at large. The focus on unfairness, therefore, almost certainly diverts attention from other causes of U.S. trade problems.

II. Presidential Discretion—Foreign vs. Sectoral Interests

The second theme in the new legislation is derived from Congress's view that presidents subordinate U.S. economic concerns to diplomatic ones. This is a perennial issue in the congressional/executive dialogue. Every occupant of the White House tries to preserve maximum presidential discretion, particularly on trade issues that affect foreign policy, while Congress always is far more sensitive to sectoral and/or constituent interests.

As Congress saw it in Section 301 of the 1988 Trade Act, the president always subordinates trade policy to geopolitical considerations and this tendency has characterized all post–World War II trade policy-making by the executive. Senator Russell Long (D-Louisiana), the chairman of the Finance Committee for many years in the 1970s and 1980s, regularly railed against "those striped pants fellows in the State Department" who would get the president to subordinate the industrial interests of the United States to diplomatic considerations. Senator Long's statement of the congressional view is worth quoting:

> It has been my view—and I think is the view of this committee . . . that from the State Department come repeated pressures to be liberal on imports, whereas in many cases, American industries are getting the worst of it. Those who try to keep the American industry in business are repeatedly being accused of being protectionist because they do that. . . . The Secretary of State likes to take the point of view—and his functionaries like to take the point of view—that all of this is foreign

policy. If they need a vote in the United Nations on some crucial issue in the Security Council, they would like to take the view that it would help to make further trade concessions or let people dump products in here and have the United States do nothing about it.

Repeatedly we are confronted with the fact that if we want the cooperation of various countries in foreign policy we ought to go along with them on economic matters, either by the way of not imposing countervailing duties or letting them dump products into our market and do many other things that work out to our disadvantage.

The only way we know how to defend ourselves against that on the Finance Committee is to try to write a law to say you shall not do this, you shall not do that, you shall make findings and make recommendations—and then the president can say that those recommended actions will not happen, but the Congress can have a chance to overrule the president on it. What we must ask for and insist on is that that Commission follow the law and that they be completely independent of the White House. . . . Have you been, at any point, asked to give any kind of assurance that you will go along with the White House on their trade policy? The President has plenty of power to defend his views without the executive branch's controlling that Trade Commission.[5]

The history of the ITC is a paradigm of congressional concerns about the attitudes of the executive toward U.S. economic interests. The Tariff Commission, the forerunner of the ITC, was created in 1917, to give Congress leverage with the White House in the trade area while shielding it from a constant stream of petitions for trade protection that Congress had previously faced directly. It was renamed the International Trade Commission in 1975, but it remains very close to the Congress and very much a reflection of congressional concerns.

In both 1975 and 1978, Senator Long legislated changes in the organization of the commission to assure its independence from the White House. The ITC budget goes directly to Congress without passing the Office of Management and Budget's scrutiny. The members of the commission are appointed to the quasi-judicial tribunal for nine years—a year longer than any president can sit in the White House. An appointee cannot be reappointed by the President, so no decision at the commission need ever be made with the thought that it might please or displease the White House or any of its diplomatic advisors. The chairmanship rotates between the parties, and the president may not designate either of his last two appointees to be chairman—

5. Hearings of the Finance Committee, U.S. Senate, Monday, September 25, 1978, 10–11.

again as a way of insulating commission decisions from diplomatic pressures that might be transmitted through the White House.

The creation of the Special Trade Representative's office (later renamed the United States Trade Representative, USTR) in the 1960s was inspired by the same sense that the president was subordinating trade issues to foreign policy concerns. The idea was to elevate the trade bureaucracy and gain its independence from the Departments of State, Treasury, and Defense, which had competing foreign policy concerns that sometimes took precedence over trade. The Congress was again asserting itself vis-à-vis the president by removing decision-making authority from officials in the traditional cabinet departments and enhancing the powers of an agency, in this case USTR, more likely to share the commercial concerns of congressional constituents.

Russell Long's views were very much a part of the debate over the omnibus trade act and Section 301 even though he had left Congress. A large group of his peers and colleagues believed that the Reagan administration was unwilling to defend the economic interests of U.S. industries. Many congressmen complained, for example, that when officials from the Commerce Department or USTR took the Japanese to the mat on trade issues, their hold was broken in deference to foreign policy objectives. One such objective often mentioned was getting Japan to shoulder a larger share of the U.S. defense burden in the Pacific.

Senator Lloyd Bentsen (D-Texas), Long's successor as chairman of the Finance Committee that drafted the 1988 bill, underscored the congressional view again in an opening salvo of the debate in 1987. The senator asserted that there was a time when we were totally dominant in trade and we could dictate on trade but that this time has long passed. Bentsen spoke for many in Congress in both parties, who believed that the Reagan administration— different from its predecessors in so many ways—like earlier administrations, failed to give enough weight to domestic U.S. economic interests.

The Reagan superdollar[6] and the seven years of record-breaking trade deficits that followed added to congressional concerns about presidents and trade. The ballooning trade deficits increased the feeling that the direction of trade policy had to be reversed. So Congress set about correcting the situation in a predictable fashion: by changing the rules of the game and rearranging the blocks in the organizational chart of the U.S. trade bureaucracy. It still eschewed direct congressional micromanagement of trade, as it had often in the past, but by changing the rules and the charts it tied the president to a still tighter leash.

In Section 301, Congress restricted the president's freedom not to retaliate if a negotiation with a foreign trading partner over market access breaks

---

6. The dollar hit its peak in March, 1985.

down. Furthermore, the president actually lost the job of deciding when and how to act on 301 petitions; the USTR was given this task. The president may still want to allow U.S. diplomatic and defense interests to override trade issues, and he can do so, but the congressional web around him is more restrictive than ever before. Among other reasons, this is because the organizations of the government more likely to share congressional concerns— Commerce, the ITC, USTR—are stronger and the rules of the road favor them to a greater degree.

III. The Reagan Administration's Execution of Trade Laws

The third theme underlying the Omnibus Trade Act and changes in Section 301 in that Act was bipartisan concern in Congress about the trade policies of the Reagan administration. In the mid-1980s, as U.S. industries staggered from the burden of a soaring dollar and burgeoning import competition, the perception was rife that the administration was not adequately or consistently using the legal authority to defend U.S. trade interests that Congress had authorized in prior legislation.

The Reagan administration's positions on trade encouraged this perception. It opposed "protectionism" philosophically, so its statements worried those in Congress with domestic constituencies to protect. It revelled in the rise of the dollar, and appeared to disregard the impact of the superdollar on almost the whole U.S. manufacturing sector, and on sectors of the agricultural economy exposed to foreign competition. Yet, the Reagan administration's antiprotectionist rhetoric often seemed only to disdain congressionally sanctioned trade remedies, while opening new areas for executive action. While the Reagan team criticized and ignored the trade laws developed by Congress over the years, it did not hesitate to use so-called voluntary restraint agreements (VRAs) or orderly marketing arrangements (OMAs), negotiated with U.S. trading partners. VRAs and OMAs were outside both the congressionally sanctioned list of trade remedies and the international system of rules for industries hurt by trade. President Reagan used them, nevertheless, to limit imports of automobiles, steel, and machine tools.

Automobiles

The automobile experience gave U.S. trade law a new trade phenomenon. The ITC ruled in 1980 that imports were not the most important cause of serious injury to the U.S. auto industry, suggesting that U.S. domestic policies and practices in the industry itself needed careful review. Faced with an automobile quota bill introduced by Senator John Danforth (R-Missouri) and keeping a 1980 campaign pledge, President Reagan disregarded the ITC finding and put in place four years of more-or-less mutually agreed upon export restraints by Japan. Since the fifth year, the Japanese have renewed these VRAs unilaterally to ward off unsanctioned protectionism.[7]

Steel

In the case of steel, the USTR announced in October, 1984 (a month before Reagan's reelection), that the President had decided to disregard the ITC's recommendation to grant steel import relief under Section 201 of the Trade and Tariff Act of 1974, which provides for relief to U.S. industries to adjust to *fair* competition from foreign companies. At the same time, however, President Reagan was telling steel executives that he had authorized negotiations on bilateral, voluntary restrictions with nations supplying "unfair" steel. In effect, he refused to use legislated means to help the steel industry; instead, he chose to launch protracted bilateral negotiations that took over a year to complete and resulted in the imposition of quotas for five years against twenty-nine different supplying nations.

Machine Tools

The Reagan Administration also granted protection to the machine tool industry in a manner not exactly contemplated by the trade rules. When the Reagan administration decided to restrict imports, Secretary of Commerce Malcolm Baldridge declined to announce the quota levels. Instead, he used the announcement that cutbacks would be sought as an inducement for the supplying nations—Japan, Switzerland, and West Germany—to cut back on their own. Baldridge correctly likened the process to the steel industry voluntary restraint agreements. However, unlike steel and autos, the machine tools investigation did not proceed from an investigation as to whether the industry had been injured by imports. Rather, the quotas were justified on national defense grounds. Section 232 provides for national defense to be the premise for helping an industry. But Congress noted that this case languished for three years with no action in spite of the defense imperative that presumably lay behind it.

The Reagan administration—because of its own commitment to free market ideology, particularly in its first four years—was reluctant to be seen

---

7. Since 1985, Japanese automobile restraints have not exceeded the annual figure of 2.3 million. In fact in the past few years, shipments have not reached or exceeded this limit. However, Japan's Ministry of Trade and Industry has kept the restraints on as a contingency in the event that the 1990 downturn in the auto industry might generate U.S. political pressure to cut back on an expected increase in Japanese market share in the United States.

helping U.S. industries injured by fair competition. Resistant to congressional pressures, it also avoided taking up Section 301 complaints about unfair measures in other countries that limited the market access of U.S. exporters. And it ignored the trade adjustment assistance powers in the law. If there was a consistent pattern to the administration of the trade laws in the Reagan administration, it was that it tended to weigh in when a powerful U.S. industry claimed "unfairness," but it did so in ways that often seemed to bypass the congressionally mandated rules. When the diplomatic stakes were judged too volatile, President Reagan hesitated to use remedies suggested by the law and instead exercised discretionary authority in various laws to negotiate politicized "settlements" or "suspension agreements" after pressure built up for action.

Examples of this pattern abound. The administration resorted to settlements in several widely celebrated Title VII cases. This title of the trade laws provides for duty relief against injurious dumped or subsidized imports, and was used to limit imports of steel from myriad nations, lumber from Canada, and semiconductors from Japan. The exporting nations agreed to, among other things, quantitative restrictions on their shipments to the United States, in exchange for which the United States did not impose countervailing or dumping duties on the products that the Department of Commerce had found to be subsidized or dumped. Likewise, the tendency to use the trade laws only when political pressures made it necessary were at play when the executive branch chose to self-initiate or review these cases in the first place.

This selective approach to the trade laws marred the administration's claims that the unfair import laws it was using were purely rule-oriented and apolitical. Likewise, when the president refused to use the laws and instead granted protection in the form of politically expedient VRAs, the country and Congress became confused about policy. Industries came to rely on political muscle and were not consistently pressured to make the adjustments necessary to merit public investment in protection. The result: the consumer paid the bill and the industries got to raise prices and/or contain losses of market share, but few of the beneficiaries of protection became truly competitive as a result.

Bipartisan criticism articulated during the 1988 trade bill debate attests to the fact that members of Congress had increasingly come to distrust the executive branch's handling of trade policy, and had decided to take matters more fully into their own hands. Senator John Danforth (R-Missouri) was one of the loudest critics of Reagan even though he was from the same party. Danforth spoke out often on the Senate floor as well as in a highly visible speech at the National Press Club.

Congressional opinion—which was never actually put to a vote on steel and autos—had pressured Reagan to protect the auto and steel sectors, so Congress focused much of its public criticism of the manner in which the trade laws were being administered on the moribund state of Section 301, the handling of the machine tools case, and the allegedly lax handling of the Multi Fibre Arrangement restrictions on textile and apparel imports.

There had always been a protectionist streak in Congress—representing as it does individual constituent interests—but actions by the Reagan administration, which bypassed sanctioned processes for gaining trade relief and politicized the process, made matters worse. And the conflict over the trade laws and their application diverted attention from fundamental problems of industries, which often were exposed in more transparent ITC hearings. During the 1980s, the need for domestic change was hidden and muffled by confusing ad hoc relief from import competition and argument over the adequacy of trade laws.

Slowly the Reagan administration began to recognize that it could not continue to carry out trade policy in its second term the way it had conducted policy in the first term. It reversed its policy toward the superdollar in September, 1985. By doing so, it hoped to counteract rising impatience in Congress and across the nation with trade deficits in particular and its trade policy in general. It hoped that a dollar devaluation would reduce the trade deficit and take the steam out of pressure for new trade legislation that Reagan called "kamikaze protectionism" in 1986.

But the fat was already in the fire. Coordinated action taken to bring the dollar down pursuant to the Plaza Agreement did not reduce the trade deficit fast enough or far enough to prevent the passage of the Omnibus Trade Act in 1988. The Congress, habitually suspicious of administration trade policy even in the best of times, had lost confidence in the integrity of the execution of the existing trade laws by the administration. It decided, as it had before in 1975 and 1979, to use its constitutional power to regulate foreign commerce to draft a new and more tightly circumscribed mandate for future presidents.

IV. Overseas Market Access for a More Competitive United States

Congressional preoccupation with "unfairness" and distrust of the executive's willingness to confront our allies over trade problems is consistent with a desire to see foreign markets opened to competitive U.S. exports. It is also consistent with a concern that some U.S. industries have lost their competitive edge for reasons that are largely domestic. There was an underlying belief in Congress that U.S. industries would export if foreign markets are fairly open to them, but that without help, many of them would not be able to do so.

The Plaza Agreement removed one major burden that American industry had had to carry during the early Reagan years. It contributed to a dramatic, 30 percent reduction in the value of the dollar, which gave American-based industries and U.S. agriculture an opportunity to be price competitive once again. And Congress, in the new trade bill, pushed the Reagan administration and its successors to focus more attention on U.S. competitiveness abroad and at home.

Competitiveness is the trade bill's fourth theme, which is highlighted in the title of the bill. It finds expression in a number of provisions, including the entire Title VI devoted to education and training for competitiveness. And the idea of competitiveness provides the thrust in the bill, when it seeks to force the executive branch to take diplomatic risks to seek better treatment for U.S. exports overseas, and to focus U.S. industry on exports rather than on the protection of its domestic markets.

The new trade law carries a message from Congress to President Reagan and his successors that they should focus more attention on U.S. access to foreign markets. Changes in Section 301 of the 1988 trade act are intended to give U.S. exporters and the trade bureaucracy more weapons to fight barriers to market access overseas, and to push the president to take diplomatic risks to open these markets. The president is no longer able to duck the issue when a firm is having problems exporting because of foreign barriers. More complex and burdensome provisions seek to force executive action.

These "forcing" changes in Section 301 are a direct reproach to President Reagan's trade policy in his first term. During that period, he kept the Section 301 window in the trade bureaucracy closed. Then, in the fall of 1985, the administration both shifted policy on dollar devaluation and initiated Section 301 cases in the hope of taking the wind out of the sails of Congress, which wanted to legislate policy changes.

Complaints can no longer languish on the president's desk. The president's authority under Section 301 to make legal determinations and decide what is the best action to take was, as mentioned above, transferred to the USTR. The amendments also set new deadlines for initiating cases, spell out new procedures and time limits for the Trade Representative to deal with complaints against trading partners, mandate retaliation for trade-related violations of the international legal rights of the United States, and empower the trade representative to pursue trade liberalization with specific, "priority" foreign countries.

In sum, amendments to Section 301 underscore all four themes in the trade bill as a whole: Congress's desire, first, to battle so-called unfair trade practices overseas; second, to reduce presidential discretion and the subordination of U.S. trade policy to diplomatic considerations; third, to gain greater consistency in the administration's enforcement of trade laws; and fourth, to push for export opportunities.

Conclusion

The changes in Section 301 in the Omnibus Trade and Competitiveness Act essentially continue a process that has spanned the past several decades in which Congress has whittled down the president's New Deal dominance in the international trade area. The pattern is familiar. Instead of legislating quotas on special products, Congress prefers to force bureaucratic changes or toy with the rules by which the executive branch or the ITC makes its decisions. The changes in the rules of Section 301 in 1988, which were a reaction to the Reagan administration's handling of Section 301 in its first term, are in many ways a replay of rule changes in 1975 and again in 1979. In these earlier efforts, Congress tightened deadlines, mandated judicial review, and shifted jurisdictional responsibility for dumping and countervailing duty cases. The changes in 1988 were only more of the same.

The Reagan administration encouraged this latest congressional effort by appearing to give low priority to trade issues in its first term, and by giving short shrift to existing trade remedies. The new Section 301 is built on this foundation of mistrust. Congressional action is therefore best understood as a reaction to the president, to whom Congress traditionally defers in foreign trade matters.

CHAPTER 6

Strategic Bargaining and Section 301

John McMillan

1. Introduction

International trade negotiations ordinarily proceed according to the norm of reciprocity, under which one country offers increased access to its own market in exchange for similarly increased access to a foreign market. Section 301 of the Trade Act changes this by having the United States threaten to limit a foreign country's access unless that country increases its purchases of U.S. goods. Under the former system the deal is "If you help me, I'll help you"; under Section 301 it is "Unless you help me, I'll hurt you."[1]

The U.S. Congress did not invent this technique of trade policy. In the seventeenth century it was used by the government of Flanders, which retaliated against England's prohibition of imports of its lace by prohibiting the importation of English woolens. This forerunner to Section 301 was successful: England removed the offending trade barrier. Section 301 is often labeled a tool of the managed traders; but Adam Smith, the supreme antimercantilist, approved of Flanders's action. "There may be good policy in retaliations of this kind, when there is a probability that they will procure the repeal of the high duties or prohibitions complained of" (Smith 1952, 199).

The pros and cons of Section 301 have been debated at length. I shall not review them here; the modest aim of this paper is to see whether game theory can help clarify the issues. No new game theory will be developed; I shall

I thank Richard Baldwin, Jagdish Bhagwati, Vincent Crawford, Joanne Gowa, Lawrence Krause, Barry Nalebuff, Joel Sobel and T. N. Srinivasan for comments and discussions, and the National Science Foundation (SES-8721124) for research support. This paper was published earlier by Basil Blackwell (Oxford) in *Economics & Politics* 2, no. 1 (Spring 1990): 45–58.

1. Section 301 of the 1974 trade act enables the president to retaliate against foreign countries' trade-restricting policies that reduce U.S. exports. The so-called Super 301 provision of the Omnibus Trade and Competitiveness Act of 1988 focuses on countries rather than sectors within countries; and it specifies a process of investigation and negotiation, to be followed by retaliation should the United States's demands not be met.

merely take some off-the-rack models and check how well they fit Section 301 negotiations.

The analysis to be developed will support the view that Section 301 can be successful, at least in its own terms. But it can have perverse effects. It cannot be implemented without some risk of generating a costly trade conflict. And the logic of the negotiation process tempts decision makers to choose actions that can be seen to be successful, rather than those that have a high social return.

2. Distributive Aspects of Section 301

The fundamental feature of all negotiations is that they are nonzero-sum games. Elements of both cooperation and conflict coexist. The sum of all players' payoffs varies with their decisions; the size of the pie is determined by the player's actions. The players have a common interest in making the pie as large as possible, but they have conflicting interests over how the pie is to be divided. A negotiation has both efficiency aspects and distributive aspects. In practice these two elements are inseparable. But in thinking about negotiations it is helpful to separate them.

Section 301 has implications for both the efficiency aspects and the distributive aspects of trade negotiations. As nonnationalistic analysts, we need not be too concerned about Section 301's purely distributive effects— although we might worry if a transfer goes from as poor a country as India to as rich a country as the United States. But Section 301's efficiency consequences, positive or negative, directly affect total world welfare.

To examine the distributive effects, we consider a simple bargaining game, due to Binmore, Rubinstein, and Wolinsky (1986), in which a pair of bargainers, call them A and B, seek to divide \$1 between themselves. If they agree to divide the dollar such that A receives z and B receives $1 - z$, then A's utility is rz, for some positive number r, and B's utility is $1 - z$. (That is, A values each cent at r times B's valuation—r can be either larger than or less than one.) Bargaining proceeds in sequence: A makes the first offer, which B can accept or reject. If B accepts, the dollar is divided as A proposed; if B rejects, then he or she makes an offer to A. This process of alternating offers can go on indefinitely, except that there is a chance that, because of events beyond the control of the bargainers, the bargaining will break down irrevocably: at each stage of the game, breakdown can occur with some fixed, small probability.[2] In the event of breakdown, each bargainer receives a fallback

---

2. The incorporation of this chance of breakdown is merely a technical device to give the modeled bargainers an incentive for early settlement; we shall focus on the case in which breakdown is very unlikely. Without some such incentive, they could rationally bargain forever.

level of utility, respectively f_a and f_b. Information is perfect; in particular, each knows the other's fallback level and utility function. What division of the $1 will the rational bargainers agree to?

An equilibrium of a bargaining game occurs when, in the words of Schelling (1960, 70), "each expects the other not to expect to be expected to retreat." Bargaining situations used to be thought to be inherently indeterminate (and are still so described in some undergraduate textbooks); theory could not predict the outcome. But it can be shown that, if each bargainer is fully rational in forming his or her expectations of what the other will accept, and knows his or her rival is similarly rational, then the game just stated has a unique outcome. From the agreement, bargainer A receives a utility level of $[r + f_a - rf_b]/2$, and bargainer B a utility of $[1 + f_b - (f_a/r)]/2$. (A proof of this is given in the appendix.)

The significance of this result for our purposes is that each bargainer's payoff is higher the better his or her own alternative is and the worse his or her opponent's alternative is. That is, A's utility increases in f_a and decreases in f_b, and vice versa for B. Alternative opportunities are a source of bargaining power. The alternative opportunities overhang the negotiations, affecting each bargainer's expectations of what the other will settle for and shaping the terms of the agreement.

In addition, A's utility increases with r (which is the ratio of A's valuation of one cent to B's). The bargainers' relative valuations of the object of negotiations shape their expectations, with the result that A's bargaining position is stronger, the larger his relative valuation.

These results look like mere common sense; they have a dog-bites-man quality. But game theory often finds that common sense is an unreliable guide through the complexities of strategic interactions. Once we start thinking through the logic of conjecturing others' conjectures, apparently intuitive results often turn out to be false. Bargaining power is a slippery concept. So it is useful to know that common sense is corroborated by this model.[3]

It follows from our simple game that one can improve one's bargaining position by taking actions that would result in a higher return for oneself in the event that the negotiations break down. And a more aggressive way of improving one's bargaining position is to worsen one's opponent's alternatives—bargainer A might try to lower f_b. This is the intent of Section 301, in requiring that the foreign country's access to the U.S. market be limited should the negotiations fail. Our model suggests that implementing Section

---

3. See, for example, the essay of Schelling (1984) on the logical difficulties hidden in the notion that a nation should weigh its own costs against the costs of its enemy in allocating its resources to defense. A different bargaining model that also supports the conclusion that worsening one's opponent's alternatives improves one's bargaining position is developed by Dasgupta and Maskin (1989).

301 increases U.S. bargaining power, in the sense that, other things being equal, the terms of agreements will be more favorable to the United States with 301 than without.[4]

How much bargaining power does the United States gain from implementing Section 301? What determines how far any new agreement will have shifted from the pre-301 status quo? According to this model, the improvement in the negotiated agreement from bargainer A's point of view is proportional to the lowering in bargainer B's fallback f_b. Thus, the larger the threatened reduction in f_b, the better for bargainer A.[5]

On the other hand, the model says that the bargaining-power effect of the reduction in f_b can be nullified by a countervailing reduction in f_a. In other words, if B is able to worsen A's fallback, then A obtains no bargaining advantage from his or her initial action. If counterretaliation is expected, there is no point in lowering the other's alternative, for there is nothing to be gained from it.

The model further implies that, given the size of the reduction in f_b, its effect in shifting the point of agreement is larger, the larger r is. The credibility of bargaining positions is the key to this result. It is credible to bargainer A that bargainer B will hold out for a favorable settlement when either A knows that B attaches a high valuation to the item being bargained over, or A knows that B knows that A attaches a low valuation to it. Thus, implementing Section 301 will tend to have a large effect when (a) the cost to the target country of conceding is small, and (b) U.S. welfare rises markedly with the country's compliance.

The worsening of an opponent's alternatives has been discussed so far as a purely distributive tactic. In the model, the rational bargainers calculate the strategic value of both their own and their opponent's alternatives, and they immediately agree on an efficient division of the gains. Lowering one's opponent's alternatives simply shifts the agreement in one's favor, without causing any loss in overall efficiency. Our analysis, so far, is therefore not pessimistic about the consequences of Section 301; the simple bargaining model suggests that, while Section 301 might cause a redistribution of world welfare toward the United States, it need not cause a net reduction in world welfare.

Whether, in fact, the implementation of Section 301 has been purely distributive is an empirical question. But there are two sets of reasons why Section 301 might not be harmless. First, the negotiators' aims, reflecting domestic political concerns, might not take account of the full social conse-

---

4. For the threat to lower f_b to be effective, it must be credible. The fact that the threat is written into legislation helps achieve credibility; more on this in section 4.

5. As we shall see in section 4, however, stronger threats may worsen the bargaining frictions and increase the likelihood of an inefficient outcome, assumed away in this simple model.

quences of their decisions. Second, game theory suggests some reasons why changing the strategies used in trade negotiations by introducing Section 301 could create bargaining frictions and resultant efficiency losses. We now consider each of these issues in turn.

3. Efficiency Aspects: Political Economy

In terms of what is being sought in the negotiations, the outcome of the simple divide-the-dollar game is efficient. But this is a narrow definition of efficiency. A broader view of efficiency would evaluate the decision makers' goals. It is not clear exactly what aims trade negotiators actually pursue. What is clear is that they do not seek to maximize social welfare as defined by trade theorists. In the 1985 Section 301 action over the South Korean insurance market, for example, "both governments approached the case with the perception that the main issue was the sharing of profits in Korea's insurance markets. In the negotiations, both governments, especially that of the United States, basically represented the interests of their insurance industries. The effect of what was being sought in the negotiations on other activities, and on the efficiency of the economy as a whole, was not a major consideration" (Cho 1987, 493).

The decision makers' objectives reflect the workings of the domestic political system and the competing claims of import-industry groups, export-industry groups, and consumers. The resulting agenda is a warped reflection of domestic interests because of the disproportionate power of concentrated interests over diffuse interests—especially producer interests over consumer interests. Thus, the negotiators do not necessarily seek outcomes that are efficient from the point of view of the economy as a whole.

Our simple model suggests some determinants of the effectiveness of Section 301 threats: it identifies various sources of bargaining power for both the United States and the targeted country. Let us now further examine these components of bargaining power, and evaluate them in the light of the decision makers' incentives.

One obvious determinant of bargaining power identified by the model is the U.S. ability to harm the targeted country in the event that the 301 threat is carried out. A 301 threat will achieve a large shift away from the status quo when the targeted country is very dependent on its sales in the United States, for then the United States has the ability to cause a large reduction in f_b. Over a third of South Korea's exports, for example, go to the United States, giving the United States large bargaining power vis-à-vis Korea.

If the target country has the ability to counterretaliate and worsen the U.S. fallback sufficiently, then the United States obtains no bargaining advantage from a 301 action. According to the model, the threat of sufficient counterretaliation, by affecting the bargainers' expectations, leaves the two parties in the same relative bargaining position as they were in initially. The possibility of counterretaliation was probably why the EC was not put on the 1989 Super 301 list of "unfair" traders, despite its having arguably more objectionable trading practices than two of the countries actually targeted, India and Brazil (Milner, in this volume). In their inability to harm the United States by counterretaliation, India and Brazil are in a weak bargaining position.

The model further predicts that 301 will have a large effect when only a small cost of conceding is incurred by the decision makers in the target country. This restates what has been noted before by trade analysts: "Whatever success the United States has attained in the Section 301 process is attributable to its flexibility in identifying barriers that foreign governments could dismantle without risking crippling local opposition" (Maskus 1987, 417). The 1989 Super 301 actions against India and Brazil, however, would not seem to satisfy this criterion, given the strength of nationalistic feelings within these countries and therefore the costs to Indian and Brazilian politicians of appearing to be obsequious toward the United States. The model has shown bargaining power to be multidimensional; in the cost-of-compliance dimension, India and Brazil actually have strong bargaining power.

The incentive for the United States to pick Section 301 cases for which the targeted country's compliance costs are small can generate a seductive tendency toward trade diversion rather than trade creation (Bhagwati 1988 and 1989). Success of a 301 action need not mean genuine market opening. Compare a foreign market in which there are imports, but few from the United States, with a market that is completely closed to imports. The political costs to the foreign government of complying with the demand to buy U.S. goods are likely to be lower in the former case than the latter. The result of the 1985 Section 301 claim that South Korea unfairly restricted its insurance market was initially merely to guarantee a larger share of the Korean market to the two U.S. insurance firms already operating in Korea; only later was the market opened to other U.S. firms and firms from other countries (Cho 1987).

Another prediction from the model is that Section 301 will tend to have a large effect when U.S. welfare, as perceived by the U.S. negotiators, would rise markedly following the foreign country's compliance with the Section 301 demands. In such cases it is rational for the foreign negotiators to accede to the U.S. demands, for they can predict that the U.S. negotiators will be prepared to bargain hard. The U.S. bargaining position is made strong by picking sectors where a change in the trade status quo would give the United States a large gain, measured by the yardstick being used by the U.S. decision makers.

The lesson from our simple game is that there are multiple determinants of bargaining power in international negotiations. Section 301 actions are likely to be successful in achieving the U.S. negotiators' aims if they are addressed at countries with small counterretaliation ability; at countries that would suffer significant harm from having their access to the U.S. market limited; and at sectors where, in the view of the decision makers, both potential gains to the United States are high and compliance costs for the targeted country are low.

If the United States chooses 301 actions according to these criteria, will 301 advance social welfare? The first two criteria—that the targeted country have little ability to counterretaliate and that it would suffer high costs if the United States invoked its threat to retaliate—are irrelevant to the existence of any social gains from a 301 action. The third criterion—that the potential gains to the United States be high and the compliance costs within the foreign country be low—ensures the existence of social gains from a 301 action only to the extent that the U.S. and foreign negotiators are seeking to advance social welfare, broadly defined. Thus there is no guarantee that the sectors chosen for 301 action—selected on the grounds of likelihood of negotiating success—are sectors in which potential social welfare gains are high.

The very existence of Section 301 might cause a change in the volume of world trade. Bhagwati and Srinivasan (1976) model a country that fears it might have future trade restrictions invoked against its exports, with the restrictions being more likely the more it currently exports. Its optimal anticipatory policy is to impose a tariff on its imports, so as to shift its domestic resource allocation away from the production of exports; thus both its exports and its imports are reduced, and world trade contracts. This model assumes a period-by-period balance of trade, and so does not account for the possibility that the country is running a chronic balance-of-payments surplus. By law, Section 301 is implemented only if there is a marked bilateral trade imbalance. If the Bhagwati-Srinivasan model were modified to encompass such a case, the optimal policy would be different, as the country could increase its imports without decreasing its exports. In fact, according to the USTR, Super 301 has caused a liberalization of trade. To avoid being named in the first Super 301 list of priority countries, it is reported, South Korea and Taiwan took steps to increase their imports from the United States (USTR 1989).

International trade negotiations are usually conducted according to the norm of reciprocity: one country rewards another country's concessions by concessions of equal value (McMillan 1989). Like Section 301, reciprocity is based on mercantilist reasoning: the belief that exports are a good thing and imports are a bad thing. In GATT negotiations, when across-the-board tariff reductions are negotiated, the reciprocity rule has the advantage that it produces outcomes consistent with liberal trade—witness the success with which tariff reductions have been achieved under GATT. Section 301, focusing on particular sectors of the economy, lacks reciprocity's fortunate feature of aligning the goals of mercantilists and free traders.

4. Efficiency Aspects: Bargaining Frictions

It is a nontrivial puzzle to understand how rational people could ever cause a negotiation to end inefficiently, when efficiency is evaluated from the perspective of those involved in the negotiations. By definition, an outcome is inefficient if there exists an alternative that would make some or all of the participants better off and none worse off. How is it possible that such an alternative is not adopted?

Modern bargaining theory offers one potentially important source of inefficiency. The model discussed in the preceding section depicted the bargainers as being fully informed. If, instead, the bargainers have private information, then they will seek bargaining advantage from it. Various game-theory models show that it is rational to pursue the strategic gains from private information so far as to risk either a breakdown of the negotiations or a costly delay in reaching agreement.[6]

In trade negotiations, each country is likely not to know exactly what aims the other's decision makers are pursuing, and therefore not to know the minimum they will agree to. The benefits to the United States from opening the foreign market are likely to be more accurately estimated by the U.S. negotiators than the foreign negotiators; and similarly the costs to the foreign government of complying with the U.S. demands might be better understood by the foreign negotiators than the U.S. negotiators (Feenstra and Lewis 1988). This source of potential inefficiency is present whether or not Section 301 exists; but it is conceivable that Section 301 has exacerbated the potential losses from informational frictions. Invoking Section 301 increases the stakes in the negotiation and may result in longer delays to agreement or more frequent disagreements, as the negotiators try to squeeze extra bargaining advantage from their private information.

Another source of bargaining breakdown is the pursuit of the bargaining power that comes from the ability to commit oneself to one's demands, first and most vividly described by Schelling (1960). A game in this tradition that has some of the flavor of Section 301 negotiations is offered by Crawford (1982). This can be described as a game of rational brinkmanship. It can be thought of as another divide-the-dollar game. Initially, each bargainer decides whether or not to commit himself to a demand, and what demand to commit

---

6. Asymmetric-information bargaining games are surveyed by Binmore and Rubinstein (n.d.) and Wilson and Kennan (1988).

himself to. Each simultaneously announces his demand to the other. The commitment is not completely irrevocable: after making it, each learns how much it will cost him or her to undo it (but does not learn the opponent's cost of backing down). Finally, each chooses whether to stick to his or her commitment or to back down. There are four possible outcomes in the second round. If the two bargainers have chosen positions that are consistent, agreement is reached; in particular, if one is committed while the other is not, the committed bargainer gets all that is demanded. But if both are committed to demands that are incompatible, an impasse occurs. The main result from this model is that rational behavior creates a positive probability of breakdown, even though there exist feasible agreements that both bargainers would prefer to the impasse: the bargainers can be stuck in a prisoners' dilemma. Thus everyone could be made better off if the use of these strategies were eschewed.

Crawford's model is relevant to Section 301 if U.S. commitment evokes a countercommitment from the targeted country. What is the nature of the bargainers' commitments in the trade negotiations context? The targeted country can write its position into legislation, so that acceding to U.S. demands would require the passage of new legislation. Politicians can further commit themselves by stirring up domestic protectionist sentiment. Their cost of backing down is the loss of their political capital. It is plausible that they do not know, at the outset, how strong the public's feelings over the foreigner's trade practices will become, and therefore what the political cost of backing down on the trade demands will be; moreover, the size of this cost is likely to be more accurately known to the home government than to the foreign negotiators. Thus the model seems to fit the facts: for example, it seems to describe the U.S.-Brazilian 301 negotiations over Brazil's informatics policy (Felder and Hurrell 1988; Odell 1989; Odell and Dibble 1988). If both countries attempt commitment, the model shows that a chance exists that, even if everyone behaves rationally, the United States will be forced to carry out its threat to introduce punitive trade restrictions.

Common sense says that the likelihood of breakdown is low when the cost of disagreement is high. Unfortunately for common sense, Crawford shows that the strategic interactions means that this is not necessarily true. A change in the disagreement outcome causes changes in the costs and benefits of attempting commitment to particular positions. For some configurations of the model, these strategic effects can result in each bargainer rationally taking a less extreme position when the disagreement outcome for one of them worsens, making impasse less likely. Another apparently commonsense result—that impasse is less likely when it is more difficult for either party to maintain commitments—also does not hold in this model. The United States might try to implement Section 301 only in cases in which impasse is unlikely. But this model warns us that it is no simple matter to choose such actions, since the probability of breakdown depends, in a complex and nonintuitive way, on the parameters of the negotiation.

A further consideration is the effects of Section 301 on the stability of the trading system. In all of the models considered so far it has been assumed that an agreement, once reached, will be maintained: there exists some mechanism for enforcing contracts. International agreements, however, have only weak enforcement mechanisms. International trade law relies on *lex talionis*. The main guarantee that an international agreement will be maintained comes from the ongoing nature of international interactions. The cost of reneging now is suffering future sanctions from the affected trading partners. In other words, cooperation arises because the players are in a repeated game.[7]

A well-known result in game theory is that cooperation can occur when a game is repeated; an equally important, but often forgotten part of this result, however, is that cooperation need not occur. Repeated games generally have many equilibria, only some of which involve the players behaving cooperatively. Other equilibria are inefficient (Aumann 1981). Any cooperation that arises from the repetition of a game is fragile. The system can instead be stuck in a low-level equilibrium.

A change in strategy by one of the players, such as implementing Section 301, will upset an existing equilibrium. There is no guarantee that the new equilibrium that emerges, after all the players have chosen their new strategies in response, will be efficient, even if the old one was. And the bigger the initial change in strategy, the more likely it is to upset the system's stability. This is just a different way of stating the point, familiar enough in trade-policy discussions, that there is a danger of retaliation breeding further retaliation (Milner, in this volume). A danger from aggressive bargaining strategies is that they risk upsetting the delicate balance on which the very ability to make international agreements rests.

No country, including the United States, is completely innocent of trade practices that could justifiably be labeled by some country as unfair. A targeted country can easily find some U.S. practice that is contrary to the spirit or letter of GATT laws, and retaliate against this practice. In the model in section 2, which assumed agreements were fully enforceable, retaliation had a purely distributive affect: it determined which of the efficient outcomes would be agreed to. But with the imperfect enforceability of international agreements, retaliation can create inefficiencies. With retaliation and counter-retaliation, the global trading system could unravel to a grossly inefficient equilibrium. The suggestion of Hudec (see chap. 4 in this volume) that the United States should make itself subject to the same standards as Section 301

---

7. For more on repeated games as the enforcement mechanism for international agreements, see McMillan 1986 and 1989.

imposes on other countries is one way of reducing the likelihood of retaliation getting out of hand.

An implication of the divide-the-dollar game in section 2 is that the stronger the threat, the more effective it will be. But this is subject to a reductio ad absurdum, providing a warning against pushing simple models too far. Why stop at trade retaliation? Why not extract the maximum bargaining advantage by threatening nuclear attack? The incorporation of bargaining frictions into the analysis shows why stronger threats are not necessarily better, for they may increase the likelihood of bargaining breakdown.

These three kinds of bargaining frictions—generated by asymmetric information, commitments, and counterretaliation—do not, of course, necessarily occur. Sometimes a new agreement is made immediately after Section 301 is invoked. Examples of this are Taiwan's 1986 agreement to change the basis of its customs duty calculations one week after the President directed the USTR to propose Section 301 retaliation and South Korea's 1986 agreement to reduce its barriers on importing U.S. motion pictures and television programs in order to avoid a Section 301 investigation. Bargaining frictions did arise in the case of the EC's subsidies of canned peaches, over which there were lengthy Section 301 negotiations (USTR 1986, 293–94). The 1985 Section 301 action against the Brazilian computer industry produced acrimonious negotiations (Felder and Hurrell 1988; Odell and Dibble 1988). In the Section 301 action against various European countries' subsidization of specialty steels, the U.S. threat was carried out: the United States imposed quotas and higher tariffs (Baldwin 1988, 84).[8] These bargaining costs—the lowered welfare when the threatened trade restrictions are actually imposed—should be taken into account in any evaluation of the costs and benefits of Section 301 and Super 301.

5. Conclusion

Extrapolating from some simple game-theoretic models, this paper has suggested that invoking Section 301 will tend to shift the terms of agreement in the United States's favor. This shift will be larger (*a*) the greater the harm to the targeted country from having its access to the U.S. market limited; (*b*) the smaller the targeted country's ability to harm the U.S. in retaliation; (*c*) the smaller the costs within the targeted country of complying with the U.S. demands; and (*d*) the greater the benefit to the United States—in the U.S. negotiators' perception—from the demanded liberalization. But these deter-

---

8. Indirect evidence on how prevalent bargaining frictions can be comes from a type of negotiation for which much more data exist, labor negotiations. The inefficient outcome—a strike—occurs in about 15 percent of contract-renewal negotiations in U.S. manufacturing industry (Wilson and Kennan 1988).

minants of the success of a Section 301 action do not identify the areas where the social gains from freer trade are largest. Thus there is a tendency to direct Section 301 actions at the wrong targets. Section 301 increases bargaining frictions: attempts to exploit the bargaining power that comes from either private information or commitments can lead to costly delays to agreement or even the possibility of a complete breakdown in the negotiations. And the use of retaliatory strategies can upset an existing global equilibrium and lead to counterretaliation.

Appendix

Because a simple proof of the Binmore-Rubinstein-Wolinsky result stated in section 2 is not readily available, a proof is given here (following Shaked and Sutton 1984). We seek a subgame-perfect equilibrium: as well as requiring that actions be rational, this requires that the beliefs themselves be rational. For beliefs to be rational, they must stand up to a series of questions of the sort: "Given what I believe he is going to do, what must this mean he believes I will do? But then what must he believe that I believe he will do?" And so on through a possibly infinite chain of beliefs about beliefs. Beliefs are rational if no contradiction is exposed in this chain of reasoning.

To find the subgame-perfect equilibrium, it turns out to be necessary for the bargainers to look three stages ahead. Suppose the game has reached stage 3 without agreement. Now it is bargainer A's turn to make the offer. Define z to be the most money that bargainer A can induce bargainer B to let him have in the third stage. Thus, by definition of z, bargainer A rationally demands z and bargainer B rationally agrees.

Now imagine we are in the second stage and mimic bargainer B's reasoning. What can he offer bargainer A that A will accept? Bargainer B knows that bargainer A knows that he, A, will get a utility level of rz if he forces the bargaining into the third stage. But bargainer A also knows there is a probability, which we shall denote p, that the bargaining will break down between his rejection of the offer and the start of the third stage, in which case he would get only f_a. Hence bargainer A will be willing to accept less money than z in the second stage. By rejecting B's offer, A takes a gamble: he gets utility rz with probability $(1 - p)$ (that is, the probability that there is no breakdown) and f_a with probability $p;$ thus he gets, on average, $(1 - p)rz + pf_a$ upon rejecting the offer. The monetary equivalent of this is $(1 - p)z + (pf_a)/r$. B correctly reasons that this is what he must offer A in the second stage; this leaves B with the remainder of the \$1, that is, $[1 - (1 - p)z - (pf_a)/r]$.

We go further back now, to the first stage. By parallel reasoning, A deduces that from his point of view the best offer to B is something less than what B would get by waiting until the second stage; B is willing to accept precisely $\{(1 - p)[1 - (1 - p)z - (pf_a)/r] + pf_b\}$. So A rationally asks for the difference between \$1 and this amount, or an amount of money $1 - \{(1 - p)[1 - (1 - p)z - (pf_a)/r] + pf_b\}$.

The final step in the argument is to observe that the third stage, once it is reached, looks exactly the same to both bargainers as the first stage did: there is still \$1 to divide; it is A's turn to make an offer; and there is an infinite stream of potential stages still ahead. Thus the best A can do in the first stage must be the same as the best A can do in the third stage, once the game reaches it. In other words, z must equal $1 - \{(1 - p)[1 - (1 - p)z - (pf_a)/r] + pf_b\}$. Solving this for z, we find that, from the \$1, A gets an amount of money $z = [1 + (1 - p)f_a/r - f_b]/(2 - p)$, or an amount of utility $[r + (1 - p)f_a - rf_b]/(2 - p)$. As the probability of breakdown p approaches zero, this approaches the expression given in the text.

REFERENCES

Aumann, Robert J. 1981. "Survey of Repeated Games." In *Essays in Game Theory and Mathematical Economics in Honor of Oskar Morgenstern,* ed. V. Bohm and H. H. Nachtkamp. Mannheim: Bibliographisches Institut.

Baldwin, Robert E. 1988. *Trade Policy in a Changing World Economy.* Chicago: University of Chicago Press.

Bhagwati, Jagdish N. 1988. *Protectionism.* Cambridge, Mass.: MIT Press.

Bhagwati, Jagdish N. 1989. "U.S. Trade Policy at the Crossroads." *The World Economy* 12, no. 4:439–79.

Bhagwati, Jagdish N., and Srinivasan, T. N. 1976. "Optimal Trade Policy and Compensation under Endogenous Uncertainty: The Phenomenon of Market Disruption." *Journal of International Economics* 6:317–36.

Binmore, Ken, and Rubinstein, Ariel, N.d. "Noncooperative Bargaining Models." In *Handbook of Game Theory with Economic Applications,* ed. R. J. Aumann and S. Hart. Amsterdam: North-Holland, forthcoming.

Binmore, Ken, Rubinstein, Ariel, and Wolinsky, Asher. 1986. "The Nash Bargaining Solution in Economic Modeling." *Rand Journal of Economics* 17:176–88.

Cho Yoon-Je. 1987. "How the United States Broke into Korea's Insurance Market." *The World Economy* 10:483–96.

Crawford, Vincent P. 1982. "A Theory of Disagreement in Bargaining." *Econometrica* 50:607–38.

Dasgupta, P., and Maskin, Eric S. 1989. "Bargaining and Destructive Power." Discussion paper no. 1432, Harvard University.

Ellsburg, Daniel. 1975. "The Theory and Practice of Blackmail." In *Bargaining: Formal Theories of Negotiation,* ed. O. Young. Urbana: University of Illinois Press.

Feenstra, Robert C., and Lewis, Tracy R. 1988. "Negotiated Trade Restrictions with Private Political Pressure." University of California, Davis, unpublished paper.

Felder, Ellene A., and Hurrell, Andrew. 1988. *The U.S.-Brazilian Informatics Dispute*. Washington, D.C.: John Hopkins Foreign Policy Institute.

Hudec, Robert E. 1989. "Thinking about the New Section 301: Beyond Good and Evil," University of Minnesota Law School, unpublished paper.

McMillan, John. 1986. *Game Theory in International Economics*. New York: Harwood.

McMillan, John. 1989. "A Game-Theoretic View of International Trade Negotiations: Implications for the Developing Countries." In *Developing Countries and the Global Trading System*, ed. J. Whalley. London: Macmillan.

Maskus, Keith E. 1987. "The View of Trade Problems from Washington's Capitol Hill." *The World Economy* 10:409–23.

Odell, John. 1989. "International Threats and Internal Politics," University of Southern California, unpublished paper.

Odell, John, and Dibble, Anne. 1988. "Brazilian Informatics and the United States: Defending Infant Industry versus Opening Foreign Markets." Center for International Studies, University of Southern California.

Schelling, Thomas C. 1960. *The Strategy of Conflict*. Cambridge, Mass.: Harvard University Press.

Schelling, Thomas C. 1984. "The Strategy of Inflicting Costs." In *Choice and Consequence*, ed. Thomas C. Schelling. Cambridge, Mass.: Harvard University Press.

Shaked, Avner, and Sutton, John. 1984. "Involuntary Unemployment as a Perfect Equilibrium in a Bargaining Model." *Econometrica* 52:1351–64.

Smith, Adam. 1952. *An Enquiry into the Nature and Causes of the Wealth of Nations*. Chicago: Encyclopedia Brittanica.

USTR. 1986. *National Trade Estimate: 1986 Report on Foreign Trade Barriers*. Washington, D.C.: U.S. Government Printing Office.

USTR. 1989. "Fact Sheet: 'Super 301' Trade Liberalization Policies." Washington, D.C.: USTR.

Wilson, Robert, and Kennan, John. 1988. "Strategic Bargaining Models and Interpretation of Strike Data," Stanford University, unpublished paper.

Part 3
Trading Partners'
Reactions to 301

CHAPTER 7

Super 301 and Japan

Makoto Kuroda

When the original form of the Super 301 provision first made its appearance
in the U.S. Congress amid the debate surrounding the drafting of the omnibus trade bill, it was frequently asserted that the provision was devised
with Japan in mind and was being drafted for the purpose of countering
Japanese impediments to trade. Then in May, 1989, when priority countries
and priority practices were designated as required by Super 301, some
people in the United States commented that if Japan had been excluded from
designation, a new trade act targeted solely at Japan would have been enacted. These lines of thinking show that there is no denying a very close connection between the enactment of Super 301 and U.S.-Japan trade relations
and trade problems.

By implication, Section 301 seeks to impose clear damage to the relationship between our two countries. Further, it diverts attention away from
what the United States should do to improve its global trading picture. This
chapter attempts to evaluate Super 301 from the standpoint of Japan—the
country most closely bound up with the development and implementation of
the clause. The chapter also considers possible future responses to Super 301
on the part of Japan and other U.S. trading partners.

I. U.S. Policy Direction and the Problems It Presents

Several observations can be made about Super 301. First, the principal danger
of the clause is, of course, its unilateral nature, which stands in conflict with
the current world trading system: that of multilateral discipline and disputes
objectively judged through a multilateral body, namely the GATT. But it must
be admitted that Super 301's provisions do not in themselves give any indica-
tions of a completely new line of thinking in U.S. trade policy. There is, in
fact, a substantial history of U.S. policy veering toward and away from
unilateral action in trade. The second observation is that it is clear that at least
certain key figures in the U.S. government are fully aware of the dangers of

unilateralism at the root of Super 301. Years of discussion about the legal and policy problems posed by 301's unilateral power have already taken place in both the executive and legislative branches of the U.S. government.

The conception of unilateralism inherent in Super 301 germinated in the insertion of Section 301 in the Trade and Tariff Act of 1974, but did not assume a relatively concrete form until September, 1985, when the Reagan administration announced its "New Trade Policy" by declaring that it would make active use of the procedures detailed in that provision and other trade remedy legislation. Previous to 1985, the U.S. government served the role of arbitrator in trade matters. The self-initiation of the DRAM (semiconductor) dumping case in 1985, with the United States serving as both judge and prosecutor, marked a new era of unilateral trade policy.

This "blame thy trading partner" policy was clearly the outcome of the political situation in the mid-1980s—an increasing trade deficit and Democrats critical of a nonexistent Reagan trade policy. Consequently, several questions had arisen in the minds of the administration: first, whether the trade deficit was something to tackle seriously, and if so, how to do it, and second, how to crack down on trading partners who employed practices that seemed not to conform to U.S. and multilateral notions of fairness.

U.S. policy became a mixture of two objectives: the improvement of the overall trade account and specific targets in specific industry cases, the latter mostly focused on Japan. Subsequent to the Plaza Accord, Congress continued to rewrite U.S. trade law. The passage of the 1988 omnibus trade bill included tougher provisions for the existing Section 301 and added the Super 301 clause and numerous other provisions similar in character to Super 301 to cover additional areas such as the protection of intellectual property rights and telecommunications trade. The fundamental concepts behind these provisions, clearly, were nothing new to U.S. trade policy.

The U.S. policy direction symbolized by Section 301 and its like has elicited numerous criticisms from other countries, and provoked debate within GATT and other forums. The Japanese government reacted to the recent application of Super 301 to Japan with the statement that the provision could do nothing but harm to the multilateral free-trade system that underpins the world economy, and that it had no intention of negotiating with the United States under the auspices of the clause. This stance is in line with the views of other nations, and it is also my personal view.

The danger of the U.S. approach can be easily imagined. The most likely scenario is a situation in which other nations resist the United States by employing 301-like provisions against their trading partners. The dire consequences of such "mirroring" are immediately obvious, but serve to illustrate several important points.

What if the EC was to assert that the U.S. patent system is discriminatory and should be repealed since it takes "first inventing, first served" as its premise for Americans and "first applying, first served" as its basis for dealing with foreigners? What if Central and South American countries were to insist that U.S. restrictions on sugar imports are clear impediments to trade and demand their removal? What if Japan and Taiwan were to claim that the U.S. requirement for voluntary restraints on machine tool exports are harmful to domestic industry and demand compensation? Would the United States enter into negotiations with these trading partners? If the United States decided not to make the required concessions and these countries responded with counter-measures or sanctions against U.S. imports without recourse to GATT procedures, what would become of the world free-trading system?

The logic behind Super 301 is currently not accepted by the rest of the world, so we are several steps away from this type of confrontation. The United States is able to enforce Super 301, despite criticism from the world community, because it is an economic superpower that other countries are highly dependent upon. This show of force is ill-timed, however. The very nature of the interdependence that has enabled the U.S. to promote its will is shifting. For many countries the relative dependence on bilateral relations with the United States is gradually declining. If the United States does not wake up to this fact and maintains its present trade policy direction, it is easy to envision the world adapting quickly to the new rules of the game. An EC version of Section 301 would occur first, followed shortly by many other nations.

It must also be remembered that larger countries have some bargaining power with the United States through initiating retaliation or accepting punishment, but smaller countries have no such recourse. This disparity of power creates an antagonistic atmosphere in which it is difficult to conduct calm discussions.

In short, the U.S. asks its trading partners to jump through hoops it would not itself attempt, and uses increasingly precious leverage to promote destructive new rules of the game that it naively hopes others will not consider using. This entire process is occurring in a progressively hostile and re-criminatory atmosphere that could clearly impede rational multilateral initiatives.

Nevertheless, perspicacious individuals within the U.S. government seem to recognize this danger, and seem to be seeking to deflect attention away from Super 301 while taking pains to ensure that the provision is applied to its minimum extent. This tactical position seems reflected in the fact that the May, 1989, official announcement of priority countries and practices did not use the word *unfair*. In fact, U.S. Trade Representative Carla Hills obviously tried not to provoke undue reaction by consciously avoiding that term as well as avoiding any mention of automatic retaliation in official statements.

Also, the targets chosen from numerous candidates seem to indicate that the United States is looking for some quick victories. Certain observers believe that the designation of priority countries and practices will again be limited next year to points on which the United States believes it can win, even if those are discussed under GATT auspices.

If the momentum of Super 301 can be held in check this way, and the simultaneous implementation of appropriate economic policies leads to progress in adjusting trade balances, it may be possible to avoid the worst-case scenario described above. Even granting the efforts of these individuals however, the problems inherent in Super 301 will not be resolved.

In respect to the application of the clause to Japan, going through the motions, however gently, is not the correct approach. The degree of media and public awareness of the implications of Super 301 are too well developed. We know that Japan is labeled, for all intents and purposes, an unfair country and that we are slated for automatic retaliation. The explanation that the administration is duty bound to apply legislation enacted by Congress, regardless of its implications, does not wash. In the case of bad legislation such as this, there should be efforts made to either abolish it or ensure that it will not actually be applied. Some say that if Japan had not been designated, worse things could have come from Congress. But what punishment could be worse? Japan has been named as if it were an enemy of the United States.

Japan and other countries that have been or will be targeted under Super 301 should stick to their stance of not negotiating under the framework of Super 301. Japan is open to listening carefully and, if necessary, negotiating on problems with trading partners, even if these discussions are outside international agreements, so long as they are outside the Super 301 framework. We try to accommodate our trading partners as much as possible. But we will not address the issues raised by Super 301 in negotiations associated with the clause, because we will not sanction a 301 process, artificial, messy, and short term as it is, being imposed upon trade talks.

II. The Roots of Super 301: Misperceptions of Economic Realities

What has caused the irritants to U.S. trade policy that lie behind the appearance of Super 301? The American trade policy in place today stems from a misreading of current economic events. Special attention should be given to understanding the perceptions of economic realities held by the U.S. Congress and the authorities in charge of trade policy that invited the emergence of Super 301. This, along with a careful look at the economic situation of the two countries, gives a clearer reading of the context of Super 301.

When discussing trade between the United States and Japan something that is frequently confused is whether the central focus should be on trade imbalances or on market access. Understandably, officials responsible for trade policy become seriously concerned about both of these problems, although from the standpoint of economic policy, the methods that these officials should adopt in order to realize these two policy goals ought to be entirely different. The trade imbalance and market access issues have been intermingled during the trade discussions that have taken place between the United States and Japan for the past year or two; or, to express this more skeptically, one is forced to conclude that the two have been intentionally confused in some cases.

For example, Ambassador Carla Hills has stated that the bulk of the U.S. trade deficit is a macroeconomic problem and that the problem with the balance of trade cannot be improved through trade policy or through the Super 301 provision. What is more, even Congressman Richard Gephardt has said that 70 or 80 percent of the trade deficit results from macroeconomic problems. On the other hand, it is frequently asserted in Washington that Japan is a special case, evidenced by the fact that neither exchange rate adjustments nor demand adjustments are preventing the persistence of the country's huge trade surplus, and that instead of employing macroeconomic policies, Super 301 must be applied across the board in order to remove the trade imbalance with Japan. To remove confusion we should therefore separately examine the problem of the U.S. trade deficit and the problem of market access in Japan.

The U.S. Trade Deficit

In 1981, when President Reagan took office, the United States recorded a $28 billion trade deficit with the rest of the world and a $16 billion deficit with Japan. By 1987 those totals had surged to a $153 billion trade deficit with the rest of the world and a $56 billion deficit with Japan. Within the United States and in the U.S. Congress, this rapidly widening deficit stimulated mounting distrust of the Reagan administration's trade policies and a swelling chorus of criticisms aimed at Japan. Without doubt this set the scene for the appearance of Super 301.

Nevertheless, it is not readily apparent that the present U.S. trade deficit warrants such a great degree of anxiety. Furthermore, the use of retaliatory measures for trade, embodied in the Section 301 approach, will certainly prove a fruitless method of resolving that deficit.

People who are concerned about the U.S. trade deficit fear that an accumulated deficit will invite an unmanageable build-up of debt, and that the inflow of foreign capital arising as a result of trade deficit will be used to buy up U.S. assets. In fact, the U.S. economy today has achieved almost full employment, and it is the United States's own excess demand, borne of economic strength, that is bringing about the trade deficit. Thus, it is not convincing to assert that domestic industry and employment are being damaged by the trade deficit.

What is problematic about the trade deficit is the anxiety and fear aroused by the corollary inflow of capital. But in the context of the current situation, is the inflow of capital and the resultant indebtedness really at such a crisis point? In 1988 the United States's external indebtedness exceeded $500 billion, as a result of which the country is frequently described as being the world's largest debtor nation. This is a misnomer, however, arising as a result of understating the value of the United States's long-term holdings of foreign assets, notably foreign direct investments by American firms. In fact, there was a net surplus on U.S. receipts and payments of investment earnings in 1988. This means that, last year at least (1988), the value of U.S. holdings of assets overseas remains larger than the United States's external obligations.

Usually surpluses and deficits in merchandise trade accounts draw attention, but little is known about services trade. How are these investment flows reflected in U.S. or Organization For Economic Cooperation and Development (OECD) statistics? Investments made in Japan by American corporations 30 to 35 years ago are only now being partially cashed in—Honeywell, Chrysler, and General Motors are just three examples of this trend—so U.S. investment in Japan may look negative in 1989. The figure will not reflect the enormous profits gathered from these investments. Shouldn't we stop publishing merchandise trade statistics, unless there are similarly detailed statistics on other transactions such as investments and services?

In light of this situation, the problem for the United States is not dwelling on deficits, but determining the possible future course of these net external obligations, and assessing whether or not they will be manageable.

There is reason to be optimistic about the future, springing from the fact that the ratio of the United States's current account deficit to its GNP has dropped sharply from its peak of 3.4 percent in 1987 to 2.8 percent in the second quarter of 1989. The wealth of the U.S. economy is approximately $36 trillion at the end of 1987, overwhelmingly greater than that of any other nation, and was still growing at a speed of over $2 trillion every year during the 1980s. Compared to this, the ratio of net external obligations this year seems either extremely small or nonexistent. Further, the speed at which external obligations are increasing is far smaller than the speed at which the wealth of the U.S. economy is growing.

If the wealth of the United States grows at the present yearly rate of $2 trillion and the ordinary trade deficit at the rate of $200 billion, then the ratio of U.S. external obligations to the national wealth reaches only 8 percent even after 100 years, and never even exceeds 10 percent. Furthermore, the ratio of the current account deficit (equivalent to the increase in external indebtedness) to GNP is continuing to trend downward, and so there is absolutely no question of the U.S. payment of debt and investment earnings becoming an excessive burden.

Moreover, over the past two to three years the U.S. budget deficit has peaked and is trending downward, the net personal savings rate has turned upward, and the increase in consumption has assumed only modest proportions. In other words, the recent inflow of capital into the United States has arisen as a result of robust U.S. investment due to the attractions of the high rate of expected earnings in the United States.

In the past there have been many countries whose current account deficits were very large in relation to GNP: Japan, Taiwan, Korea, and Singapore are examples, as are Mexico and Brazil. Some of these became surplus countries—the example of Korea, which suffered chronic current account deficits until around 1985, should be borne in mind—while other countries ground to a halt, strapped by massive indebtedness. The basic cause of this disparity was that in Taiwan and Korea, for example, the capital inflow took concrete shape in the form of increased productive capacity, which prevented the emergence of a supply-demand gap and positioned these countries to meet future growth in demand, whereas in Brazil and Mexico this type of productive investment was lacking. Given these precedents, if the inflow of capital into the United States is utilized for productive purposes it is nonsense to say that the present deficit constitutes a problem.

The 1986 revisions to the U.S. tax structure brought major improvements to the economy by encouraging investment in the United States and generating housing construction and consumer spending. The amount of investment that strengthens production capabilities has also been growing gradually. Provided there is not another rapid widening of the budget deficit and investment opportunities for the private sector are not undermined, we will see progress being made in enhancing productive capacity and, with that, a narrowing of the current account deficit. If policies to encourage productive investment in the United States are introduced, this scenario would accelerate.

In this context, it is sensible to view capital inflows from Japan as a contribution to the revitalization of the U.S. economy. The expansion of the U.S. economy in the early 1980s was carried out under the economically extraordinary conditions of super-high interest rates and huge fiscal deficits. The expansion, which occurred without causing a lack of private investment money or reinflation, was made possible, to a considerable degree, by foreign money in the form of capital inflows. As a complement to the relatively small amount of available domestic investment capital in the United States, capital inflow from overseas was necessary or perhaps inevitable. The important point is to pay attention to whether such money was effectively used, not to question the origin of the inflow itself.

Japan's own trade balance can be taken into account at this point. Permit me to use yen values to focus on the reality of the Japanese economy and to avoid describing the disturbances caused by exchange rate fluctuations. Japan's present trade surplus with the rest of the world is approximately ￥ 10 trillion, while in 1980 Japan had a trade deficit of ￥ 3 trillion. This means that Japan's trade shifted toward a surplus to the tune of ￥ 13 trillion during the 1980s. Now, taking a look at the imports of fuels and materials, the import of oil decreased by ￥ 10 trillion from ￥ 13 trillion in 1980 to ￥ 3 trillion in 1988. Further, the total fuels and materials imported decreased in value ￥ 13 trillion: from ￥ 21 trillion in 1980 to ￥ 8 trillion in 1988. Thus, it is apparent that the decrease in the imports of fuels and materials became the trade surplus of Japan. It is essential to realize that Japan's surplus is linked with fuel imports, not just bilateral terms of trade, sentiment, or emotion.

At the end of 1973, when the first oil shock occurred, Japan's terms of trade worsened greatly. A period of adjusting the Japanese economic structure to aggravated trade conditions began, with prices of primary products increasing rapidly from that point until the second oil shock. Here the great difference between the U.S. and Japanese financial circumstances should be noted. The Japanese yen is not a key currency and the Japanese economy cannot be an investment haven for the people who want to maintain the value of their assets. Therefore, market forces tend to work rapidly, with Japan's policy positions quickly reflected in current account balances. In the 1970s, the terms of trade worsened quickly, reflecting the price increases of primary products.

Concurrently, a strong force existed to compensate for this economic pressure through the increase of Japanese exports of manufactured goods. Japan's economic and industrial structures changed accordingly and the appreciation of the dollar in the early 1980s also worked to support this structure. In other words, Japan's present economic and industrial structure has been formed in the course of fifteen years with the aim of adjusting itself to the cheap yen and expensive primary products. Even though in the early 1980s everyone believed the yen was undervalued, it took almost five years for currency adjustment to take place.

After the Plaza Accord, Japan's economic structure changed rapidly again, but this has been only a four-year process so far. Structural changes have not yet caught up with the new environment and it is inevitable that there is still a considerable amount of trade surplus. Oil prices and exchange rates can change rapidly in the short term, but the real economy cannot change in a day.

In the United States it is conceived that Japan is a strange country since, even with appreciation of the yen, the bilateral deficit has not shown any significant changes. Europe is used as a comparison because changes did show up in European-U.S. bilateral trade flows. However, statistics show that U.S. exports are increasing much faster to Japan than elsewhere, and this is indeed a reflection of the new exchange rate regime. U.S. exports to the world were still going up in 1989, and U.S. exports to Japan are growing at even a faster rate than that.

It must also be remembered that the relative rate of change in the Japanese economic structure is very high. Manufacturing industries are relocating their international production bases rapidly and the aging of the Japanese demographic structure is also rapidly progressing. Thus, neither of the U.S. nor the Japanese external imbalances will probably last long, and this is a source of optimism. The structure of trade is highly developed and apparently beneficial overall: it should be the subject of careful and unemotional analysis as a basis for policy decisions.

Access to Japanese Markets

The other reason offered to support Super 301 is that "although Super 301 is not the last resort to solve the trade imbalance problem, it is a means to open foreign markets. The problem lies in the lack of access to the Japanese market." This is a blatantly untrue assertion.

First of all, before the Plaza Accord, the U.S. dollar was greatly overvalued and exports from the United States could not compete in the international marketplace. The exchange rate that reflected proper U.S. purchasing power (though it is preferable to avoid using this concept since there are various meanings and understandings of purchasing power), was said to be 170 to 180 yen to the dollar. At that point the actual rate was 240, handicapping by approximately 30 percent the real competitiveness of American export goods. Under such conditions, it is no wonder that imported goods from the U.S. were uncompetitive, regardless of the degree of openness of foreign markets.

After the Plaza Accord, as the exchange rate adjusted, Japan's imports expanded rapidly. The average yearly import expansion rate from 1986 to 1988 exceeded 20 percent and for manufactured imports exceeded 30 percent. Expansion rates of imports from American sources were 31 percent in 1988, and 19 percent in 1989 so far—higher than any other developed nation in the world. Incidentally, the expansion rate of merchandise imports by the United States as an average for the five years before the Plaza Accord was around 20 percent, meaning that the current import expansion rate of Japan is far higher than the United States's was at a time of "peak import penetration." With such an import expansion rate, how can the Japanese market lack access? If it is claimed that the market lacks access, then the U.S. market in the early 1980s should be considered to have lacked access too.

It should also be noted that Japanese enterprises are making great efforts to adjust structurally to exchange rate fluctuations and other environmental changes. The decline of energy prices and import prices reduced the average input price level of Japanese manufacturers by approximately 20 percent, and they are taking further actions in order to maintain their competitiveness in the world marketplace. A well-balanced conclusion concerning Japanese market access cannot be made without paying attention to these fundamental changes as well as the balance of trade.

Some may claim that Japan's import expansion rate is naturally high because the absolute level was so small. Others may claim that Japanese merchandise imports as a ratio to GNP did not go up at all and have stayed at a low level. However, the ratio of total imports to GNP to Japan in the first half of 1989 is approximately 7.1 percent: this is larger than the American historical standard of approximately 6.5 percent in and before the 1970s when the U.S. trade account was roughly balanced. Total imports by the United States as a ratio of GNP is currently slightly larger than 9 percent, which is larger than the historical standard.

Japan's ratio of manufactured goods imports to GNP is running at 3.8 percent in 1989. It is true that this is a smaller figure than Europe's or the United States's, but this number has been growing pretty fast recently. Furthermore, it should be noted that such figures take into account factors such as the distance to other countries that have similar industrial structures, which determines the pattern of horizontal division of labor between countries. Such factors may explain why the manufactures import ratio of the United States is approximately only one-third of that of European countries. Does it make sense then to use that comparison to say that the United States is less open than these European countries?

If product import ratios are to be used to criticize Japan's trade practices, Japan can also use statistics selectively to illustrate various points. For example, on a per capita basis, U.S. exports to Japan are 50 percent higher than U.S. exports to the EC, and U.S. exports of manufactured goods are at an almost equal level to both Japan and the EC. Does this not imply that the EC is as "unopen" as Japan is alleged to be? Such forms of argumentation can never lead to meaningful dialogue and fruitful conclusions.

Attention should be paid, instead, to recent progress rather than spending time on pointless debate. Japan's imports are growing the most rapidly in the world, and U.S. exports to Japan are increasing even more rapidly. These facts seem to show that the macroeconomic measures taken in 1987 and 1988 have, in fact, been very effective. Even when evaluated from a results-oriented viewpoint, which Americans seem to prefer despite its lack of economic sense, these figures seem to show the good performance of policies. If we neglect these achievements and try to pursue different but wrong policies, the results would be hazardous.

III. Adopting the Proper Perspective

Super 301 and the recent U.S. unilateral trade policies are not realistic or effective measures to solve existing trade and economic problems. However, what is of great concern is not the statutes themselves, but the fact that an emotional confrontation may be building between the people of the United States and Japan over their use. This could lead to the adoption of even less effective or realistic U.S. trade policies.

The media reporting on these questions, and on Japan's alleged sins, is seriously distorted. It is also rapidly disseminated by foreigners. We are unfortunately slow to respond to this flood of charges. Part of the problem is also our belief that eloquence doesn't bring a gold medal, silence does: for example, there is a traditional belief that talking about one's own hard work is unnecessary and even indiscreet, because the level of a rice harvest is believed to expose the level of work put out. But surely Japan is not the odd man out here. If a society is stable and traditional, silence is given more weight.

Thus, elementary communication between our two countries is not so easy because we are very different. The United States was created by those with different social backgrounds from different countries who wanted to be Americans. The articulation of their individual positions was quite routine—not so in Japan and Europe. We have to learn to deal with Americans since they are unique and strange. On the other hand, our intentions and aims are difficult for you to discern. We can articulate them more clearly if you wish, but that may cause new conflicts. Going by U.S. standards, this may be a positive development in our relationship, although it might have to wait. Gradually the export of information and intentions will be promoted by a newer, more linguistically facile generation of Japanese.

Japan has been fairly lucky—the appreciation of the yen and a substantial decline in commodity prices, especially oil, have moved in tandem with economic growth. It seems to Americans that Japan is twice as big all of a sudden, but without the exchange rate conversion, the change is not as dramatic; the real growth of Japan between 1982 and 1987 is identical to that of the United States. Still, U.S. perception is driven by this. In Japan things don't seem terribly different and there is still an awareness that the oil price and exchange rates can change again overnight. Americans must remember that even as economic conditions change rapidly, traditions, culture, and language acquisition do not.

As discussed above, the economies of both countries changed for the better in 1987 and 1988. The ever-expanding U.S. trade deficit and Japan's trade surplus are reaching a turning point: America's exports and Japan's imports are expanding rapidly. These improvements are apparently related to Japan's domestic demand expansion policy in 1987 and U.S. actions to hold down the fiscal deficit. They are evidence that such macroeconomic policies are firmly effective. Despite the existence of such evidence, why does the United States try to go in different directions, rather than attempting to solve problems through this existing policy mode?

This is not to say that the Japanese fail to understand the political situation in the United States. But political situations exist everywhere, including Japan. Certainly there has been intense political revulsion in foreign countries toward U.S. trade policies since Section 301 began to be used more frequently. In light of the efforts the United States has been making to promote world economic and political development, is it sensible to adopt policies reflecting short-term political pressures, policies that are not even adequate to the taxes imposed on them?

The crucial case of this self-defeating exercise is the Uruguay Round. If the United States would like to discuss market access questions, there exists a suitable forum in GATT. The U.S. government has repeatedly expressed its support for the multilateral, free-trade system, and made efforts to strengthen GATT. The adoption of a unilateral trade policy by the United States obviously contradicts the basic position of the U.S. government, and will largely undermine U.S. leadership at GATT negotiations.

As trade tensions have mounted, Japan's own position on using GATT is shifting slightly, as can be see in Japanese resistance to U.S. allegations on semiconductors. That retaliatory action had begun to be contested through the GATT system, but was stopped. Japan did not call for a panel at that time because of concern that using this tactic may bring up an agriculture issue, and no country wants to appear hypocritical. Now Japan is moving toward the idea of using the GATT framework.

Calmer heads must prevail at this stage. Officials who clearly understand what their country's long term national interests are must take over. What they must do is decide whether trade and access problems actually do exist and, if so, to think of ways to solve them without bias and without interruptions caused by political pressures. In such delicate circumstances, neither side should resort to the excuse that "political situations do not allow it." Too much is at stake for short-term, political factors to be allowed to dictate trade policy and related issues between Japan and the United States.

Now the two countries are engaging in bilateral talks on domestic problems under the heading of "Structural Impediment Initiatives." This discussion has very special features because both sides are making suggestions that would have previously been considered to be undue interference in each others' domestic affairs. This can become a useful exercise if it is recognized that increasing interdependence between countries now requires a better understanding of each others' systems and moves must be made toward harmonization of those systems to the maximum extent possible. In this sense, it would be wise to put Europe and Asia into the scope of such talks, which would also serve the purpose of making the discussion more objective and less emotional.

Commentary

Henry R. Nau

In his contribution to this conference, Makoto Kuroda makes four points that I would like to respond to: (1) that the new features of Section 301 of the U.S. trade law can only do harm to the multilateral free-trade system, (2) that the trade problem in U.S.-Japan relations is not lack of access to the Japanese market, (3) that U.S. trade and budget deficits are on their way to solution, and (4) that all countries have their domestic politics. Taken together, Kuroda's points are too sanguine about the direction of macroeconomic policies in the United States and Japan and too pessimistic about the prospects for domestic, bilateral, and multilateral trade negotiations.

301 and the Multilateral Free-Trade System

In May, 1989, Carla Hills, the U.S. Trade Representative, stated that, "Super 301 and Special 301, like other trade tools at our disposal, will be used to create an ever expanding multilateral trading system based upon clear and enforceable rules."[1] Kuroda, on the other hand, says that Section 301 can do nothing but harm to the multilateral trading system. How can two reasonable people disagree so completely on the likely effects of Super 301 on the multilateral trading system?

The fact is, of course, that the jury is still out on the consequences of 301 for the free trading system. At this point, in my judgment, it is impossible to say whether 301 is good or bad. As I have argued elsewhere, unilateralism is not always bad.[2] It depends on where it takes the system. In the case of Super 301, it can be argued that negotiations in spring, 1989, leading up to the

---

1. See Statement of Ambassador Carla A. Hills, Office of the U.S. Trade Representative, Executive Office of the President, May 25, 1989.

2. See *International Reaganomics: A Domestic Approach to the World Economy,* Significant Issue Series, vol. 6, no. 18 (Washington, D.C.: Center for Strategic and International Studies, 1984); and Henry R. Nau, *The Myth of America's Decline: Leading the World Economy into the 1990s* (New York: Oxford University Press, 1990). Robert Hudec makes the case for unilaterally breaking the law of GATT in his contribution to this volume.

identification of priority practices and countries in late May achieved significant further opening of foreign markets, particularly in the case of South Korea. At the same time, as Robert Hudec points out in his chapter in this volume, the 301 provision, prior to revisions in the 1988 trade bill, resulted in U.S. retaliation or market closing steps on seven different occasions (six in response to treaty violations and one against unreasonable practices), and the revised provisions may bring about more frequent retaliations because of its strict deadline requirements.[3] So far, however, the United States has applied the provision very sparingly, as Kuroda himself notes. On balance, therefore, 301 has probably opened rather than closed markets—at least so far.

It is true that such tough unilateral bargaining may tempt other countries to adopt similar policies. But this is true of all policies in trade negotiations. It could just as easily be argued that by running a trade surplus, Japan is encouraging other countries to do the same. That is exactly what countries tried to do with their beggar-thy-neighbor policies in the 1930s.

On the other hand, all trade surpluses, like all 301 actions, are not necessarily bad. For the past couple of years, Germany has run a trade surplus with its EC neighbors; this has served the interests of the latter countries as well as those of Germany. German surpluses have been the mechanism by which excess savings flowed from Germany to other EC countries and fueled industrial restructurings in France, Italy, Spain, and other countries. To some extent, Japanese surpluses have served the same purpose in the United States. Excess savings have moved from Japan to the United States to fuel a remarkable economic expansion that is going into its eighth year at the time of this writing and has involved, as Kuroda correctly points out, a resurgence of American investment and productivity, particularly in the manufacturing sector. U.S. productivity growth rates in manufacturing have averaged 3.9 percent annually throughout the decade of the 1980s, some 50 percent higher than manufacturing productivity growth (2.7 percent per year) during the postwar boom years of American economic hegemony from 1948 to 1973.

Trade surpluses, like 301 actions, have to be evaluated in context. The difference between Germany's surpluses with Europe and Japan's surplus with the United States is that the German surplus is accepted, while the Japanese surplus is not. Germany's surplus is viewed as serving the interests of all countries, Japan's is not, at least not by many groups in the United States. This raises a big question for Japan. Why is this so? It has nothing to do with discrimination, as some Japanese may be inclined to think. It has, rather, to do with the larger purposes that Japan is perceived to be pursuing. Germany is pursuing common objectives with its EC partners toward closer economic,

---

3. See Hudec's chapter in this volume.

monetary, and eventually political union. Its larger purposes and internal social and political purposes are well understood and widely accepted by its partners. Japan, unfortunately, is not perceived to be pursuing common objectives but narrow, self-interested, mercantilist objectives, and its internal social customs and political processes are still poorly understood in foreign countries. Some of this is due to Japan's own attitudes toward foreigners. And it raises a larger issue of access to Japan which goes well beyond access to the Japanese market.

Access to the Japanese Market

Kuroda is particularly offended by arguments that Japan's market is closed. There is some statistical evidence to support his view. As he notes, Japan's import-to-GNP ratio in the first half of 1989 was 7.1 percent, somewhat, but perhaps not significantly, below America's average of a little more than 9 percent, and that the ratio of product (manufactured goods as opposed to commodities) imports to GNP, although low, is rising—according to Kuroda, to 3.7 percent in 1989. But in 1987, Japan's manufactured imports amounted to only 2.8 percent of GNP, compared with 7.5 percent in the United States and 14.8 percent in Germany.[4] To be sure, as Kuroda notes, there are structural factors that account for some of these differences. (Australia and New Zealand have similarly low ratios.) But price and other realities suggest that there are still formidable informal obstacles to imports into Japan. Recent studies conducted jointly by Japan and the United States in the context of the SII found that, with respect to some 122 products, prices were higher in Japan than in the United States on 84 of these products and, in many cases where Japanese prices were competitive, the products were not widely available in Japan, confined to special discount stores or novelty shops.[5]

The best evidence that Japanese markets are still not fully open are the view of an increasing number of Japanese citizens themselves. Japanese consumers are clamoring for more foreign goods and more convenient and price-competitive distribution outlets. And some Japanese producers, especially the smaller ones, are up in arms about the bidding practices of large Japanese firms that practically give away products to win government procurement contracts.[6] These are the same practices that discriminate against foreign firms in the Japanese market.

Japan is becoming a more open market. Let there be no mistake about

---

4. See OECD, *Economic Surveys: Japan 1988/1989* (Paris: OECD, 1989).

5. *Washington Post,* November 8, 1989, sec. A.

6. Recent examples involved a Fujitsu and NEC bidding as low as one yen (less than a U.S. penny) for several local government contracts. *Washington Post,* November 2, 1989.

that. Unlike revisionist views of Japan, I do not conclude that Japan is so different from the United States that it can never change significantly. Let Japan continue to increase manufactured imports at a rate of 30 percent per year, as it has for the past several years. In a decade, that will make a significant difference. But Japan still has a way to go. It cannot take refuge in structural or cultural differences. Even if Kuroda is right about Japan's market being fully open, why do trade policy officials the world over not believe it is open? Apparently, Japan is failing utterly to explain itself effectively or convincingly to the rest of the world.

Indeed, the fact that foreigners believe Japan is still insufficiently open and Japan cannot understand why they believe this to be the case illustrates the huge gap that remains in making Japan transparent to the rest of the world. This point goes beyond the specific statistics that may indicate that the Japanese market is open, at least in terms of conventional tariff and nontariff barriers. It concerns the fact that Japan is known worldwide far more by its external commercial interests than by its external or internal social purposes or political personality. Japan exports commercial products, but not clear and acceptable political purposes. It has a stunted profile internationally. Foreigners see its dynamic economic power, yet understand little about its society, politics, or culture. And, curiously, Japanese tell us little about these aspects of their national life. We learn about Japanese society from foreign journalists, not from best selling books by Japanese authorities.[7] In the largest sense, Japan is not open enough for the world to get to know it, for foreigners to get inside Japanese society, to touch it, feel it, absorb it, and become comfortable with it. Some of this, to be sure, is the fault of foreigners. The United States and other Western countries have made too little effort to get to know Japan. But the burden of responsibility lies with Japan. With power comes obligation, an obligation to justify and legitimize power, an obligation to make foreigners feel that Japan cares about them, about the world, about the system. Japan, in my view, faces a much larger challenge to its world role than simply opening its trade markets. It needs to do the latter too, but, as the trade barriers become more informal and less tangible, it also needs to give foreigners more access to the society in general.

Japan does not have to export its culture, as the United States has done during its period of economic power. Many Japanese consider their culture unique and, therefore, not exportable. But Japan has to import greater understanding of its culture. That means it has to open up to foreigners all around— its schools, universities, neighborhoods, trade associations, farming commu-

---

7. A case in point is the highly critical analysis of Japanese society offered by the Dutch journalist Karel van Wolferen, *The Enigma of Japanese Power* (New York: Alfred A. Knopf, 1989).

nities, etc. Japan should spend some of its huge trade surplus on a massive "Get-to-Know-Japan" campaign—bringing foreigners to Japan for extended stays, teaching foreigners Japanese, bringing exchange students to Japan, and sponsoring sister cities and sister community relations. Here is where Germany has built up a much greater bank of political capital and credit in Europe—capital that softens and humanizes its economic power and capital that it may now need to draw upon as it reasserts its national interests in East Germany and Eastern Europe. Japan has much less political goodwill in the bank. It should start collecting some now. It is Japan's fault as much as that of the United States that it lets its openness be measured primarily in terms of technical trade barriers rather than a broad acceptance of foreign access and involvement in Japanese society.

It bothers me, therefore, that Kuroda and other Japanese officials and businessmen do not see this larger issue of openness. For even if the trade balance were righted, the issue of Japanese political leadership and Japan's social openness to the world would remain. No great power can command respect through its economic presence alone.

U.S. Trade and Budget Deficits

The importance of a nation's role going beyond its economic power is illustrated today by the policies of both the Soviet Union and the United States. With his economic house in bankruptcy, Mikhail Gorbachev has been able to appeal to the liberal political values in both the Soviet Union and Eastern Europe that have won him the acclaim of the rest of the world. Similarly, the United States, despite its relative decline in economic power, is witnessing the spread of its democratic and pluralist values such as it has never seen before, even when it exerted much greater political and economic dominance. The purpose of wealth and power (whether the latter are used for liberal or illiberal ends) seems to be as important to the people of the world as wealth and power themselves.[8]

This point needs to be recalled by the American people, who have been entertained recently by cynics characterizing America as just another great power in decline.[9] For America's purposes are not constrained by trade and budget deficits; rather, trade and budget deficits reflect American purposes for much of the 1980s. America was much more concerned about reducing the role of government in the economy—by both lowering taxes and deregulating—and increasing the role of government in defense than it was about

---

8. On the role of national purpose as well as wealth and power, see Nau, *The Myth of America's Decline*, especially chap. 1.

9. See, for example, Paul Kennedy, *The Rise and Fall of the Great Powers* (New York: Random House, 1987).

government or national borrowing. The result was that we invested more than we saved and thus ran an unprecedented current account deficit during the decade. Japan and others accommodated our deficits, both because, as Kuroda notes, borrowed money was often used to boost productivity in the United States, and because other countries continued to accept American political leadership.

But substantial borrowing from abroad and stimulation of consumption and investment activity in the United States can continue without inflationary consequences only if the United States retains excess productive capacity, which it has done since the recovery began in 1983, at least until recently. Today, however, the economy has reached nearly full employment. Now, the United States must add to productive capacity at a pace consistent with demand pressures and the availability of supplies (e.g., labor, etc.), or it can expect prices to rise. The budget and current account deficits, therefore, have become potentially damaging to the American economy—that is, threatening excess demand—only in recent months just as most American economists and other commentators have concluded, after years of forecasting disaster because of the deficits, that the deficits are being resolved and no longer threaten America's economic future.

Kuroda joins this group of sanguine forecasters when he argues that U.S. macroeconomic policies are on track and, if sustained, will prevent any swelling of the current account deficit and damage to American industry and employment. It is true, as he points out, that macroeconomic policies in both Japan and the United States took a turn for the better in 1987–88. The current account imbalances of both Japan and the United States have narrowed somewhat as a consequence—Japan's surplus from 4.3 percent of GNP in 1986 to an estimated 2.5 percent in 1989 and America's deficit from 3.1 percent in 1986 to an estimated 2.4 percent in 1989.[10] But the adjustments have not been commensurate with the enormous realignment of exchange rates that has occurred between the dollar and yen (and other currencies, such as the deutsche mark). Current exchange rates, therefore, may not be sustainable in the absence of further adjustments. The U.S. current account deficit, for example, has declined in absolute terms from 1987 to 1989 by only 13 percent (from $144 billion to an estimated $125 billion), although the dollar has depreciated on a trade weighted basis since 1985 by approximately 50 percent. The reason: the United States has failed to reduce absorption in its economy. At nearly full employment, the budget deficit remains 3–5 percent of GNP (the higher figure if you exclude the social security surplus and include the off-budget expenditures for the rescue of the savings and loan industry). Private

---

10. IMF, *World Economic Outlook,* (Washington, D.C.: IMF, 1989), 105. Other data in this section also come from this source.

and public investment remain too high given the level of public and private savings in the economy. Either the United States increases savings by boosting private savings and/or reducing public dissavings (i.e., the U.S. budget deficit), or it must reduce investment. There are no other alternatives. The current account deficit cannot be lowered by trade protectionism, as many in Congress appear to believe, or by further depreciation of the dollar, as some economists advocate, unless these measures increase U.S. savings or decrease U.S. investment. If savings remain the same (i.e., no lowering of the federal budget deficit and no increase in private savings), these measures will most probably reduce investment, either by recession or by inflation.

With fiscal policy immobilized, hopes for avoiding either a recession or inflation in the United States focus increasingly on monetary policy. Already in 1989, the administration and the Federal Reserve Board were locked in repeated quarrels over monetary policy—the administration concerned about recession and seeking lower interest rates, the Fed concerned about inflation (and the value of the dollar) and cautious about lowering interest rates. This tension will only grow in the Congressional election year of 1990. The strain on monetary policy from the fiscal deficit is probably greater than it has been since 1981–82 when the emerging fiscal deficit undoubtedly compelled the Fed to pursue a much tighter monetary policy to lower inflation than would have been otherwise necessary, driving the economy in that period into a steep recession.

Hence, I do not see the continued improvement in the U.S. fiscal and current accounts that Kuroda predicts. Nor do I believe Japan can rest on the laurels of its own macroeconomic policy adjustments. While the macroeconomic policy changes have been more substantial in Japan than in the United States (for example, real total domestic demand, which had to increase in Japan to reduce the current account surplus, grew from an annual rate of 4.1 percent in 1986 to 7.7 percent in 1988; while this demand in the United States, which had to decrease to reduce the U.S. current account deficit, stagnated at an annual rate of 3.3 percent), these changes have not been matched by sufficient microeconomic or structural adjustments to permit Japan to import more manufactured goods. Informal barriers to imports, most important Japan's overall reluctance to let foreigners penetrate its society and culture, remain substantial.

All Countries Have Domestic Politics

Thus, the domestic political struggle must go on in both Japan and the United States to achieve greater economic policy adjustments and preserve open international markets. Indeed, as Kuroda rightly argues, all countries have domestic politics and such politics cannot become an excuse for unilateral or bilateral trade policies that damage the free trading system (the danger with 301, at least potentially). But to avoid unilateral or bilateral solutions, the critical fronts on which the two countries must progress are domestic policy and the Uruguay Round. Sadly, Kuroda is complacent about the direction of domestic policy and says very little at all about the Uruguay Round.

The Uruguay Round of multilateral trade negotiations is scheduled to peak in 1990. It offers a means to influence domestic politics in such a way that export interests increasingly gain advantage over import-competing or protectionist interests.[11] It turns attention to opening foreign markets and potentially pits export interests that stand to gain from trade concessions abroad against import-competing interests that might prefer to see retaliation or closing of home markets (since they have little to gain from opening foreign markets). The struggle between these interests is currently focused on 301. But 301 promises too few gains for export interests to turn the battle against import-competing interests. As Kuroda correctly notes, even if the United States got everything it wants in the current bilateral negotiations with Japan, it would increase U.S. exports, at most, by $5 billion, assuming the United States got 100 percent of the relevant Japanese markets. A more realistic estimate would probably be about $2 billion. The current bilateral trade imbalance between the United States and Japan is more than $50 billion. Thus, 301 is valuable as a trade liberalizing inducement only if it can leverage opening of markets more generally. That can happen only in the multilateral trade round. The potential stakes for exporters have to be raised, and only the opening of all foreign markets, not just selective ones through 301, can raise these stakes sufficiently to permit export interests to defeat powerful import-competing pressure groups (e.g., in textiles).

In terms of their own interests, therefore, both Japan and the United States should focus less on 301 than on the Uruguay Round (and domestic economic policy). Japan should test American motivations behind 301 by proposing market-opening initiatives in the Uruguay Round that support the interests of its own exporters as well as those of other countries. For example, if Japan has political difficulty with its import-competing agricultural sector (which it clearly does), why not propose bargains in the Uruguay Round for its industrial exporters (e.g., phasing out of voluntary export restraints and other export-restricting measures on Japanese exports in automobiles and electronic products, as import liberalization measures are phased in, in agriculture) that lead these exporters to come out even more strongly against

---

11. For a full development of this argument, reflected in case studies of eight countries (United States, EC, Japan, and five key developing countries—China, Korea, Brazil, India, and Mexico), see Henry R. Nau, ed., *Domestic Trade Politics and the Uruguay Round* (New York: Columbia University Press, 1989).

Japanese agricultural policies? (Keidanren, the industrial trade organization in Japan, has already come out in principle against the maintenance of Japan's protectionist agricultural markets, including the sensitive rice sector.) This is the kind of intersectoral bargaining that becomes appropriate and feasible in the end phases of multilateral trade negotiations.

For its part, the United States should take similar initiatives designed to strengthen exporter enthusiasm in the United States for the final package coming out of the Uruguay Round. It should also make clear that the United States will discipline the use of unilateral (e.g., U.S. antidumping and countervailing duty laws) and bilateral (e.g., 301) measures if the Uruguay Round results in satisfactory outcomes for overall U.S. interests (i.e., not the interests of every specific sector that 301 encourages). In fact, the United States should go so far as to state clearly that it will suspend Super 301 and Special 301 provisions of U.S. trade law for several years and ultimately for good, if the Uruguay Round ends successfully. Some in Congress may have even anticipated such a possibility, since the mandatory deadlines and action provisions of the Super 301 measure apply only to 1989 and 1990 and would have to be renewed to apply beyond December, 1990, the date for the completion of the Uruguay Round.

Conclusion

In sum, it is time for both the United States and Japan to come back to the main problems affecting their bilateral trade and broader political relations. These problems are the necessary further adjustments of domestic macroeconomic policies, particularly in the United States, and microeconomic structures, principally in Japan. If it is unrealistic to expect much progress in these areas in 1990, with Congressional elections in the United States and perhaps a reelected but weakened Liberal Democratic Party (LDP) government in Japan, the two countries should focus on achieving far reaching and successful market-opening results in the Uruguay Round. If these multilateral negotiations are carried out effectively, they will help to strengthen market forces in both countries that may then facilitate further domestic adjustments in macroeconomic and microeconomic policy areas. In any event, this strategy promises much greater potential benefits for both countries (not to mention the rest of the world) than the current preoccupation with Super, Special, and ordinary 301.

Commentary

Hugh T. Patrick

Makoto Kuroda, former MITI Vice-Minister for International Economic Relations, has something of a reputation for being unusually frank and, at times, combative. I appreciate the stimulating and provocative views he presents in his chapter; they force us to listen and to think, if not always to agree. Although he speaks only for himself, I consider his comments to be reflective of much current Japanese thinking; his chapter provides a nice lightning rod in framing the issues I consider here. We need to hear and understand much better the full range of Japanese views. While silence may be golden to the Japanese, as Kuroda intimates, the lack of Japanese explanations of their behavior, goals, and views is doing Japan a real disservice at a time when the policies of the United States and other nations are fueled by ignorance and misperceptions about Japan. This is not to say that knowledge will make these problems go away; the problems are substantive and real. Yet knowledge is essential if the United States is going to make good policy decisions rather than bad.

My purposes here are, first, to comment on some of the specific issues raised by Kuroda, and, second, to expand on them by making several, more general comments on the political economy of the U.S.-Japan economic relationship. I argue that while Kuroda makes a number of valid and important points, he is (perhaps self-servingly) optimistic, and ignores the broader political economy realities of the bilateral relationship that have shaped the passage and implementation of Super 301.

Super 301 and Japan

The gist of Kuroda's argument is that Super 301 and related American unilateral trade policies are costly, ineffective, and unnecessary. They are costly because: they divert attention to, and indeed undermine, the Uruguay Round of GATT multilateral negotiations in this crucial final phase; they result in strong negative, at times emotional, reactions in Japan and elsewhere so as to diminish prospects for cooperation; and they invite retaliation as other countries engage in similar policies. They are ineffective because: even if successful, they will only marginally reduce the U.S. global and bilateral trade deficits; Japan and other countries will refuse to negotiate under the Super 301 rubric; and the EC and Japan, and perhaps others, will probably counterretaliate against any U.S. retaliatory actions. They are unnecessary because U.S. and Japanese macroeconomic and exchange rate policies *are* working to reduce their respective trade imbalances and to generate rapid increases in U.S. exports to the world and especially to Japan.

Kuroda implicitly dismisses as a dangerously short-run domestic political sellout the U.S. government position that Super 301 will indeed open foreign markets and that the United States had to take such unilateral actions to protect itself since the other major industrial nations had delayed in starting the Uruguay Round negotiations. Indeed, Kuroda's chapter combines a sanguine optimism about the future course of U.S.-Japan economic relations and implicit threats that Japan will, in the future, take issues to GATT or even counterretaliate against any future U.S. 301 retaliatory actions. He provocatively asks what could Congress really do, rhetoric aside, that could be worse punishment than designating Japan as an unfair trading partner, as many Japanese interpret the May, 1989, citing of Japan as a priority country for negotiations under Super 301.

Many American economists share a number of Mr. Kuroda's economic policy views. First, Super 301 is not a good instrument of policy: its unilateralism and potential use of retaliation by restricting imports go against the basic tenets of the GATT-based, open, multilateral trading system the United States has worked so hard to craft; and it gravely offends and invokes anger, resentment, and possible retaliation from America's trading partners. It substitutes U.S. power for mutually agreed-upon rules; that is neither a desirable nor a sustainable system. Second, the U.S. global trade deficit, and Japanese global surplus, are essentially separable though related macroeconomic phenomena to be resolved by macroeconomic policies. In essence, the United States spends more than it produces, invests more than it saves, and has to borrow from foreigners to cover the difference; and Japan saves and produces more than it invests and spends at home. Super 301 and other trade policies to open foreign markets or to restrict imports will make only a minor contribution to the reduction of the U.S. trade deficit. This basic truth has been well enunciated by Carla Hills, the U.S. special trade representative, and other administration officials. Third, focus on the U.S. bilateral deficit with Japan, large though it is, does not make economic sense in the context of a multilateral trade and payments system; it is most efficient to buy from the cheapest sources and to sell in the most profitable markets. It is a global, not a bilateral, balance that should be the objective of policy.

However, policy is not legislated and made in a vacuum. One of the important atmospherics in the debate leading to the 1988 Omnibus Trade and Competitiveness Act was that many congressmen intended Japan to be a major target. This is evident in the many legislative proposals that were directed specifically at Japan, as discussed elsewhere in this volume. Perhaps that is not so surprising.

After all, Japan had emerged in the 1980s as the most important economic and technological challenger (some would say threat) to the United States. Japan is by far the world's second largest economy; $500 billion bigger than numbers three and four (West Germany and France) combined. Japan, with the United States, is at the frontier of a far wider range of civilian goods technologies than any of the Western European countries. It has demonstrated immense competitive strength in a number of industries important to the United States—including automobiles, steel, consumer electronics, office equipment, and semiconductors. Japanese products, many of them brand name, are highly visible in the American market. Japan not only has developed an increasingly large global current account surplus but also a huge bilateral trade surplus with the United States, up to two-fifths of the burgeoning U.S. global trade deficit. And Japan suddenly emerged as the world's largest creditor, and main financier of America, at a time when the United States was rapidly becoming the world's largest debtor. Importantly, Japan has not been well known, much less understood; and Japanese behavior, practices, institutions, business and negotiating styles, and basic values have seemed even more different from the United States than they are in reality. Moreover, despite the clear evidence of declining and low Japanese tariff and quota barriers on most goods, the perception has become increasingly widespread that the Japanese market is somehow closed, and unfairly so.

Moreover, the way Japan had chosen to manage its trade issues with the United States over the previous decade must have contributed to the congressional perception that the Super 301 provisions would be a useful instrument for dealing with Japan. What lesson had Congress learned from the series of bilateral trade negotiations between American and Japanese officials from the 1970s on? First, the Japanese negotiators were not forthcoming; indeed, they were resistant to U.S. proposals (which always involved liberalizing changes in Japanese policy, without concomitant U.S. concessions). Only after the American negotiators pressed with increasing vigor and with threats of retaliation of one kind or another, in what was a lengthy and frustrating process, would Japanese negotiators make substantial concessions. Moreover, they never seriously threatened counterretaliation, and in the one case (semiconductors) where the United States did impose retaliatory tariffs on selected imports from Japan, Japan neither retaliated nor pursued the issue at the GATT. The lesson: set time limits in negotiating with Japan; be prepared to retaliate and have in place mechanisms to do so. The payoff: Japan would make concessions to open its markets and would not retaliate.

Apparently the administration in spring, 1989, felt it had no choice; it had to designate Japan as one of the priority nations with which to initiate negotiations under the Super 301 provisions. Otherwise it would lose credibility with Congress and face the prospect of aggressive congressional legislation aimed specifically at Japan. In practice, the USTR adopted a narrow interpretation of Super 301. It cited Japan for government procurement practices in satellites and supercomputers and for certain restrictions retarding wood products imports, three sectors that merited consideration in any event; and U.S. government officials were careful not to label Japan as an "unfair trading nation" despite that apparent intent in the 1988 Act.

Symbolically, however, this action was perceived in Japan as a major, qualitatively new and different attack by the United States. The Japanese press and general public not surprisingly deemed that its major ally now regarded Japan as an "unfair trading nation." Kuroda may be exaggerating only slightly when he says, "Japan has been named as if it were an enemy of the United States." Such resentment and recriminations have been expressed openly and vocally, by the Japanese government and by the public. It has exacerbated Japanese perceptions that America "unfairly" scapegoats Japan as an excuse, instead of solving what are essentially its own domestic problems. The U.S. Super 301 action against Japan, at the least, increased substantially the already high tensions in the U.S.-Japan relationship; it remains to be seen whether it has added a new and difficult dimension.

Of course, in pragmatic negotiating style, while the Japanese government refused to negotiate under the Super 301 rubric it agreed to consider these three sectors under existing bilateral negotiating arrangements. And Japan agreed to the SII talks outside Super 301 to consider long-run structural and institutional barriers to economic openness in Japan (and U.S. barriers to its own more successful economic performance, such as the federal budget deficit, U.S. private savings rates, corporate competiveness, and the like).

Japan's Trade Surplus

There are several important points to be made about the sudden emergence of Japan's huge trade and current account surpluses in the 1980s. First, Japan's industrial structure and export performance between 1973 and 1985 dramatically changed as a consequence of the first and second oil crises and the low exchange rate of the yen for most of the period. To simplify, in macro terms the Japanese economy geared up to generate enough exports to pay for needed imports predicated upon a high price of oil. Second, in fact the terms of trade have moved sharply in Japan's favor since 1980, and particularly since 1985 when the yen appreciated and oil prices (in dollars) dropped sharply. Kuroda's assertion that Japan's surplus since 1980 is overwhelmingly attributable to the sharp decrease in the yen price of oil and other minerals is only a moderate exaggeration. Third, sharp yen appreciation between 1985 and 1987 is bringing changes to Japan's economic structure that are still under way. Japan's current account surplus has declined from its peak, though more so in yen and real terms and as a percentage of GNP than in dollars due to the exchange rate measurement effects. The current account surplus peaked at $87 billion in 1987 and was about $57 billion in 1989; however, it is not at all clear that this measure will decrease much further in the early 1990s.

Much depends on the currency and base year chosen for comparison. For example, even though the yen appreciated 47 percent on a nominal trade-weighted basis between 1985 and 1988, Japan's trade surplus increased by $39 billion; yet Japan's export volume rose by 4 percent and import volume by 41 percent. In yen terms, Japan's trade surplus declined by ¥ 974 billion ($8 billion). If 1986 is chosen as the base year, then by 1989 Japan's trade balance had decreased by $20 billion (based on second and third quarter annualized data). Changes in Japan's trade surplus are well explained by conventional economic factors: demand growth in Japan and abroad; changes in relative prices and terms of trade; increase in export prices in dollar terms but decreases in yen terms (and decreases in the previously extremely high profits from exports); and relative unit labor cost behavior. The fact that in 1985 Japan's exports were 47 percent higher than imports (in dollars) has meant that imports must grow much more rapidly than exports to reduce the absolute trade deficit. [1]

Kuroda is probably too sanguine, and overly optimistic, in asserting that neither Japanese nor U.S. external imbalances will last long. As a percentage of GNP, Japan's current surplus will probably decline to a reasonable level (say about 1.5 percent) within a few years, though without a major increase in oil prices I doubt it will return to zero. More disquieting to some congressmen is that the absolute surplus measured in dollars is not likely to decline much farther; this, however, is a political rather than economic issue. However, I am much less optimistic about the willingness of U.S. policymakers to take the needed actions to result in a major sustained reduction in the U.S. trade and current account deficits soon.

Kuroda states the argument of some economists that the U.S. global trade deficit and attendant transfer borrowing is not a serious problem so long as those resources go into productive investment in the United States and that the

---

1. For a careful analysis, see Susan Hickok, "Japanese Trade Balance Adjustment to Yen Appreciation," *Quarterly Review,* Federal Reserve Bank of New York (Autumn, 1989): 33–47.

debt continues to be sufficiently small relative to GNP to be readily serviced. However, this misses the point: the problem is not one of economics, but of economic power. I share the common American political judgment that U.S. power is reduced by persistent current account deficits and increasing foreign indebtedness.

Moreover, Kuroda does not directly address the real and deep American unhappiness about the very slow decrease in the U.S. bilateral deficit with Japan. In large part that is because it is not an economic issue; however, as discussed below, it has become a major American political issue. Movements in the bilateral balance are well explained by conventional economic factors, supplemented by a more microanalysis of Japanese and American trade structures and sectors with declining competitiveness relative to imports. It is not surprising that Japan's recent major growth in manufacturing imports is of labor-intensive goods from developing countries, and that the bulk of American imports from Japan continues to be cars, trucks and parts, and a wide range of industrial electrical goods, from semiconductors, telecommunications equipment, and office equipment, to VCRs. Even so, U.S. exports to Japan have risen rapidly, more rapidly than to the world as a whole. The base year problem is particularly severe, however. In 1985, U.S. imports from Japan were 2.96 times its exports to Japan, so that exports will have to grow more than three times as fast as imports, or absolute levels of imports will have to decrease, in order for the bilateral deficit to decline significantly.

Access to the Japanese Market

Kuroda incorrectly and disengenuously dismisses the issue of access to the Japanese market out of hand. His basic argument is that, since 1986, Japanese total imports have grown rapidly (at more than a 20 percent annual rate), manufactured imports even more rapidly (at a rate of over 30 percent), and imports from the United States equally rapidly. This is correct, but it is not sufficient. Rapid growth rates from the very low initial base of imports, especially manufactured imports, are not particularly surprising or impressive. While Japan's import performance since 1986 is indeed very good and to be commended, the real issue is whether the amount of imports will continue to grow rapidly in the future.

Actually, Kuroda could have told a much stronger story about market openness, though in any advanced, complex industrial society including the United States, it is never a simple story. Every country has its distinctive features, yet, private enterprise, free-market democracies share essential commonalities. In many institutional respects, Japan and continental Western European countries are closer to each other than they are to the United States. In general, Japan is not an outlier, outside the range of OECD nations' institutional arrangements and economic behavior.

This is clearly the case in terms of governmental barriers to imports. Japanese tariff and quota barriers are low, below those of the EC.[2] As with the OECD countries in general, Japanese tariffs and quota restrictions on manufactured imports are very low, with occasional exceptional spikes of higher tariffs, as well as government procurement and other regulatory restrictions. Japan has imposed far fewer "voluntary" export restraints (VERs) on its imports than the United States and the EC. The percentage of imports affected by these and other nontariff barriers are marginally lower in Japan than in the United States, and considerably lower than the EC, though the measures are too crude to have great meaning. Japanese agriculture continues to be highly protected by quotas, tariffs, and state trading that imposes high domestic prices on consumers. Yet agriculture is so inefficient and unproductive that Japan is also the largest importing nation of agricultural exports. Even so, the total burden of restrictive agricultural policies on consumers and taxpayers as a share of GNP is higher in Japan (3.2 percent) than in the EC (2.6 percent) or the United States (1.6 percent).

There are, however, other arguments that suggest Japan's markets are less open to imports than analysis of official barriers would indicate. One commonly cited complaint is the still small share of imports, and especially manufactured imports, to GNP. The other is the persistence of high prices of many imports in Japan following the sharp yen appreciation; the reduction in yen costs has by no means been fully passed through to consumers.

Are Japan's imports, particularly of manufactures, "too low" in comparison with other advanced industrial nations? Is Japan an outlier in import performance? This is the question posed in empirical tests by Saxonhouse; Leamer; Bergsten and Cline; Balassa; Barbone; and Lawrence—studies that have attracted attention because of their policy implications. The results are contradictory. The recent evaluation by Srinivasan of the theoretical and econometric foundations of these studies find most are flawed, some seriously so.[3] There is no convincing evidence that the small share of imports in Japanese GNP is due to informal barriers against imports; the Leamer and Saxonhouse studies, which exonerate Japan from the onus of being a low-imports exception to the experience common to other countries, receive higher marks than other studies.

Srinivasan goes on to point out that even if such tests were done rigorously and correctly, and indeed did find that Japanese imports are "too low," the results would be difficult to interpret because the tests are only indirect. There is no way to know whether the results are due to a pervasive

---

2. For a recent evaluation of market openness comparing Japan, the United States, and Western Europe, see OECD, *Economic Surveys—Japan, 1988/1989,* (Paris: OECD, 1989), chap. 4. Note particularly tables 23, 24, and 25, from which the following data are drawn.

3. See Koichi Hamada and T. N. Srinivasan, "The U.S.-Japan Trade Problem," paper presented to the Columbia Conference on U.S. Trade Policy, September 8, 1989.

set of informal import barriers or myriad other possible explanatory factors. Importantly, as Bhagwati, Saxonhouse, and I have argued, it may well be that Japan imports too little on the average because it exports too little, since its exports (especially in automobiles, VCRs, and other products in which Japanese companies are highly competitive) have been held down by foreign barriers against them.

The persistence of high Japanese prices relative to world prices for traded or tradable goods is a more compelling concern. A number of recent studies have documented the degree to which domestic prices have, or have not, fallen as the yen appreciated. The explanations vary depending on the product. Government regulation is an important part of the story, resulting in high prices for food products, electricity, cigarettes, and the like. A high-price, low-volume, high-profit marketing strategy is pursued by some importers and indeed their foreign suppliers; yen appreciation gains have been taken as profits rather more than as an opportunity to compete through price reductions. We do not yet have clear understanding of these price effects. What are the time patterns of adjustment? Does Japanese price behavior under currency appreciation differ significantly from other countries? What are its causes? Why are Japanese consumers so quiescent in paying higher prices for their consumption basket than are people in most countries? I suspect consumer behavior in Japan, as elsewhere, is asymmetric: more quick to notice and respond to price increases than to potential price decreases that have not occurred.

Every country has its own deep-rooted structural impediments to more efficient economic performance; many impinge on imports. Japan certainly has many such impediments. They show up in two broad ways. The gap between efficient and inefficient sectors (agriculture, very small-scale production and distribution, unskilled labor-intensive manufacturing) is substantially wider in Japan than in the United States, though closer to Western Europe. More important, Japan, in contrast to the United States at the other extreme, is not an outsider-friendly society—even to other Japanese. It takes time and effort and skill to penetrate many Japanese markets even after the product is competitive in price and quality. The bilateral SII talks aim at reduction of fundamental barriers to market access in the long run, in principle in both countries, but in practice clearly aimed mostly at changes in Japan. In theory, such talks are desirable, but as discussions, not negotiations. In practice they are likely to be dangerous at a time when Congress is very impatient with Japan and seeks results as measured by a reduced bilateral trade deficit with Japan. Expectations that SII talks will produce such results in the short run are misplaced, as the USTR clearly understands and articulates but Congress at times may not accept. Over the longer run it may well make sense, as Kuroda suggests, to develop such discussions on a broader national participation basis rather than purely bilaterally.

The SII final report of June 29, 1990, was successful politically, and in providing a framework for further consideration of structural issues. The interim report in spring, 1990, together with successful negotiations on the three sectors designated under Super 301, made it possible for the administration not to renew its Super 301 priority designation of Japan in May, 1990.

Yet, to ask the question whether Japan's market is less open than, say, that of France, or of other major industrial nations is to miss the point. Even if Japan is not an outlier—not so different in trade behavior and performance from other industrial countries—that does not mean Japan should rest on its laurels and be lax in pursuing further market-opening policies. Neither Japan nor any other major industrial nation has eliminated all trade barriers. The commonly shared objective is to create a system of open, multilateral trade with a minimum of barriers, where those minimum existing barriers, such as national security, in turn are justified and transparent. In my view, countries with good growth, low unemployment, and a current account surplus have a special obligation to reduce their import barriers, though this has not yet been articulated as a formal rule for the international system (as Bhagwati has also argued should be done). This is the reason Japan should be eliminating its remaining trade barriers, not because its markets are "less open" (especially since the actual evidence on comparative degree of openness is unclear).

The U.S.-Japan Economic Relationship: A New Game

The United States does have a Japan problem, though many Japanese seem unwilling to acknowledge it. It is a problem of both reality and perception. And if the United States has a problem, then so, too, does Japan. The relationship is too important for either to ignore such concerns. Most important, the problem is new, qualitatively different, and much more profound than earlier problems in the bilateral relationship. The key lies in the new reality of Japan's comprehensive economic power and its external projection, particularly into the American economy. And, while economic transactions are typically a positive-sum game, power is relative.

This new reality is very simple: it is Japan's now-great economic power that creates the fundamental source of tension in the bilateral relationship. Note that the tension is generated in the United States, not Japan. It is the United States that is being challenged and is on the defensive. This is not because Japan is different or Americans are racists. It is not even because Japan as a nation exercises its economic power badly or wants to challenge the United States; on the whole, the Japanese government thus far has tried to accommodate Japan's growing economic strength to American national interests. It is simply that Japan has become an overwhelming global economic power, second only to the United States. Moreover this power is manifested disproportionately in the total sum of its bilateral economic relationships with the United States.

And it is the sum, synergistically greater than its parts, that makes Japan seem so economically powerful. Japan is now second to Canada as the largest source of U.S. imports, while remaining a distant second to Canada as a market for U.S. exports. By a substantial margin, Japan is first as the source of manufactured imports, first as the import source of automobiles, steel, semiconductors, machine tools, and consumer electronics. Japanese products are more visible in the American market than those from Canada or any other nation. Japanese businesses are a distant second to the United Kingdom in ownership of American business and other real assets; yet, it is more Japanese than British entrepreneurs that are perceived as "buying up America." It is in finance and technology that Japan is perceived as by far the most important foreign player.

To put it this way overstates the case for national economic power. No government can harness and focus its nation's economic power the way it can its military power. Market economies are highly decentralized. They are made up of myriad discrete individuals, families, companies, and industries, with private ownership of capital and finance, operating in private markets. There is no Japan Inc., nor any America Inc. Indeed, the huge U.S.-Japan economic relationship consists of multitudinous transactions among individual companies and persons; it is the interpenetration of these business relationships at the most microlevel that makes the economic relationship so beneficial and strong—and so costly to lose.

Given this new reality, how should the United States and Japan manage their economic relationship? Very carefully. And in ways different from the way it has been managed in the past. A key issue is not simply how to accommodate the Japanese economic powerhouse as the major new player in the world economy, but how to make Japan a responsible leader in the international economic system.

The American postwar paradigm for dealing with Japan is no longer valid. However, the paradigm has continued to dominate American policy formation until fairly recently, even as the conditions justifying it have been eroding. That paradigm was initially based on a patron-client relationship in which Japan was regarded as having a small and weak economy to be nurtured. By the 1970s, Japan, as a consequence of its rapid economic growth, came to be referred to as a junior partner in an alliance that was deemed of exceptional importance, as its economic performance made it an important new economic player.

Japan's very economic success, together with the relative slowing of U.S. economic performance, undermined and eventually made outmoded the basic economic assumptions of the postwar paradigm for U.S.-Japan relations. This was, however, an evolutionary process; its implications became clear only in the 1980s. Moreover, as noted, the recent major transformation of the U.S.-USSR relationship has substantially reduced U.S. security concerns, making its economic concerns and objectives even more important.

The United States is now debating two new, competing models to become the new paradigms for its relationship with Japan. These models can, somewhat simplistically, be labeled the revisionist model and the mutual dependence model. This is not the place to elaborate the logic of each model and assess their relevance in terms of how best to advance American national interests. Both differ in major respects from the earlier paradigm. To engage in such a debate is healthy, though recourse to "guilt by association" arguments rather than substance is appalling and should be rejected. We do need to evaluate the ideas of each model in terms of the American national interest. We have muddled along too long based on outmoded and inaccurate premises and perceptions. My prediction is that the mutual dependence, joint leadership model will win the day. Containment is too costly, and probably not attainable.

Yet, how the United States and Japan move from where they are today is unclear. The path certainly is difficult. Indeed, the U.S.-Japan economic relationship is fraught with danger. Both nations lack vision; both are beclouded by emotionalism and misperceptions. But beyond that, both nations have severe problems both in managing the relationship and in managing themselves. The great challenge in the relationship for the United States is whether it can learn how to share power as well as burdens with Japan. The respective national interests overlap but will not be identical; compromise will be necessary, but will be difficult for the United States. For Japan the crucial issue is what sort of vision it will develop of itself and the world; and how it will exercise power responsibly.

But perhaps the greater challenge lies within the domestic economic, political, and social order in each nation. For the United States, the great challenge is how to get its own house in order: raise the domestic saving rate; reduce the Federal budget deficit; improve the educational system; increase civilian, goods-oriented R&D; enhance corporate competitiveness; expand exports. For Japan, the domestic challenge is equally great and equally difficult: how to transform itself into an open society.

CHAPTER 8

Super 301 and the World Trading System: A Korean View

Chulsu Kim

Super 301 requires the U.S. Administration to condemn the whole trading regime of another country, usually a friendly country and a GATT contracting party. The advantages possibly gained by using this policy tool, I think, are more than offset by disadvantages such as creating resentment against U.S. products and jeopardizing the commercial interest that the United States hopes to promote. In terms of foreign policy, it creates problems for the United States in the designated friendly countries where the U.S. image will be hurt considerably. It also provides ammunition to elements that oppose close relations with the United States.

Furthermore, if this practice continues, other countries will begin to use the same policy tool, and they will have their own priorities and yardsticks. If all countries did that, it is quite obvious that the multilateral trading system would completely break down, and the law of the jungle would prevail.

Despite these objections, why then did Korea negotiate with the United States? It was clear in the early months of 1989 that the chances of Korea being designated a priority foreign country (PFC) appeared to be high. We think that Korea's reputation as an open market was, unjustifiably, not good. Because of the large and growing trade surplus we had with the United States, about $9 billion the year before, Korea was a likely target. The fact that the Korean import market had grown by nearly 30 percent in the previous three years, due to import liberalization measures taken since the beginning of the decade, ironically appeared to increase the probability of designation since the potential for further opening due to pressure seemed more likely. Our pessimistic assessment of the situation in the early months of 1989 was accentuated when, in March, in accordance with the provision of the law, U.S. industry filed trade complaints with the USTR. Of the thirty-nine submissions made, Korea topped the list with twenty-three.

Indeed, there were those in the Korean government who argued strongly that we should not make concessions to the United States even if we were designated a PFC. Since there were twelve to eighteen months to negotiate after designation anyway, Korea would lose nothing by waiting until May 30, the original deadline. But after careful and exhaustive deliberations at home and extensive informal contacts with the USTR, Korea opted for the negotiation route.

There were several reasons and motives why we made such a conscientious and sober decision to seek a negotiated settlement. First and foremost, it was clear that the PFC designation would have fueled anti-Americanism at home. In the tumultuous process of democratization in Korea, anti-Americanism was gaining ground, particularly among radical students. We had, clearly, an important stake in seeing that such a movement was kept in check.

Second, the designation would have jeopardized our own liberalization effort, probably one of the fastest in the world at the time. Except in the field of agriculture, less than 1 percent of manufactured products were subject to nontariff barriers in Korea as of January, 1989. The average tariff rate was 12.7 percent on all products; scheduled to go down to 7.9 percent by 1993 according to a five-year autonomous tariff reduction schedule approved by the National Assembly. And in the field of agriculture, Korea's trade regime was not more restrictive than that of some industrial countries. How could we defend and pursue our liberalizing policies at home when our foremost trading partner branded us an "unfair trader"? The political consequences of having been so designated would have been highly detrimental to the trade-liberalizing achievements already made in Korea and our ability to continue that progress.

Third, the designation would have created tremendous commercial uncertainty. Given the overriding importance of the U.S. market for Korea, commercial certainty had to be preserved for Korean traders as well as for U.S. importers of Korean products. We, of course, could have negotiated after designation, but we felt that the damage would begin to occur at the time of designation.

Fourth, we genuinely believed that the branding of Korea as an "unfair trader" would be unfair. Thus, it was a challenge and opportunity for us to prevent or at least mitigate this unjustifiable stigma in the United States. Many of the industry complaints lodged against Korea in March, for example, were based either on inaccurate and outdated information or false charges that could be easily repudiated.

I would argue that the agreements themselves represent the policies that were already being pursued by the Korean government and would have been accomplished perhaps a year or two later in the absence of Super 301.

The officials of the two governments met and negotiated on three major issues of concern to the United States: namely, agriculture, localization, and foreign investment policies in Korea. In the field of agriculture, where Korea has serious sociopolitical difficulties, we held firm except for a few tariff cuts and removal of technical barriers, particularly sanitary regulations. The Korean insistence on resolving the rest of the agricultural issues in GATT was finally agreed to by the United States. Korea agreed that six months later (in early November), it would disinvoke the balance of payments cover that had provided the justification of agricultural restrictions and accepted the GATT beef panel report.

In the field of what the U.S. negotiators called "localization policies," we agreed to remove border closure provisions in Korean laws for reasons of promoting local production, an authority that has not been widely used in recent years. Korea also agreed, under this heading, to simplify import procedures and abide by the GATT standards code with respect to standards, technical regulations, quality controls, and testing and certification. These agreements could be made because of the ongoing Korean efforts to modernize and streamline import-related laws and regulations in line with relevant GATT provisions. Therefore, the agreements in this area were reached in the early part of the negotiations.

In the foreign direct investment area, Korea committed itself to terminating the performance requirements on foreign investment as a term or condition of permitting an investment, or as a condition for receipt of any incentive. In recent years, Korea did not impose such requirements except for a few cases. Korea also agreed to move from the current "case-by-case" investment approval system to an automatic approval system on a gradual basis by January, 1993. Given the fact that we began to liberalize foreign investment in 1962, the timetable agreed to in the negotiation was a reasonable one.

Now, returning to U.S. trade policy, to say that Super 301 erodes U.S. credibility and undermines the U.S. goal of opening markets does not mean that the United States cannot or should not establish priorities and pursue an activist policy. In fact, such initiatives and leadership are required to achieve global trade liberalization. Most of the rest of the world also shares that objective.

But it seems to me that the means chosen must be consistent with the goals. This is why GATT must be strengthened along with the dispute settlement mechanism. It is the only current means available to constructively resolve bilateral disputes through a multilateral procedure. In those areas not covered by GATT, new rules must first be negotiated in the Uruguay Round.

With the Uruguay Round entering a very critical phase, the aggressive use of Super 301 is likely to upset the delicate balance of the negotiations. This would run counter to the stated objective of the United States.

CHAPTER 9

The Point of View of an Emerging
Trading Nation: Brazil

Marcilio Marques Moreira

I will try to bring forth the point of view of an emerging trading nation—
Brazil—that has been a privileged target of threats, actions, and retaliations,
characterized at the time of their proposition as "natural or necessary measures," within the framework of Section 301 of the U.S. trade law.[1]

The opening of three regular 301 procedures has been announced. Brazil
does not acknowledge them formally since they pertain strictly to the realm of
U.S. domestic laws. To behave otherwise would be tantamount to accepting
the extraterritoriality of a partner's internal laws. The two first actions involved shoes (later not pursued) and informatics. The latter went on and off
for more than four years and was only terminated in October, 1989.

A list of products potentially subject to retaliation was published in the
Federal Register. It covered products whose average annual imports (upwards
of $700 million) amounted to many times the alleged damages to the U.S.
computer industry that the eventual retaliations were supposed to "expiate."
A second list was in the making, but was finally not published, encompassing
the products that would have effectively been targeted by the retaliation.
Although actual retaliations were never activated, the damage to Brazilian
sales to the United States of products included in the *Federal Register* list was
substantial. The most abrasive case was that of Brazilian commuter planes: its
manufacturer, Embraer, had several significant contracts with U.S. airlines
suspended. For many months, it still had to post bonds on the delivery of
planes, at a substantial cost, "guaranteeing" to U.S. purchasers the reim-
bursement of a 100 percent tariff if it ever came into effect. Pleas to exclude
the possibility of the retroactive effect of eventual retaliations went unheeded.

The third case was linked to the alleged infringement of patents on

---

1. I speak as an academic rather than in my current, official capacity as Brazil's Ambassador to the United States. The economic reform package, introduced on March 16, 1990, has
changed the situation since this presentation was made at Columbia University; the presentation
has been left intact, however, to convey the thoughts and sentiments as of an earlier date.

products and processes of U.S. pharmaceutical companies. Patents on food and pharmaceutical products—whose unimpeded supply to the population was considered an issue of public priority—had ceased to be granted in Brazil, as allowed by the Paris Convention, as early as 1945 for products and 1969 for processes, that is, well before most foreign companies (that today control around 85 percent of the Brazilian domestic market) had established themselves.

Notwithstanding Brazil's solid legal position, retaliations were imposed in the second half of 1988 on products from Brazil in two areas—pulp and paper and electronic appliances—whose potential for expansion in the U.S. market is considerable due to our relative competitive advantages in those sectors.

Within the country's tradition of using multilateral dispute settlement procedures, Brazil's reaction was to submit the case to GATT. It took us, however, almost one year to have the United States agree to the formation of a panel.

Meanwhile, trade in a range of products, chosen in an arbitrary way, is being impaired, hurting both Brazilian private export companies that were legitimately doing their best to sell to the U.S. market, and U.S. importers. A shadow is also cast on the whole concept of multilateral trade rules while the bilateral relations between Brazil and the United States are strained by unnecessary and discretionary attrition. Furthermore, it inhibits the Brazilian government's margin of maneuver in the area of intellectual property, a crucial link in the chain leading to the country's access to advanced technology and in its quest for modernity.

More recently, Brazil was included, with Japan and India, in the scope of Super 301 as well. Our mechanism of import licensing and other quantitative import restrictions were, despite recent steps toward gradual liberalization, among the items objected to. Now, Brazil maintains its firm position not to consult or negotiate in the framework of 301s of whatever generation. But we have agreed to discuss, in GATT, the legitimacy of the alleged practices. We maintain that they are consistent with the balance of payments waiver granted to Brazil, in view of the country's stringent financial constraints, aggravated by the debt crisis. The mammoth trade surpluses that we have been able to generate since 1984 are actually engulfed and more than fully absorbed by payment for services, interest, and other debt-related payments.

Brazil was also included on the priority watch list of Special 301 on intellectual property related to four different areas that go from adequate patent protection for all classes of inventions to local printing requirements for theatrical and television films. A later finding, on November 1, neither upgraded nor downgraded us on the list: that remains as one additional question mark in our bilateral economic agenda with the United States.

Analysts have tried to identify why Brazil has been targeted so often with 301-related actions. Different reasons have been mentioned, among them the especially aggressive lobbying posture of a few business associations. Some have, however, stressed the paradigmatic character of the choice of Brazil that also applies, albeit in different contexts and dimensions, to India and Japan.[2] A contributing factor appears to have been the assessment that Brazil is too small as a market for U.S. products to wield any counterretaliatory power, but large enough as a country of continental dimension to be noticed and to be credible as the target of exemplary deterrence.

A second dimension of the paradigmatic character of Brazil derives, in part, from a perverse comparison between the dismal 1980s (marked by the debt crisis, inflation, and slow economic activity) with the previous fifty years of very encouraging growth.

To understand Brazil's quandary we must take a closer look at the country's recent development, especially from 1950 to 1980, and at the adverse phenomena that in the 1980s played havoc with a formerly vigorous growth. The average real rate of GDP growth from 1950 to 1980 was 7.4 percent; exports grew from $1.3 to $20.1 billion in the same period; imports from $0.9 to $23.0 billion; the stock of foreign direct investment from $1.0 to $17.5 billion; and the accumulated debt stock from $0.6 to $54.0 billion.

The almost uninterrupted growth of fifty years, however, ground to a sudden halt with the advent of the dismal 1980s. A peculiarly perverse convergence of the second oil shock, skyrocketing interest rates, price collapse of nonoil commodities, and a severe global recession led inexorably to the debt crisis.

The effect on the Brazilian economy was devastating. Annual GDP growth fell to 3.1 percent in the period 1982–88. The debt service was multiplied by real interest rates that went from 0.7 percent in the precrisis period to 6.6 percent, and it incided on a debt stock that had doubled in three years in the effort to finance skyrocketing interest expenditures and higher oil costs.

In the seven years from 1983 to 1989, the Brazilian interest bill on foreign debt reached the staggering figure of $71.5 billion. Even taking into account the net inflow of loans of $13 billion during the period, we are left with a net outflow of $58 billion in financial resources from 1983 to 1989.

This brief outline seems to be clear evidence that an objective analysis of the degree of openness of any economy has to broaden its scope, going beyond the trade balance, to current accounts if not to the full balance of

---

2. See, for instance, Peter B. Evans, "Declining Hegemony and Assertive Industrialization: U.S.-Brazil Conflicts in the Computer Industry," *International Organization* 43, no. 2 (Spring, 1989): 207–38.

payments. In bilateral trade with the United States, for example, despite the large surpluses we were able to muster since 1983, only in two out of eight years since 1982 have we presented modest bilateral current account surpluses.

And yet, dogmatic politicians and zealous technocrats, when attributing the blame for the crisis of the 1980s, ignore the forces beyond Brazil's control and concentrate exclusively on Brazil's own "lapses" in the shape of earlier "ideological deviations." To "correct" such "sins" they preach a policy that would unqualifyingly embrace the lofty virtues of the market and of an open-borders stance. Section 301, in their eyes, would work as a crowbar to help implement this "new economic policy," regardless of the economic "straight-jacket" Brazil is restricted by and oblivious of the country's progress in the direction of more market-driven policies and closer insertion into the world economy.

Unfortunately, Brazil's economic situation, its perception that its trade and intellectual property policies are entirely consistent with established international laws and obligations, and its willingness to have multilateral determination (in appropriate forums like GATT) of any dispute concerning her rights, are in conflict with the U.S. approach that is driven by unilaterally determined views of what Brazil's policies and the bilateral trade profile ought to be. In the resulting contest, the United States is resorting to tools such as threats, crowbars, and sanctions. This approach does not square with respect for the symmetry of rights, fairness in trade, and the spirit of multilateralism. This is a matter of regret.

CHAPTER 10

A European View of the 1988 U.S. Trade Act and Section 301

Corrado Pirzio-Biroli

Regarding the three major ongoing trade reforms—Uruguay Round, Europe 1992, and the U.S. Omnibus Trade and Competitiveness Act of 1988—only the last has raised worries worldwide that are greater than the opportunities it offers.

To many countries, the Act appears to be a sign of "mépris" of the GATT, for it facilitates the breaching of the standstill agreement in Punta del Este and encourages unilateral U.S. measures against alleged "unfair traders." Any such measures would be taken outside GATT jurisdiction and some might possibly be taken before the relevant issues became part of GATT jurisdiction at the conclusion of the Uruguay Round. As Mr. Krenzler said recently, our American friends have often claimed that the objective of Section 301 is merely to open third markets, and retaliation is only a last resort for exercising leverage. But the reality is quite different: trading partners are given no choice but to negotiate on the basis of an agenda set by the United States, on the basis of U.S. judgments, U.S. perceptions, U.S. timetables, and, indeed, U.S. legislation. All this is a departure from the rule of international law.

World trade problems cannot be solved through forced settlements based on a unilateral determination of unfairness, unilateral time tables, and the threat of unilateral trade action if no agreement is reached. In particular, this cannot be done with respect to countries that possess substantial retaliatory power. Were the rest of the world to respond with their own 301s, GATT would seriously face collapse and the U.S. Congress would, to be sure, be up in arms.

If U.S. action simply led to retaliation by the EC and possibly by some other powerful countries, this would affect America's markets. And the EC is its most promising one. In 1985–88, U.S. exports to the EC alone grew so much that the growth alone was as large as the total Japanese market for U.S. exports in 1987 ($28 billion). Besides, how does the United States expect to reduce its current account deficit without the European market absorbing much of that reduction?

I hope that Special 301 and Super 301 are not harbingers of tomorrow's world. Once a major trading partner gives "legitimacy to unilateralism," as Bhagwati said, we must worry. Just as with Smoot-Hawley in the 1930s, critical aspects of the U.S. trade act may have been proposed with the best intentions. If only they had known what this act triggered, Smoot and Hawley would presumably have refrained from introducing it.

The risk is particularly large at a time of reduced security tensions, for this is likely to restrain the impact and voice of the Defense and State Departments in the trade debate concerning major allies.

Fortunately, the Community, which possesses the greatest retaliatory power today because it represents the greatest world trading power, has embarked, for internal reasons, on its Single Market Program, which will lead to opening up the EC markets internally and worldwide. It is hard to see how the USTR could succeed in implementing the 1988 trade act vis-à-vis the EC without prompting the most serious trade war since the 1930s.

I understand, of course, the motivations of Congress in passing the 1988 act. They reflect internal economic policy problems and frustrations with GATT weaknesses.

Unfortunately, there is no attempt to produce a better macroeconomic policy mix in the United States. As to GATT's weaknesses, let us not forget that it was Congress that voted down the International Trade Organization. It is Congress that has included in the trade act aspects that other GATT partners consider GATT illegal. And it is Congress that has difficulties agreeing to act on GATT determinations that U.S. laws are discriminatory (e.g., super import quotas, Superfund, customs user fees, Section 337).

So, Congress, wanting a weak GATT in order to preserve its margin of maneuver, now believes that GATT weaknesses force it to take unilateral measures. But congressional action is a reflection of the country, of its institutional setup and economic problems. Where trade power is in the hands of the legislative branch, it is far more difficult to resist pressures than when it is in the hands of the executive (as in Europe). George Kennan recently said "I do not think that our U.S. political system is adequate to the needs of the age in which we are now moving." This quote applies well, it seems to me, to U.S. trade policy structures in an increasingly interdependent world.

The EC has supported the positive features of the act, such as trade negotiating authority and implementation of the harmonized tariff nomenclature system. At the same time, it has criticized a number of amendments to U.S. trade laws as dangerous, unnecessary, and untimely. For it felt that the panoply of prior U.S. trade laws was already the most extensive and far-reaching of any Western nation. But, we exerted restraint and said that we would watch closely to see how the administration would interpret and apply the new trade laws.

The USTR is fully conscious of the policy dilemmas the U.S. trade act gives rise to. In a testimony in May, Ambassador Hills said "When we fail to negotiate bilateral solutions in 301 cases, we often face Hobson's choice: inaction, or retaliatory action that is likely to be inconsistent with our GATT obligations." It took courage to tell this simple truth to Congress. Ambassador Hills has also said that she will employ the act's 301 provisions and other negotiating tools to strengthen and expand the rules of the international trading system and pry open foreign markets.

But she has also made it clear that the chosen means to achieve U.S. trade policy goals encompass multilateralism, bilateralism, and unilateralism. This approach cannot give, it seems to me, the necessary emphasis where the United States claims she really belongs, i.e., the multilateral level. There is a basic contradiction here.

The USTR has certainly done its very best to navigate between two contradictory laws and procedures: GATT and the U.S. trade act. Notably, it has skillfully chosen 301 candidates and practices. The EC was identified as a Super 301 target for telecommunications, while four member states were identified as potential targets on intellectual property. And USTR believes that it can continue to reconcile the irreconcilable through "a balanced mix" of the multilateral, bilateral and unilateral tools in its trade policy arsenal, whereby each type of action should complement, not undermine the other types.

Sustained success in this approach would be tantamount to the squaring of the circle. Some U.S. administration officials draw satisfaction from recent examples of perceived "successful" implementation of Section 301: Japanese concessions on cellular mobile telephones, EC-Japanese and Korean commitments to negotiate on shipbuilding subsidies, concessions by several countries in advance of the Super 301 list (Korea, Taiwan) and Special 301 list (Indonesia, Saudi Arabia, Taiwan, Colombia, and the PRC).

These signs that 301 may be working may encourage a tightening of 301 rules in the future. Unfortunately, it is more difficult to measure the wider damage that could be done by 301 action, both in terms of U.S. relations with the rest of the world and in terms of the Uruguay Round's outcome.

With the United States trying to force others to roll back trade barriers before the round's conclusion, the question arises: why is the United States not doing likewise with its own barriers? The more successful 301 is, the more it will require a Uruguay Round package to be weighted to the detriment of the United States insofar as the latter would have obtained unilateral concessions by others beforehand.

Another potential damage is that if Congress sees 301 as a successful instrument, it will tend to be reluctant to replace it with reinforced multilateral trade opening instruments, the more so as 301 does not require U.S. compensation, while international liberalization requires equivalent moves by the United States.

The importance of the latter point will appear obvious to those who know Congress. We will have to use the end of the Uruguay Round to pressure the United States to bring its trade laws into full conformity with the letter and spirit of the GATT agreement.

Any Uruguay Round package will have to include an agreement on a stronger dispute settlement system. This would presumably require altering Section 301, under the fast-track procedure. For, if one can solve the problem of blocking a GATT panel report, 301 loses its only rationale. At a minimum, the act's tight deadlines, unilateral determination of unfairness, and mandatory requirements for action would have to be abolished.

As long as most congressmen believe that the U.S economy is vastly more open to imports and foreign investments than those of other countries and that the 301 instrument is a success, they will persist in seeking unilateral concessions by others, for they do not require market opening measures by the United States: they come at no political cost.

An example of the difficulties the United States will face in pushing excessive requests for trade liberalization by others is what happened, I am told, in the context of the U.S.-Canada Free Trade Area negotiations on subsidies.

The U.S. request to Canada to abolish all subsidies for industrial investment led Canada eventually to cave in, provided the United States did the same with similar subsidies by American state and local authorities. As the United States could not accept this, a compromise had to be found: a dispute settlement system concerning countervailing duties, and a study on investment subsidies in the United States and Canada. No partner should start trade negotiations from the double assumption that its market is perfect and that a perfectly open market can be achieved on a world scale soon. Both such assumptions are unrealistic.

Quite to the contrary, major partners must recognize that they are partners in sin. According to the World Bank's 1987 *World Development Report,* substantial shares of the imports from industrial countries were subject to "hard-core" nontariff barriers (NTBs) in 1986: 13 percent for the EC, 15 percent for the United States, and 29 percent for Japan; average figures for imports from less developed countries affected by hard-core NTBs were generally even higher: 23 percent in the EC, 22 percent in Japan, and 17 percent in the United States. Since 1981, the United States, which had been a force for trade liberalization, from 1945 until 1974 saw its hard-core NTB increase substantially faster than those of the EC, while Japan's remained constant in terms of Japanese imports. The precision of those calculations, and the relative sinfulness of different nations, may be debated. But there is no doubt that there is no nation here suffering from excessive virtues that justify self-righteousness.

My last point is this. Are the potential damages of 301 action worth the candle? Will U.S. exports grow sufficiently to reduce America's focus on unfair trading practices abroad and lead it to accept repeal of 301? I doubt it, at least as long as the United States remains addicted to overconsumption.

The next step down the protectionist road could then be trade-outcome or import-performance criteria. And this would be a disaster for the United States and for the world system, especially since some other powers may be tempted to follow suit. In fact, as Bhagwati has reminded us, there is no plausible way to calculate "fair" shares for the Japanese, in any market. Any attempt by the United States to impose specific import commitments on Japan may strengthen temptations by others to do likewise, as they would suspect that Japan would indulge in import manipulation to please the United States and thus drive trade from them to the United States by imposing what Bhagwati has called Voluntary Import Expansions (VIEs).

On the other hand, nobody could guarantee that market opening measures by Japan and the Four Tigers would primarily or sufficiently benefit the United States. If this did not happen, new reasons could no doubt be found to hit Japan even harder, while the critics continue to underemphasize domestic problems that are the primary source of America's trade imbalance: the U.S. budget deficit, high cost of capital, low productivity, and, last but not least, low propensity to export due to historic and cultural factors.

Contributors

Claude E. Barfield, Jr., is coordinator, Trade Policy Studies, and director, Science and Technology Studies, at the American Enterprise Institute for Public Policy Research, Washington, D.C.

Judith Hippler Bello is a practicing attorney in Washington, D.C. She was formerly general counsel with the Office of the United States Trade Representative and chairman of the interagency Section 301 Committee.

I. M. Destler is professor at the University of Maryland's School of Public Affairs, director of its graduate program on Public Policy and Private Enterprise, and visiting fellow at the Institute for International Economics. His recent books include *American Trade Politics* (1986) and *Dollar Politics* (coauthored, 1989).

Geza Feketekuty is senior policy advisor to the United States Trade Representative and a resident scholar at the International Trade Commission. He has played a key role in developing trade policy for a number of years and recently wrote a book on that topic entitled *International Trade in Services: An Overview and Blueprint for Negotiations.*

Alan F. Holmer practices trade law in Washington, D.C. He previously served as deputy United States Trade Representative and also as general counsel with that office.

Robert E. Hudec is Melvin C. Steen Professor of Law at the University of Minnesota. His major work in the international trade area is *The GATT Legal System and World Trade Diplomacy* (1975, 2d ed. 1990).

Chulsu Kim is currently commissioner of the Korea Industrial Property Office and former assistant minister for trade with the Korean Ministry of Trade and Industry. He has served as principal trade negotiator for the Korean government and in other high level positions since 1973.

Makoto Kuroda, currently a director of Mitsubishi Corporation, was special advisor to the Japanese Ministry of Trade and Industry, formerly serving as vice-minister for international affairs with the MITI. His articles on Japan's economy and U.S.-Japan economic relations have been widely published in Japan and the United States.

Robert Z. Lawrence is a senior fellow in the Economic Studies Program at the Brookings Institution. His recent books include *Can America Compete?* and *Saving Free Trade: A Pragmatic Approach.*

John McMillan is professor of economics at the Graduate School of International Relations and Pacific Studies at the University of California, San Diego. He is the author of numerous journal articles and three books.

Helen Milner is associate professor of political science and a member of the Institute on Western Europe at Columbia University. She is the author of *Resisting Protectionism: Global Industries and the Politics of International Trade* and of articles on international trade policy.

Marcilio Marques Moreira has been Brazilian ambassador to the United States since 1986. He is the author of numerous books in Brazil and *The Brazilian Quandary,* published in the United States.

Henry R. Nau is associate dean and professor of political science and international affairs at the Elliott School of International Affairs, George Washington University. He is the author most recently of *The Myth of America's Decline: Leading the World's Economy into the 1990s.*

Douglas Nelson is assistant professor of economics at the Maxwell School at Syracuse University. His recent research on the political economy of trade policy has been widely published in academic journals.

David Palmeter, a practicing attorney in Washington, D.C., has published widely on international trade law and policy. He is chairman of the Customs and Trade Law Subcommittee, Antitrust and Trade Law Committee, International Bar Association.

Corrado Pirzio-Biroli serves as deputy head of the European Community delegation in Washington, D.C. He has written a number of articles and reports on West European integration, international economics, and East-West, North-South issues.

Paula Stern is president of the Stern Group, an international trade advisory firm in Washington, D.C., and a fellow at Johns Hopkins University's Foreign Policy Institute. From 1984 to 1986 she chaired the International Trade Commission, serving as commissioner for nine years.